The Third Millennium:
Reflections on Faith and Reason

The Third Millennium:
Reflections on Faith and Reason

David Walsh

GEORGETOWN UNIVERSITY PRESS / WASHINGTON, D.C.

Georgetown University Press, Washington, D.C. 20007
©1999 by Georgetown University Press. All rights reserved.
Printed in the United States of America
10 9 8 7 6 5 4 3 2 1 1999
THIS VOLUME IS PRINTED ON ACID-FREE OFFSET BOOKPAPER.

Library of Congress Cataloging-in-Publication Data

Walsh, David, 1950–
    The third millennium : reflections on faith and reason / David
Walsh.
        p.   cm.
    ISBN 0-87840-749-9 (cloth)
    1. Civilization, Christian.   2. Faith and reason—Christianity.
3. Christianity—Influence.   I. Title.
BR115.C5W27   1999
230—DC21   99-18234
                                                                    CIP

To His Holiness, John Paul II

Contents

Acknowledgments

IT IS A PLEASURE to record here my gratitude to those whose assistance has made this book possible. Financial support was provided by the Earhart Foundation as part of their funding of my larger project on "The Transparence of the Modern World." I benefited greatly from the careful reading that Brendan Purcell provided at an early stage of the manuscript. Steve Millies was an able and congenial research assistant, and Bill Byrne kindly undertook the compilation of the index. I am grateful to John Samples, Director of Georgetown University Press, along with Gail Grella and Ivan Osorio, for the efficiency with which they brought the work to publication. Copyediting was skillfully provided by Northeastern Graphic Services.

The book is respectfully dedicated to Pope John Paul II, who has led the world in celebration of the jubilee year of the birth of Christ, and whose *Fides et Ratio* has shown the way toward the deepest convergence between faith and reason in our time.

The Third Millennium:
Reflections on Faith and Reason

Introduction

THE MILLENNIUM is the most momentous calendar event any of us will live through. Yet despite the attention lavished upon it, nothing is more certain than that its true significance will be missed. This misperception is itself evidence of the intellectual fog under which we labor. We are incapable of apprehending the meaning of the most massively obvious events. How can our public celebrations bear any meaningful relation to the knot of time through which we are passing, if we have no credible sense of what is being marked? Are we celebrating a merely empty numerical sum? Or does something of more consequence lie behind that intriguing row of zeros? We know how to celebrate the new year, the new decade, even the new century. But a new millennium? There we are in unfamiliar territory, and the impending arrival is more than a little intimidating. No proximate generation will have such a moment to inaugurate.

What if we are not up to task? For more is at stake than throwing the party of a thousand years—an unnerving enough idea. It is what we must do afterward that is most sobering. This generation is charged with beginning a new age. We have been granted the opening of the third millennium of our history, thereby stamping it with a character that will remain more visible than the imprints of many less strategically placed cohorts. Thus, it is not the celebration that is so daunting, but its aftermath. How will we enter upon the third millennium? A peculiar detachment seems to characterize our mood of drifting toward the calendrical pivot. Business as usual reassures us that life will continue pretty much as it has. Little of the apocalyptic excitement we know from the beginning of previous millennia seems to be in the air. Or perhaps it is merely building subterraneously to be unleashed in a volcanic eruption. An eerie calm seems to characterize our lack of preparations. Sooner or later, however, that will be shattered as we are gripped by the stature of the historical shift we are entering. The advent of a new millennium cannot be overlooked forever, and eventually it will take us into its grip. Then our disorientation will be complete. How will we be able to sustain our precarious entry into a new era if we have lost our sense of what the transition means?

Of course, there will be the voices of pragmatic reason reassuring us that nothing of such cosmic import is transpiring. They will point out that it is just the beginning of another year, no different than any other. Our greatest problem is how to reprogram all the computers that had so confidently been constructed to accept all date combinations except a double zero. Surely there is something a little disturbing in this demonstration of human nescience. It is almost as if we were ready for every prospect except the void. Even the most practical level seems to remind us of our reticence before the abyss. Why were our computers programmed to so blithely ignore a year in which everything came up zero? Then we remember that it is only a number and that we can easily accommodate ourselves to it. Besides, we recall that the start of the third millennium is itself in dispute. A good case can be made for its inception in the year 2001 rather than the numerically more ominous 2000, or it might be 2003 or even 2033.[1] Other calculations have their justifications as well, and, as we reflect upon them, we find ourselves back in the familiar territory of our irresolvable debates. It is a land in which the very multiplicity of perspectives assures us that everything is relative and that it is up to us to make of them what we will. There is nothing whose objective reality provides the measure for our own. We are in charge. Yet "the millennium" shakes free from all our efforts to corral it. Somehow it remains bigger than us. It forces itself upon us irrespective of our choices and efforts to subsume it. We are not moving through the millennium, the millennium is moving through us. This is what is finally so unsettling about the event. It reminds us that time is not a medium at our disposal, but that we are subordinate to the structures that emerge through time. History is what makes us. We do not make history.[2]

The millennium imposes itself on us because it reminds us of what we can usually forget. We are part of a cosmos whose cycles include and embrace our existence. Our mastery is a limited purview over the domains that the order of the cosmos permits. We are not absolute. We are not in charge. It is the rumble of time itself that eventually rolls over us, and if we want to live we must accommodate ourselves to its inexorable rhythm. That is why the turn of the millennium remains so fascinating to us. We are still subject to the unfolding of the cosmos. The casual debasement of new year rituals, reassuring us of our blissful superiority to the vicissitudes of existence, cannot so easily be sustained in the face of such a signal turning point. Despite it all, we remain susceptible to awe. The proportions of the cosmos overshadow us, and we are held in reverence of the mystery in which we participate. Even the most blasé among us cannot remain unaffected by the promise of a new beginning contained in the millennial opening. It is as if we are back in that most magical first day of creation. We have leapt into a qualitatively different time, and unlimited new possibilities open before us. Of course, we still know that really nothing will be changed. It is just that we cannot resist the pull to believe in new birth when the cosmos itself seems to be drawing us so strongly toward it.

The magic of the millennium works its inexorable effect. It is the fertile source of the excitement that increasingly pervades the air with expectations of novelty. Once we subject our intimations to examination, however, we realize that the cosmic stretch is only one dimension. Of more importance is the extent of history that reaches out behind and before us. We no longer live simply within the rhythms of the cosmos. Our time is the open horizon of history in which singular events structure lines of meaning in various directions. This is, after all, the focus of our interest in the millennium. Cosmic revolutions may be the prereflective context from which we begin, but the foreground is firmly occupied by the historical revolutions that create our world. Our attention is captured by the sense of a new historical era. The moment may derive some of its magic from the coincidence with the cosmic return, but its substance consists of the actions that shape the world in which we live. Although created by history, we too take a hand in shaping that history. Now the question becomes more intractable: What is the meaning whose historical beginning will shape the era of the third millennium?

At this point our minds draw a blank. Beyond the cosmic magic of numbers, we have difficulty defining what the significance of the millennium is. What is it the millennium of? Everyone knows it is the third millennium of the birth of Christ, but how are we to regard a date whose principal validity is confined to Christians? What is the significance of the third millennium for a world that has politely altered the Christian demarcations of B.C. and A.D. to become "Before the Common Era" and the "Common Era"? Can we celebrate the third millennium of our common era? No wonder we sense the hollowness lurking behind the contrived jubilations. Are we to toast the arrival of the third millennium of universal calendar convenience? This is surely a utilitarian cleansing of the magic of numbers. But then we are struck by an odd realization. Despite the most single-minded efforts to evacuate all Christian reference from our periodization, we still live in a historical time that is structured by the advent of Christ. Without noticing it, we live in an anonymously Christian world, a world that is perhaps more pervasively Christian by virtue of its very anonymity.

These are rather strange suggestions, but I hope to show in this book that they are not as far-fetched as they appear at first glance. On the contrary, they point us toward the central meaning of the millennium we celebrate. We do, after all, need some starting point from which to number our reckoning of time. However, it is not entirely a matter of indifference as to what turning point we choose, and clearly different civilizations and religions number time differently. They all sense that, as far as possible, the beginning of our numbering must be rooted in what is truly the beginning for our existence. The fact that modern civilization has, unwittingly, adopted the Christian calendar pulls it inexorably in a Christian direction. Not only has global modernity derived from a Christian orbit, but it carries within it the imprint of its Christian past that cannot be ignored so conveniently. Christianity is not merely the empty husk sloughed off by a modernity now capable of standing on its own feet. It is much closer to the inner code that pervades a civilization secular in appearance but still deeply Christian in its soul. The advent of the third millennium is surely the occasion to contemplate afresh the degree to which a civilization in search of meaning continues to find it within the only spiritual order it has ever known.

In this sense the turn of the millennium is a dangerous time. Of course, there are all kinds of religious celebrations and excitations, from the conventional to the bizarre. However, the revolutionary possibility lies outside of the explicitly religious area and is at the heart of modern civilization itself. We are on the verge of rediscovering what lies embedded in this curious modern world of meaning—a civilization so successful that it has swept the globe and yet so empty that it is perpetually in search of new infusions of purpose. The millennium comes at the worst of times for this hollow modern triumph. It arises at the moment of maximum vulnerability when the emptiness of modernity has become transparent. Millennial uncertainty is itself one of the factors that tips it over the edge. From the modern point of view, we are asked to celebrate the third millennium of what? More of the same?

Here a faint realization begins to dawn. Meaning in history is not created by the accumulated achievements of our efforts within time. Work is certainly meaningful, but it is not the ultimate source of meaning. What we do is only meaningful within a whole that is defined by a higher purpose. Otherwise we have merely an aggregation of small meanings that accumulate to a slightly larger construct, but that never amount to a whole. Without a transcendent meaning, the whole is empty. It is the dark, cold universe that eventually consumes all our hopes and dreams without a shred of consolation. Nothing we do can reverse it. Yet here we are asking about the meaning of the millennium, the whole. In the question we begin to glimpse from whence it derives. The meaning of the millennium is not about the meaning of the next thousand years, because that would raise the question of what happens in the succeeding millennium, and in the next, and so on. We would end only with the last millennium, which is the end. Our universe has an end. But, if there is only a full stop, then all our aspirations are tinged with futility, and that is not the spirit in which the question of the millennium is raised. It emerges within a context already structured by faith in the whole. Reflection on the millennium is not really about meaning within time, but about the meaning of time itself as a whole. It is a question raised from the perspective of an eternity whose meaning is complete.

In this sense, the question of the meaning of the millennium is still infused with Christian expectations. Our concern with the meaning of history as a whole, which is what the question of the millennium raises, is possible only because of the sense that history has a meaning. We still have faith in the question. Even when we are counselled not to ask such questions because we are no longer able to answer them, it is only to assuage a deep-seated need that will not fall away on its own. Whether we like it or not, we still live within a context shaped by the Christian differentiation of the end of history. The question of meaning looms so sharply because it once seemed so completely known. We recall that even the focus on the millennium is quintessentially Christian. The expectation in the Book of Revelation (20:1–6) of the reign of Christ on earth has shaped the Christian imagination for two millennia. Its most stable formulation was given by Saint Augustine when he identified the present age as the millennium (*City of God*, XX, 7, 8, 9). Christ already reigns on earth through his presence within the church. The extent of the millennium, one thousand or many thousand, was no longer relevant. What was important was that history from the time of Christ to its end was comprehended as a whole. Our own millennial speculations are still tinged with the uncertainties of rival millennial visions. In either the Augustinian or apocalyptic form, the question arises from the sense of moving toward the consummation of time.

If time is just to continue indefinitely or toward a finite dissolution, then it has no meaning. Only if we still sense that it is illumined by a transcendent goal is it possible to ask about the meaning of the millennium. Even if we no longer have a strong sense of what that meaning is, we possess the residual expectation that compels us to wonder about the whole. We do not in fact live toward the future. Rather, we conceive the future as a qualitatively different time and are almost incapable of imagining the most remote future as mere repetition of the present. We cannot follow our own sober advice to forget about such metaphysical meaning and be satisfied with the finite satisfactions pragmatically attainable. Stop chasing rainbows—the biblical surety of the divine covenant with man. It is not that we cannot see the logic of such counsel. Surely a great deal of aggravation, not to mention religious conflict, could be spared if we could abandon all theological frames of reference. But we cannot—not because we do not wish to, but because we are congenitally incapable of it. Our practical world itself would collapse if it lost the halo of unattainable mystery surrounding it.

Our problem is that we lack the words to admit this to ourselves. We are neither religious nor irreligious enough. Like Ivan Karamazov, a continuing emblem of our age, we have neither the faith to affirm Christ nor the resoluteness to deny him. We gravitate toward terms like "post-Christian" or "postmodern," but what do such epithets designate if not the awareness that we still carry within us what we thought we left behind? As a result, we oscillate between moments of secular self-assertion, mounting even to titanic professions of self-sufficiency, and outbursts of devotional excess, culminating in a profusion of fundamentalisms. Is it not strange that the most technologically advanced civilization should also be prone to the most irrational spiritual eruptions? Cults such as the Heaven's Gate community are only the most dramatic expression. How is it possible to work with supreme rationality by day, designing Web pages for the Internet, and plan by night for a mass suicidal rendezvous with a spiritual spaceship?[3] On the world scene, religious fundamentalism is by far the single most important disturbing factor. It is at the core of many of the most intractable political conflicts. A milder form is more pervasively present in the fideism of much contemporary religiosity that, as Nietzsche recognized, would rather believe anything than not believe at all (*Genealogy of Morals*, Third Essay, section 28). No wonder sensible observers are inclined to discard religion as more a source of nuisance than of social remedy. However, dismissal is equally shortsighted because, when repressed, the religious impulse returns with a vengeance.

What is needed is a healing of the civilizational schism that afflicts our world. We cannot regard reason as a self-contained instrument to be used for whatever purpose we choose, because then reason itself cannot provide the direction in which it will be applied. If reason is instrumentalized, then we lack any rational source of direction. It is this contradiction that gives the air of irrationality to our most impressive technological accomplishments. Television or the Internet, for example, are marvels of communication but are employed to pander to our most elemental urges or even worse. How is it possible for a civilization capable of organizing a global marketplace and delivering an unprecedented abundance of goods to human beings everywhere to remain so helpless before the more essential task of ensuring that the goods are used well? Why this endless proliferation of products and choices that only confuse and exhaust us? Why should so much attention be lavished on comfort and appearance and so little on the inner development of the person? Every purpose is served except for the happiness of human beings. Such irrationality arises not from an excess of reason, but from its defect. Our reason is bounded by the requirements of instrumentality, of rational efficiency; it is not permitted to contemplate the ends themselves. We fail to recognize that our reason is already embedded in an order of ends that it is capable of disclosing, if we permit it. It is a constriction that results because we have cut off reason from faith.

The cause is not hard to find. Faith cannot be the context for reason because it has already shrivelled to the fideistic covering that hides our nakedness. Instrumentalized reason correlates with a truncated faith. It is because we are so painfully aware of our lack of illumination, of the hollowness of our claim to rationality, that we grasp so uncritically for a fundamentalist assurance that comes from we know not where. This is by no means a proclivity of the uneducated and unwashed. Even the most sophisticated minds are susceptible to such spiritual naiveté. They sense their lack of a mooring and, rather than drift precariously on the ocean of existence, latch on to whatever authoritative text or institution impresses them. It is not the simplicity of such faith that is the problem, for all faith is ultimately simple. Rather, it is the refusal to contemplate the source of what draws them.[4] It is as if such fideistic respondents sought to remain frozen in time at the moment of their first spiritual inkling. A suspended faith of that kind can only become more brittle. It has no life and eventually breaks, to be captured by a new frozen moment of stillbirth. Gone is the possibility of an expansive contemplation of the divine drawing that reveals itself in the movement of faith itself. Without that spiritual flexibility, there is no possibility of gaining the intellectual flexibility that would make it possible to rebuild the bridge to a rationally technocratic world. Frozen in time the tension between reason and revelation cannot unfold its creative dynamic.

Perhaps the millennial moment might be the occasion for a dissolving of such long-hardened conceptions. Surely it is the project of a millennium to rediscover the unity of symbolisms whose emergence, integration, and separation was the work of the preceding two millennia and whose roots reach into the millennial distance of the human race. Normally we shy away from considering such vast historical perspectives, but the turn of the millennium thrusts their contemplation upon us. Providentially, this opening coincides with an exhaustion of the arrogant self-assurance of the modern world, a mere blip in the expanse of recorded and unrecorded time. With our modern hubris temporarily humbled and our imagination stretched by the contemplation of millennial meaning, we are in the best position in a very long time to rediscover the richness that has been bestowed upon us. The dried bones—the truncated fragments of traditions, both rational and spiritual—that have come down to us can be recovered in their living breathing unity, so long as we are prepared to follow the intimations we possess. Such an enlargement of horizon is the task I propose for this meditation. It is a first step on the millennial journey that resumes the human effort to found an order within history while recognizing that we are incapable of consummating the order of history.[5]

The opening of a new millennium in which we as a civilization are peculiarly bereft of grand visions is a most auspicious beginning. It reminds us that all our achievements, prowess, and brilliance are ultimately not our own. We have been gifted by the process that has brought us forth, and the equilibrium of our existence is crucially dependent on that recognition. The twentieth century has been a bitter reminder of the catastrophe of such spiritual amnesia.[6] By contrast, our challenge today is to initiate the long-restorative effort of recollection. In that process we will discover that we are not who we thought we were or at least not what we appeared to be. In place of the long-familiar landmarks of reason, science, religion, history, and technology, we will discover the gap in our understanding of who we are and our place in the order of things. Dropping the overweening self-confidence that everything can be mapped by us, we might open toward the mystery of the realization that we are searching for our way from within the map. Our reassuringly familiar labels stand exposed for what they are—abbreviations for realities we do not fully understand. Instead of seeing ourselves as outsiders to the process, we will rediscover our place within it, including the mysterious boundary that holds us all and refuses to be captured by our "raids on the inarticulate." The condition for such a reorientation is that we shift attention from the familiar foreground to the peripheral background of our awareness.

The first level of this reflection is historical. To gain a millennial perspective we must be prepared to move beyond the taken-for-granted parameters of contemporary life. The great complexes of meaning that dominate our world—the science-technology axis and the liberal-constitutional order of rights—have emerged within the specific historical setting of the Christian West. Despite the familiarity of this observation, its significance is not properly grasped. What, for example, is the reason why Christian civilization generated such intellectual forms and other civilizations did not? It is not that other civilizations lacked the genius to move in such directions, for technical and scientific accomplishments flourished in China long before Western Europe had even been civilized. Similarly, conceptions of law and the attendant notion of rights are widespread political developments. Why did their modern elaboration begin only in medieval Christianity? There are of course many factors that converge to make such historical developments possible, and it is not my intention to explore the question comprehensively. Rather, I will investigate the interior link between such complexes of meaning and the overarching spiritual evocation of Christian society. It is relatively easy to identify the external factors—material, social, political, and so on—that contribute to the birth of science and the definition of rights. But to reflect on their inner dependence on a Christian worldview is both more essential and more difficult.

It is more essential in disclosing something about the nature of science or rights as such, and it is more difficult in that such a dependence is contrary to the received understanding of these contemporary thought forms. Natural science and liberal rights emerged to assert their independence of any religious traditions. This is the principal source of their authority in the modern world. Not entangled in theological presuppositions, they can stand on their own feet as the undisputed exemplars of the modern mind. Science and rights constitute the universal language of our world to which all cultures and civilizations are expected to submit. Having transcended their own cultural origin, they can now lay claim to the position of unconditional arbiter of truth and right in the contemporary pluralist community. Occasional murmurings are heard from Islamic or Eastern or tribal societies who resent this intellectual imperialism of the West. But what can they do? Even their objections are peculiarly couched in the language of Western self-determination or appeal to the empirical arguments of Western science. It seems as if the globally modern civilization of the West, which has been institutionalized in its sponsorship of international organizations, has won the day.

But has it? Everything depends on maintaining the perception that modernity is a civilization that has transcended its own historical particularity. If we wish to examine seriously our place at the turn of the millennium, we cannot take such claims at face value. Our Western inclination to deconstruct the sources has taught us to suspect what everyone takes for granted. Usually it conceals an uncomfortable realization that few are prepared to confront. The objectivity of scientific method, as well as the myth of expertise it sustains, barely suppresses the awareness of the lack of understanding it contains. Our science is a science of phenomena and their relationships, confirmed by our capacity to manipulate phenomenal realities successfully. But why reality is organized in the way it is or how it is ultimately ordered remain questions beyond the reach of our methodologies. We lack a science of substantive reality, of being, and for this reason are deprived of any means of ordering our purposes in relation to the whole. Occasionally, we even attempt to hide this self-awareness behind the conceit that such philosophical questions are not real since they are not amenable to the scientific methodologies. But this is only to render our poverty blatant. We know that phenomenal science presupposes the relativity of all perspectives. How is that possible except from the awareness of what is not relative?

In historical terms, avoiding this question takes the form of refusing to investigate the degree of dependence of empirical science on its Christian background. The reason for this reluctance is obvious. If we were to admit that science is peculiarly attached to a Christian differentiation of reality, then it would be tantamount to surrendering its claim to unlimited independence. Yet this is what is at issue. If there are presuppositions to experimental science that can be validated only in (or most fully in) the Christian perspective, then to be true to itself science would have to acknowledge its spiritual presuppositions. It would no longer be science as we know it, but rather science as we suspect it to be. That is, a way of viewing reality that is itself dependent on a more embracing perspective, which is in turn not the final viewpoint but one that can claim some definitiveness only because it relates to the absolute viewpoint on the world. Only God knows reality in this adequate sense; our knowledge consists of knowing the distance we are from it. But that presupposes that the divine knowledge of things has been definitively differentiated from the human perspective.[7] This is the achievement of Christianity, yet it has received scant attention from modern intellectuals.

Our contemporaries understandably shudder at the prospect of acknowledging religious dependency. The prospects are unsettling for science, just as they are for the distinctive modern political enterprise. A secular public order anchored in respect for individual rights also finds it difficult to accommodate the admission of its dependence on a transcendent spiritual orientation. Yet the same inexorable conclusion is indicated. Respect for the inviolable dignity and worth of each human being is incompatible with the utilitarian calculus to which we subject all things. From the perspective of the marketplace, the value of each person is what an employer or customer will pay for their service. Organizational efficiency demands that each individual member be rated in terms of his or her productivity. The logic of the rational exploitation of resources demands that nothing be allowed to stand in the way of the most efficient manipulation and distribution. Everything, it seems, has its price, even the human beings who are the putative beneficiaries of this vast rational enterprise. Only in one sphere do we make explicit rejection of this scale of measurement. Politics is finally not organized to serve the imperious demands of rationality. As with the implicit spheres of the family and social relationships, here we seek to call a halt to the juggernaut of technical efficiency. We recognize that such rationality is ultimately irrational if it does not serve the good of human beings who must be regarded as irreplaceable ends in themselves. But from where do we derive that conviction? It exists as a picturesque residue of an earlier age in which nobility and sacrifice seemed the highest aspirations of human life. Yet, astonishingly, it works, more or less. In the midst of this feverish technocratic civilization, we cling to the transcendent faith that each human being matters more than the whole universe. No wonder we shrink from contemplating our predicament.

The relentless flow of events, however, makes it impossible to ignore, and the opening of the third millennium reminds us of the larger perspective within which we might make more sense of our modern world. We are not forever condemned to remain within the schizophrenic confines of our past few centuries. Merely adverting to the tension is already an expansion of horizons that invites us to surmount them. What is required is the reassurance that it does not entail an abandonment of all that is best in our achievements. The point of raising the question of the contextual spirituality of our science or noting the transcendent presuppositions within our language of rights, is not to make us any less scientific or respectful of others. On the contrary, the point is to deepen and extend such attitudes. The greatest threat to scientific rationality derives from ignorance of the presuppositions and limitations of scientific method. Scientific arrogance leads toward disaster. In the same way, the endless confusion concerning rights-talk, the gnawing suspicion of its vacuousness, and the inability to render an account of the order of rights tend to undermine what we want to preserve. An honest admission of the transcendent character of rights commitments cannot erode their intelligibility any further. It can only lead toward a realistic perception of their true nature, a reconsideration that can only deepen and strengthen such convictions. The enlargement of horizons invited by the advent of the new millennium can be the means of placing the modern world on a firmer foundation than any it has hitherto enjoyed.

The great hurdle to overcome is the incomprehension of the way in which the Christian differentiation might provide the overarching meaning for a world composed of a plurality of religions and a diversity of perspectives. How can Christ be the apex of a world that is not fully Christian? Either a Christian meaning will be imposed on the experience of individuals and societies who would themselves reject it or else the Christian differentiation will retain its validity for those who have submitted to its order alone. In one case, freedom is disregarded; in the other, meaning has been abandoned. The task is difficult, but the millennial opening invites at least an attempt by one small book. On the one hand, the millennium is shared by all who are part of the modern world, and yet it is peculiarly rooted in one spiritual tradition. Do we relate to one another entirely at the level of utilitarian convenience, or can we find a deeper common bond between us? The factors that provide hope for the latter are the twin features of the common civilization we share, with its commitments to scientific rationality and respect for individual rights. Despite the immense cultural and social differences that distinguish the peoples of the world, a real convergence has also occurred in the defining features of modernity. The question is whether this elemental conversation, exemplified by such institutions as the U.N. with its half-century-old Universal Declaration of Human Rights, can be nudged further in the direction of a substantive spiritual community.

The suggestion here is that there is the possibility of such deeper dialogue, but only if we are prepared to acknowledge the Christian derivation of the world we share and confront the consequences for truth across the spectrum of spiritual traditions. If Christianity is the source for the intellectual and moral developments of modernity, then it is in some sense integral to the truth of all the great spiritual traditions of mankind. To believe otherwise would be to abandon the notion of authoritative truth. This we cannot do without relinquishing the contemporary faith in the authority of science and the justness of respect for human rights. Once we have accepted truth in one area, we cannot resist its expansion to others. There cannot be a plurality of truths in theology while admitting a univocity in science or morality. We may not be capable of explaining how the multiplicity of perspectives are one, but we cannot assert their incommensurability in principle. Truth is one, even if it remains hidden to us. Acknowledgment of the mysterious unity of truth may not seem like much of an advance, but it underpins the only possibility of serious dialogue among human beings about what is important.

Inquiry and exchange are worthwhile only if we believe in the existence of truth. One of the principal obstacles to conversation across the world's religions has been the prevailing misimpression that tolerance requires a relativization of perspectives. The only problem with this attitude is that it undermines not only truth *between* religions but *within* them as well. If the most important questions must be consigned to the black hole of ignorance, then nothing serious can be said at all. Ultimately, everything shades off into a context in which everything is relative. But this, however, is precisely what we deny when we insist on the objectivity of science and the inviolability of rights. What I want to point out is that this millennial convergence of mankind presupposes in practice an implicit spiritual convergence on truth as well. The challenge is to find a means of articulating it across the spiritual traditions. How can we find a way of expressing our common faith in truth that is not fully known by any of us, but that underpins the capacity we exemplify to elaborate our partial hold on truth?

The question has already answered itself. We exemplify a faith in the practices that constitute modern civilization. That means that a spiritual orientation is implicitly present and must in some sense represent a convergence of the great spiritual traditions of our history. Otherwise it would be impossible for the diversity of cultures to find even the elemental meeting ground represented by contemporary science and universal human rights. However, this means that the spiritual tradition most explicitly generative of such practices must also find itself already within a dialogue with the other such principal traditions. Christianity must in some sense be contained within them just as they are contained within Christianity. But how can we find a means of relating them to one another that does not either reduce their diversity to a homogenous jumble or impose a violent uniformity on their differences? The first thing to note is that there is no perspective outside of such spiritual perspectives. They are the most embracing horizons of meaning available to us. Even our secular science and morality derives from and silently depends on such an overarching framework. The consequence is that spiritual traditions can only be related from within themselves—that is, from the perspective of the most differentiated, because only such will possess the conceptual means to comprehend what is only compactly expressed in the less articulate forms. Aboriginal peoples do not develop theologies. But which is the most differentiated? In some sense, the world religions have their respective differentiations and this is the great source of their durability. However, it is precisely for this reason that they can be related to one another. They are partners in the differentiation of meaning. What is relatively undeveloped in one tradition may be found to be more fully elaborated in another and vice versa. The conversation does not have to be initiated, for it is already underway once they are present to one another.

It is quickly discovered that no one perspective has a comprehensive hold on truth. Each has a different perspective on the one truth. This is what makes their dialogue most fruitful, a prospect slowly coming to realization at the dawn of the third millennium. Traditions that have had only intermittent contact with one another now are engaged in establishing a continuous conversation across a range of issues, both spiritual and practical. The amazing wealth of insight generated by such juxtaposition arises from the recognition that each partial perspective on divine truth can be deepened by the enriching presence of others. Interest in other religions is now so constant that we might regard it as a feature of contemporary spirituality. It is hard to be a faithful Christian or Jew or Muslim or Buddhist without contemplating how one is completed by the perspective of other faiths. This is not to suggest that the world religions will eventually be absorbed into one syncretic whole. Their amalgamation would be tantamount to their destruction. Besides, the plurality of perspectives seems too much a part of the providential ordering. But their interrelationship must go deeper.

In this exchange, Christianity plays a crucial role. Not only is it the spiritual background of modernity, but it lays claim to the most differentiated realization of order. This is a claim that does not go uncontested, notably by the other Abrahamic faiths—Judaism and Islam—who regard it as having collapsed the differentiations they articulate. The situation is even more complex with the Indian and Chinese traditions, whose differentiation follows a markedly different emphasis. No attempt will be made to resolve such divergences, and there are good reasons for believing them to be irreducible. The conversation must continue. However, it must now acquire a self-consciousness about its underlying assumption—that is, that the unity of truth means the equivalence of meaning within the great symbolic forms.[8] Not only are they directed toward the same truth, but there is a fundamental continuity in their apprehension of it. They can enter into conversation because they are already related to one another. Each is already contained in the other, and they differ only by the degree of recognition of that interrelationship. The more differentiated tradition has the advantage of greater articulateness, but it does not replace the less articulate. Every perspective is needed because they are all partial apprehensions of a reality beyond our reach. Western Christian interest in Eastern spirituality, for example, arises from the awareness of the difficulty of sustaining the most differentiated horizon and the sense that wisdom may be contained in traditions of a more holistic character.

Yet, neither the East nor the West can avoid the recognition that modern rationality is a product of the philosophic Christian encounter. An understanding of the world we interdependently inhabit requires an appreciation of that connection. Only by connecting science and rights with their intrinsic spiritual source will it be possible to appreciate the way in which they are universally representative. In practice, tribal and Confucian and Hindu and Buddhist societies recognize the authoritative intellectual forms of the modern world. What other option do they have? But to relate these intellectual forms to their own indigenous traditions is a considerable challenge. It requires first an appreciation of the derivation of the scientific and rights perspectives within their proper philosophic Christian sources. Then it becomes possible to locate the modern rationality, to which they give rise, within the broader historical streams of spirituality. It is because of the equivalence of truth across the great religious traditions that such practical convergence is ultimately possible. Now is surely the moment to reflect more thematically on the spiritual unity of mankind, which furnishes the possibility of their actual unity.

Such a reflection must explore why Christian civilization has given rise to the rationality of the modern world. There are many extrinsic factors that play a role, but the intrinsic source lies in the maximal degree of spiritual differentiation of the Christian experience. It is within the Christian perspective that nature is fully differentiated as a realm for empirical rational investigation, and it is within Christianity that the transcendent finality of each human being receives its most complete elaboration. Why this is so will be explained in the relevant chapters, for now it is noted as the context within which to understand why the millennium remains a Christian symbol of periodization, even in a pluralistic world. It is because the significance of Christianity extends beyond the self-identified believers. In an important sense, Christ is the truth of all the world religions, just as they are the truth realized in Christ. The degree of civilizational interpenetration we have reached makes it finally impossible to avoid confrontation with the question of equivalence. The unity of mankind, which is practically operative and which makes possible the dialogue of civilizations, arises from our participation in the one reality.

The term "anonymous Christians" arises in such reflections. It goes all the way back to the Church Fathers, who sought a way of expressing the sense of continuity with those whose openness to reason makes them participants in the divine Logos.[9] In this sense, all who live the life of reason are in some way contained within the Christian orbit. It is the horizon that underpins the limits of rationality within all traditions, including the modern. It is not merely that *Logos,* as discovered by the Greeks, is integrated with the Christian vision, but that it finds its consummation in the Logos of Christ. This is not some abstract concept of universality. It is in the quite concrete sense of what sustains the operation of reason, maintaining it within its equilibrium and directing it toward its final fulfillment. There is no higher perspective within which human reason can operate. What is in order within all spiritual traditions of mankind finds its culmination in the Christian affirmation. This is not to say that they are definitively superceded by Christianity or that they do not contain dimensions insufficiently developed within the Christian. It is that they cannot advance beyond the differentiation or rationality afforded by the Christian perspective. No higher elaboration of order has been vouchsafed to us. It is therefore the Christian dispensation that most completely sustains the impetus toward reason within the manifold elaborations of order within human history.

All of this has here merely been asserted. Its establishment requires a specification of the way in which rationality finds its culmination within the Christian philosophy of existence. That is the purpose of this book, for now we need only conclude this overview by noting the most significant corollary also to be explored. It is that, if Christianity is the fullest differentiation of the horizon of reason, the operation of reason is peculiarly dependent on the presence of a worldview that is at least intuitively Christian. Rationality is in conflict with spiritual visions incompatible with Christianity. In particular, reason is jeopardized by the threats most endemic to Christianity. The achievement of differentiation is not tantamount to perfection. In many ways the advance in rationality heightens the tension of existence, which becomes more difficult to sustain. It means that a recognizable range of heresies emerge to exert their attraction over the differentiated mind. But the direction is not back toward the earlier compactness; rather, it is in the path that seeks to escape the tension of existence altogether.

At the center of such movements for the past two millennia, we find a heretical tendency that, while it is not tied exclusively to Christianity, has remained an abiding feature of the Christian world. It goes under a variety of names in different ages, but its core may be identified as Gnosticism. The deepening of the mystery of existence within Christianity intensifies the questions that have always bedeviled human beings. Why should the cosmos contain evil and suffering, especially innocent suffering? If the ultimate purpose is to recover unity with the divine Beyond, why should there be a cosmos in the first place? Now that transcendent divinity has taken upon itself the burden of suffering redemption, the mystery has not been diminished. Rather, it has deepened. Gnosticism, in its myriad variants, has always provided an answer to all of these concerns. This has been its principal achievement and its principal limitation.

In solving the problem of existence, Gnosticism turns its back on it. History is over. No more goals or struggles are of consequence once the gnosis of the means of escaping or transfiguring it has become available. It is one of the curious ironies, most manifest by the age of secular Gnosticism we are leaving behind, that the great activist projects of the modern ideologies pointed ultimately toward the end of progress as we know it within time. This is why the twentieth century has been the century of death. The secret of European civilization, Camus remarked, is that it no longer loves life ("Beyond Nihilism," in *The Rebel*). Our great spiritual explorers like Nietzsche and Dostoevsky sought a way of reaffirming life in the midst of its suffocation. Now that the worst of the ideological mania has passed, we are once again in a position to accept life on its own terms without imposing impossible conditions. Rationality has returned to much of our world as politics is once again regarded as a realm of finite expectations. However, the struggle for spiritual equilibrium has not ceased, because balance is by definition the fruit of resistance against imbalance. Even the renewed affirmation of the mysterious divine goodness can itself derail into the Gnostic impulse toward spiritual superiority.

Our millennial moment is enormously susceptible to such temptations, which now tend to assume more recognizably religious forms. The quest for millennial significance is itself part of the Gnostic genre. Contemporary fascination with angels, near-death experiences, and varieties of paramystical occupations move in the same direction of attempting to pierce the veil of mystery denied to all mortals. Religious revivalism of all types can readily mask the impulses to leap outside of the human condition. The more conventional appearance of such projections as religious, albeit in often crudely debased forms, should not delude us about their harmfulness. Our history is sufficient testimony to the pervasiveness of Gnostic temptations never far from the surface. Its defeat in one form has generally resulted, not in its disappearance, but in its metamorphosis into a different guise. Even those whose learning informs them of the deeper roots of such impulses, such as the literary critic Harold Bloom, have proved just as vulnerable to the Gnostic vision. While disdaining the vulgarly superficial form the impulse assumes in contemporary society, Bloom cheerfully declares his own deeper Gnostic predelictions [*Omens of the Millennium* (New York: Riverhead, 1996)].

Again the inclination would be relatively harmless if it did not lead to disastrous practical consequences. Most central is the arrest of the moral and intellectual life gnosticism engenders. Once convinced of the superiority of one's vision, there ceases to be a need to inquire further or to grow in virtue. Both science and morality are complete. Revulsion at the closure of such a life is what eventually sets us on the path of spiritual sobriety. It was the lack of progress in the Manichean worldview that ultimately turned Saint Augustine against them (*Confessions*, Book V). He eventually sought the deepening of the mystery of life within Christianity as he came to the realization that beckons us all. We are not called to leap over the vicissitudes of existence, but to deepen our fidelity within them. In the words of Victor Frankl's luminous Auschwitz account, a point had been reached in which the prisoners no longer sought escape from their fate [*Man's Search for Meaning* (New York: Washington Square, 1963), 124]. Rather, they took it up in the recognition that suffering was something on which they no longer sought to turn their backs. Now, why redemption is the flower of suffering still remains impenetrable within such a perspective, but the distorting "why" has lost much of its insistent force. No insight is gained into the process in which we find ourselves, but its structure has again returned to form the order of the soul.

It is in this sense that Christianity is the source of the most rational, differentiated, and balanced horizon available to us. Mystery remains undiminished, but its awareness is enhanced. The limits of our human participation are emblazoned as we behold the divine participation within existence as well. The other spiritual traditions are not negated, rather, their truth is revealed in its most differentiated manifestation. Human participation in the divine life is the fruit of the divine participation in human existence. This is the great realization glimpsed even by those outside all formal spiritual symbolisms. Drawn by the love of life, they intuit the direction in which life is to be found. Endlessly repeated experience teaches us that life is only to be gained by those who do not cling too absolutely to it. Existence is worth having only under the condition that it not entail the loss of what outweighs mere survival. The truth of Christ is not a strange or unfamiliar piece of information. It is confirmation of what we have always known, as far back as we care to trace the human memory. What Christ adds is the full disclosure of its dimensions and the revelation of the divine outpouring that has made it all possible. This is reminiscent of the answer to Saint Thomas's question as to whether Christ is the head of all men, including those who have never heard of him (*Summa Theologiae* III, Q.8, a.3). He answers with a resounding yes: that indeed it is Christ who provides the possibility of life for all human beings. In this book we will explore the way in which that affirmation might be reached by those for whom Thomas presumes to speak. It is only in this perspective that we can recognize the universality of the celebration of the third millennium of Christ.

Notes

1. The only thing on which considerable consensus exists is that the start of the third millennium will be 2001, the first year of the new century. This is not only because we number the beginning of a new cycle from the start of its first year rather than the last of the previous one, but even more because the Gregorian calendar took over the assumption of the preceding Julian system by numbering the birth of Christ as the year 1. There are no 0's in Roman numerals, a problem that even generated uncertainty for the Roman historians' reckoning of time from the founding of the city (*ab urbe condita*). Dionysus Exiguus (ca. 523), a Scythian monk in the Roman curia, took over the convention of reckoning the first year, *Anno Domini*, as 1. All of this presupposes that "Little Denis" was correct in his calculation of the date of the birth of Christ, an assertion that was even disputed in ancient times and with good reason. The gospel dating of Christ's birth during the reign of Herod the Great would fix the event as before 4 B.C., the year of Herod's death. Of course it is equally possible to consider the millennium as beginning not with the birth of Christ, but with the inception of his public ministry at age 30 or as the reign that begins with his resurrection in the year 33 A.D. It is

perhaps noteworthy that the Catholic Church has focused its attention less on the beginning of the new era as on the "Jubilee of the year 2000," which must be preceded by three years of preparation. See John Paul II, *Tertio Millennio Adveniente* (1994), which places its emphasis on the approach of the third millennium.

2. Despite the rationalist overtones of his essay, Stephen Gould exemplifies and explains the impossibility of shaking the sense of overarching significance attached to the millennium. See his accessible and informative *Questioning the Millennium: A Rationalist's Guide to a Precisely Arbitrary Countdown* (New York: Harmony, 1997).

3. Hayden Hewes, *Inside Heaven's Gate: The UFO Cult Leaders Tell Their Story in Their Own Words* (New York: Signet, 1997). Bill Hoffman and Cathy Burke, *Heaven's Gate: Cult Suicide in San Diego* (New York: Harper, 1997).

4. A good example of the difficulty is the recent spiritual autobiography of William F. Buckley, *Nearer My God: An Autobiography of Faith* (New York: Doubleday, 1997), which is articulate about all questions except the central movement of faith that inspires it.

5. The most encouraging recognition of the need to profoundly rethink the character of our civilization has been the encyclical *Fides et Ratio* (1998), in which John Paul II argues forcefully for the mutual interdependence of faith and reason, philosophy and revelation. So far it is a project of breathtaking ambition that has found only faint resonance within the hidebound intellectual framework of our time. But its conception and proclamation at the heart of the Church is surely indicative of deeper currents at work.

6. The great literary figures of our century, from Thomas Mann to Alexander Solzhenitsyn, have struggled mightily to lift the veil of forgetfulness of our historical unfolding. Among philosophers, none has focused more single-mindedly on the problem of balance in existence than Eric Voegelin. See his monumental *Order and History*, 5 vols. (Baton Rouge: Louisiana State University Press, 1956–87), especially volume 4, *The Ecumenic Age,* with its magisterial delineation of the tension between the spiritual exodus and the concupiscential exodus.

7. Socrates recognizes, in the *Apology*, "that the god alone is wise and human wisdom is of little worth" (23a). *Philosophia* was coined to

express this love of the divine wisdom by which humans became participants in it, but the limits of that participatory opening had still not been differentiated. Some, as Aristotle suggested, might become like gods while others sink below the human level to become like beasts. Participation in transcendent Being as a pure gift—a gift that makes all men radically equal in their helplessness—had still not been differentiated.

8. For a good, brief description of the problem of equivalences, see Eric Voegelin, "Equivalences of Experience and Symbolization in History" in Voegelin, *Published Essays: 1966–1985*, ed. Ellis Sandoz (Baton Rouge: Louisiana State University Press, 1990), 115–133. It is interesting that Voegelin's great meditation on the structures of compactness and differentiation was inspired by the example of Jean Bodin, who, at the height of the French wars of religion in the 1580's, wrote his dialogue between the world religious known as *The Colloquium of the Seven About the Secrets of the Sublime,* trans. Marion G. Kuntz (Princeton: Princeton University Press, 1975). The spirit inspiring Bodin's mystical acceptance is best captured in the letter he sent to Jean Bautru, acknowledging their religious differences but urging a mutual effort to transcend them. "From this one may learn that they are mistaken who think agreement on divine matters is necessary in a friendship. For even though Justice, one of the finest virtues, and the good faith between men in society which arises from it, scarcely seem able to exist without religion or dread of some divine powers, nevertheless, the strength and goodness of mens' natures are sometimes so great that they are able to draw together into mutual affection men who are unwilling and quarrelsome. . . . I had written to you in prior letters to this effect: do not allow conflicting opinions about religion to carry you away; only bear in mind this fact: genuine religion is nothing other than the sincere direction of a cleansed mind toward God." The letter is printed in Paul Lawrence Rose, ed. *Jean Bodin: Selected Writings on Philosophy, Religion and Politics* (Geneva: Droz, 1980), 79–81.

9. St. Paul establishes the pattern when he proclaims to the Athenians, in the significant location of the Athenian Areopagus, that the "unknown god" they worship is really the God revealed in Jesus Christ (Acts 17: 22–34). Justin Martyr affirmed in his *Apology* (c. 150):

"We are taught that Christ is the first-born of God, and we have shown above that He is the reason (Word) of whom the whole human race partakes, and those who live according to reason are Christian, even though they are accounted atheists. Such were Socrates and Heraclitus among the Greeks, and those like them. . . . Whatever has been uttered aright by any men in any place belongs to us Christians; for, next to God, we worship and love the reason (Word) which is from the unbegotten and ineffable God." See also the negative view expressed by Tertullian. *Documents of the Christian Church* ed. Henry Bettenson (New York: Oxford University Press, 1963), 5–6.

1

The Christian Enlargement of Reason

ONE MEASURE OF OUR DISORIENTATION is the degree to which even the most elemental concepts are misunderstood. What could be more familiar than "reason"? Our whole world seems to be based on rationality, yet we have only the vaguest sense of whence it derives or on what it depends. Like everything that is close at hand, we have difficulty distancing ourselves sufficiently to bring it into focus. Even to become aware of the need to understand it, to make the effort of standing apart from it, requires us to raise our gaze beyond the immediate preoccupations of our world. Reason must become a question to us. Enlarging our horizon sufficiently to make as familiar a conception questionable is already the crucial step. We have begun to view things from a different viewpoint. What that viewpoint is may for the moment be postponed, although it is worth a later return.

Philosophic Revelation

We may simply notice that reason, although a capacity common to human beings in every age, has a definite moment of self-discovery.[1] It is a differentiation of classical Greek philosophy, which is itself the fruit of a long unfolding pursuit of the divine ground.

A speculative, mystical quest for the *arche*, or source of all things, reaches its culmination in the revelatory outbursts of Parmenides, Heraclitus, and Xenophanes in the sixth century B.C. We can still detect the momentous character of the event in the exclamatory force of Parmenides's formulation "Is!" Being had reached its recognition within time. The intensity of the reality encountered can be measured in the symbols emerging from the experience. A definitive rupture had occurred between Being and non-Being, a category that would later be identified with the beings of changing existence. The difference between that which is and the manifold of things that flow through generation and perishing could not be more dramatically experienced. Its closest parallel must surely be the equally dramatic rupture in the Mosaic revelation of the abyss of divine transcendence enunciated by the "I Am" (Exodus 3:14). In each case, the order of the cosmos has been decisively severed from its divine Beyond.

Once Being has thus made its astonishing revelation, the correlative movement of wonder must turn toward the instrument by which the apprehension is made. Man discovers himself. More precisely, he discovers his *nous* or the point at which his speculative reach can transcend time in greeting the self-disclosure of transcendent *nous*. The astounding irruption of extra-cosmic Being carries along with it the no less astounding realization of the being in whom the awareness has emerged. We discover our participation in the radically transcendent perspective of Being. No longer bound to the flow of time—the inexorable march of generation and perishing—humanity is constituted by the glance of eternity beyond it all. From this illuminative core, the self-understanding of human nature unfolds into a wealth of definitional formulae. Their source is still visible in Aristotle's summary designation of man as a rational animal, or more correctly "the living being possessing *nous (zoon noun echon)*" (*Metaphysics*, 994b15). Continuity with the inexpressible transcendence of Being identifies the core. It is *nous*, or reason in this preeminent sense, that is the star by which mere *Logos* is guided. Discursive unfolding presupposes a point of reference from which it takes its start and toward which it makes its return.

Despite the degree to which the radiance of *nous* was soon covered over in Greek consciousness and in all subsequent understandings of rationality up to the present, the connection with a luminous source could never be eliminated. It is this that inspires the great modern efforts to lift the veil of forgetfulness from Being.[2] The suspicion cannot be dislodged that the bounded rationality of efficiency cannot be the ultimate source of illumination. Complaints about the iron cage of necessity cannot forever continue, without raising at least in passing the awareness of the perspective from which the complaint itself is lodged. Only from a vantage point beyond necessity can the limitations of instrumental rationality be recognized. As a result, we live in a world that is torn by the tension between the massively evident force of technique and the irrepressible awareness of the character of technique as such. However fleeting, the supra-technical vantage point is ineluctable. At its deepest level, our reason remains embedded in the illuminative encounter of *nous*. Reason is hardly reason without it.

Rather, reason is the truncated instrument now detached from the opening that constituted it. All the formal features remain in place, but they no longer have reference to the experiential context from which reason has emerged. The stage is set for the runaway elaboration of technology without reference to the good of its purported masters. To the extent that we are still capable of being stirred to consciousness of that gap, we have not entirely lost touch with the origins of reason itself. Its discovery is tied to the loving movement toward and self-disclosure of Being. The movement of recovery must involve a comparable reconnection with the source from whence we have been constituted. But it is not simply a matter of returning to the past of the Greeks. However enticing their sunny youthfulness, we are further separated by the infinitely greater depth of Christ. Our world has been marked by the impenetrable mystery of the cross and the resurrection, the epiphany of incarnate divinity. We cannot reverse course by ignoring the changes effected in our reality. It would certainly make philosophy a much tidier enterprise if we were allowed to overlook its expansion through revelation. This has been the long-standing preference of philosophy since the seventeenth century. But we are entitled to ask with Hegel whether it is faithful to the calling of philosophy itself?

We have only to consider the changed understanding of reason emerging from a Christian world. What Aristotle apprehended as the defining characteristic of human nature—the possession of *nous*—remained confined in reality to a small segment of the race. Those who possessed the full actuality of reason were a handful within the population of the polis, and one of the abiding problems of Aristotelian political thought centered on just this contradiction. If the polis existed by nature, why was it in principle incapable of effecting the fulfillment of most of the human beings who composed it? The response that those without the full possession of reason participated in it through subordination to the command of those who did possess reason went some way toward answering the objection. But it eventually fell short of the claim that the full range of virtues would be actualized in the polis. Even in the best constitution, the good man and the good citizen overlapped only in the case of the ruler (*Politics,* 1277b). For all others, down to the level of slaves, the virtues actualized were relative to their station. The universality of the life of reason seemed peculiarly attenuated.

Aristotle's human nature is perpetually on the verge of disintegrating into a variety of human natures. The *Rhetoric* was composed as a response to the situation in which the philosophic truth about man could no longer be presented in public. Instead, teleology had to be reshaped to accommodate the plurality of human types empirically present. We are pressed to wonder if Aristotle had a genuinely universal notion of human nature. Or was it a nature that applied only to the philosophic souls? If the latter, then what was their connection with the unphilosophic types and by what right did the philosophic truth claim to rule? Was there any way in which the philosophic differentiation of virtue was authoritative? In particular, how could the philosophic paradigm maintain its normativity for a nature that seemed so persistently and extensively incapable of recognizing it? Plato too struggled with the obstreperous human material of the polis, but it is only with Aristotle that the tensions become conceptual. His scientific interest brings the limits of the instruments of analysis to attention.[3]

Solutions that appear obvious to us remain unattainable within Aristotle's perspective. Despite his formidable intelligence, he cannot break through to a transcendent human nature and, as a consequence, struggles to fit such a conception within the boundaries of an intramundane order. It is a notable reminder, not of our own intellectual superiority, but of the greater philosophic differentiation from which we begin. Ours is no longer Greek philosophy, but the greatly expanded philosophic reach made possible through the advent of Christianity. Rather than argue about the possibility or impossibility of Christian philosophy, we ought to recognize more clearly the impossibility of philosophy today without Christianity. We are all Christian philosophers because that is what Greek philosophy has become in its succeeding differentiations. It is impossible to do philosophy today except in light of the Christian enlargements.[4] That is, of course, not the same as being a Christian, but it does raise interesting questions of the truth of philosophy, to which we will return.

For now, we need only recognize the extent to which our rationality is the fruit of differentiations beyond the range of Greek philosophy. We have no difficulty conceiving the universality of a human nature whose actualization remains as disturbingly narrow as it was in the days of the polis. Not only is talent still distributed parsimoniously within the species, but the number of fools in Aquinas's quip is depressingly infinite. Most of us fail to measure up even to the modest level of excellence attainable. For a great many, the blandishments of a consumer society prove too much. They succumb to the manifold addictions that define the Aristotelian "slaves by nature." Yet we have no difficulty in recognizing their common partnership in the human race. None are excluded. Our whole way of life is premised on the irreproachable dignity and worth of each one, a commitment most vividly expressed in the guarantee of liberty irrespective of conditions or consequences. Only lawbreaking justifies its suspension. Mere incompetence, as in the case of the mentally ill, must rather be weighed against the greater insult of deprivation of self-responsibility.

We are more capable of accepting the failure of self-actualization, not because we are more realistic, but primarily because we are more acutely aware of how much even the very best human beings fall short. A universally equal conception of human nature is more convincing to us because we do not have Aristotle's problem. We are not seeking to compress the transcendent finality of the person into the self-realizing citizen within time. As a result, we can more rationally acknowledge the situation of finiteness and failure that confronts human beings everywhere. It does not lead us to the distorting attempt to incarnate perfection within political reality, as with Plato, or to the increasing tendency for the categories of political science to dissociate from their referent, as with Aristotle. One should never forget that Aristotle's *Politics* was composed while the death knell of the polis was sounding. Despite its monumental analytic achievements, the limits of its rationality were increasingly apparent. Aristotle's problem was that the limits were ineluctable. Without the life of the polis, the life of human virtue (*arete*) was impossible.

It is the differentiation of the transcendent depth of each human life that unlocks the constraints on rationality. Without the burden of teleological fulfillment, politics can be analyzed on its own terms and the citizens are confirmed in their equal rational dignity. Not only can finiteness and failure be acknowledged without imbalance, but the darkness of evil can be confronted without dilution or diminution. The unintelligibility of evil is adverted within the classic analyses, most notably in Plato's incomparable depiction of the soul of the tyrant (*Republic*, Book VIII), but it is never confronted as an irremovable dimension of the human condition.

As a result, the portrait of the philosopher-king, or the statesman, can be presented as a savior figure securing order at least for the present cosmic aeon. We never arrive at the picture of radical suspicion that attaches to all human beings or at the awareness that it is precisely in the exercise of greatest nobility that the greatest temptations lie. Plato and Aristotle are often not far from such intimations, but they finally cannot break through because of the profound revision in philosophy such realizations would require. It is nothing less than the awareness of how far short every human being falls from transcendent divinity and how radically incapable we are of the redemptive restoration of all things to their divine source. As a result, reason is again confined through its incapacity to apprehend the full irremediability of the world it inhabits.

The enlargements of rationality we have mentioned, the recognition of the full universality of human nature, the removal of the burden of intramundane fulfillment, the equal distance of all human beings from divine perfection, and the ineradicable presence of evil in life all derive from the Christian differentiation. Nothing prevents their emergence from the background of classical or Hellenistic philosophy. Indeed, the universalistic aspects are already underway in Stoicism. But the full emergence of reason in this comprehensive sense—the one we recognize as our own—is peculiarly dependent on the epiphany of Christ. It is only through him that their full amplitude can be illumined. This is because it is only in the revelation of Christ that a central realization concerning order can be grasped. Nothing previously prevented such an apprehension, although the Hebrew prophets come strikingly close. However, all fell short of the radiant proclamation of the truth evident in him—that is, that participation in Being, the transcendent source of all, is attainable only through the gift of divine participation in human life. The encounter with Being, which was always sensed to depend entirely on the movement of Being toward us, is now acknowledged in its full ramification. Divinity is attainable only through the self-outpouring of divinity.

Conquest of evil and supersession of finitude in general is possible only through the redemptive suffering of infinite Being itself. Only such a one could reconcile the world with itself.

One does not have to be a Christian to acknowledge the logic of this recognition. It is quite possible to hold that such requirements are determinative while withholding the affirmation that they are fulfilled in Christ. In some sense, all of the world religions point in this direction. This is the sense in which they are all contained in one another. Of course, their divergences are also evident. But their disagreements are precisely over the degree to which such a common set of requirements are met by their respective claims. Inevitably, the differences extend even to how the expectations are to be framed, for there are no questions outside the traditions themselves. It cannot be denied that the preceding reflections point toward a Christian culmination, and there is no necessity to preempt the perspectives of the other spiritual traditions. All that needs to be noted is that the Christian differentiation provides an opening to the conversation, because it has extended the bounds of rationality emergent within the Greek philosophic discovery of *nous*. For the moment it is enough to take note of the degree to which the universally accepted conception of rationality remains dependent on these twin sources. In particular, the Christian extension of Greek reason remains definitive.

We will examine the consequences of this derivation of rationality from such illuminative experiences of Being later in the chapter. But first we must direct our attention to the conjunction of these two traditions—the Greek and the Judaic-Christian—on which our modern conception of rationality rests. Whether we subscribe to the Christian affirmation of the transcendent constitution of the human soul or not is less significant. What is decisive is our presupposition of it in practice. Without the acknowledgment of inexpressible personal depth, we would not be able to sustain a commitment to liberty as the indispensable principle, nor acknowledge our partnership in the open horizon of history with all human beings living and dead. In the absence of that transcendent openness, we would forever seek a finite realization within time. The result would be the elimination of the endless restless striving that is the essence of our historical unfolding. Indeed, by conceiving of ourselves entering a home within time, the perspective of history itself would fade into oblivion. How can time retain its significance when it is merely an anteroom to a perpetual present? Only if something of significance in itself is transacted within it does the dimension of history rise to consciousness. But, most of all, it is only in light of the transfigurative movement toward the Beyond that the full awareness of imperfection and the ineradicable taint of evil can be fully recognized. Preservation of a clear-eyed apprehension of ourselves and our place within reality is crucially dependent on maximal spiritual openness.

This is surely the sense of continuity that drew the world educated by Greek philosophy to follow the upstart figure of Jesus of Nazareth.[5] He pointed the way toward the further opening of the soul that had already begun within philosophy. There was still the lingering awareness of the character of philosophy as rooted in a spiritual outburst. Reason still carried the reverberations of its source in transcendent illumination, and philosophy was still not detached from its relation to the mystery religions. If anything the Hellenistic philosophic movements of stoicism and skepticism moved more explicitly within a religious orbit. But it was a spiritualization that was in danger of losing the great philosophic breakthrough to Being, of falling back into the preceding compactness of myth. Stoic hypostatizations and the inevitable skeptical responses were in danger of settling down as a permanent condition of inconclusiveness. It is a state all too familiar from the decline of philosophy to a mode of technical analysis in our own time. Nor is it accidental that stoical and skeptical alternatives have recurrently exercised their attraction at various points in our history. They represent the great alternatives within a philosophic differentiation in which tension toward the transcendent ground has eroded. It is no accident that our language of alienation, of anxiety, of boredom, and of irrational imbalance all derive from this setting. In the ancient world, the decline of philosophy was arrested by the advance in transcendence represented by Christianity.

Christian Expansion of Philosophy

It was an irruption that blew away the musty conventions of the school philosophies. But not because it was something radically new. Christianity's impact arose precisely because it was in continuity with the divine irruption at the heart of the philosophic breakthrough. It was a further revelation of the divine depth beyond the cosmos. Through Christianity, the break with the myth, which had begun with philosophy, became definitive. No longer could the cosmos itself be regarded as an adequate *eikon theou* or likeness of God (*Timaeus*). The only adequate intracosmic manifestation of God is God himself. This is the meaning of the epiphany of Christ. It is a recognition that the New Testament writers struggle to formulate, but it is the conviction whose significance pervades the good news. In Christ "the fullness of divine reality" (*theotes* of Col. 2:9) dwells bodily. Conventional formulae of "Son of God" did not quite capture the novelty of the experience, although they could readily be expanded to include it. Indeed, the extent to which Son of God has come to be exclusively applied to Christ is a measure of the extent to which this ancient symbol has been fully appropriated for its Christian culmination.[6] But it is in the gospel of John that we get the most theoretically self-conscious formulations. At the very beginning, Christ is identified with the *logos,* the word that was with God from the beginning and through whom everything was made. However, the denouement is when John appropriates the symbol of Exodus to identify who Christ is. The dispute with the Pharisees is the occasion for the full confrontation in which Jesus proclaims, "Before Abraham was, I AM" (8:58). The transcendent I AM of the Mosaic revelation has become incarnate within time.

Now, whether one recognizes Christ as God is a separate issue from the implications of such an acknowledgment. They are nothing less than the radical de-divinization of the cosmos itself. With the advent of Christ, the transcendence of God is fully differentiated because the insufficiency of all manifestations becomes inescapable. Only God can reveal God. This is, of course, an implication present from the very earliest glimpse of divine transcendence, but it does not become blindingly clear until the appearance of Christ. In him is beheld the depth of divinity that can have no other exemplar. The essence of transcendent reality has always been that it transcends all finite modes of expression, that it cannot be known through any immanent chain of events. Revelation is an irreducible component to all the transcendent illuminations, because Being can only be known insofar as it opens itself in freedom toward man. There is nothing that can be done from the human side to reach up toward it. But the utter ineluctability of this condition had never been fully differentiated. At some level, it required the advent of the divine fullness within time to make the distance of all finite reflections unmistakable. This is why, after Christ, there is no other mediator between man and God.

The break with the cosmos, begun in philosophy and the other revelatory symbolisms, is carried to its conclusion in Christianity. Not only are the intracosmic divinities regarded as unseemly, but they are utterly shorn of their reality. The opening of the soul in partaking of transcendent life reaches its unambiguous conclusion as the movement toward eternity occupies the foreground. The consequent relativity and sense of finitude attaching to all immanent reality is the final elaboration of the impulse that began with the discovery of a life beyond the political. Now the whole world is apprehended in its factual contingency, both natural and political, and we are on the verge of a fully analytic perspective on reality. The discovery of reason is confirmed when it is anchored definitively in the awareness of its transcendent source. No longer a momentary glimpse precariously at the source of reason, now transcendent Being is differentiated in a way that is not easily dislodged. The advance in differentiation of Greek philosophy is rendered definitive.

At the same time, the deadweight of the partial breakthroughs of philosophy are finally lifted. The philosophic theophany had broken the compactness of the intracosmic myth and, with it, the cohesiveness of the particular political community. It was not only the ecumenic empires of Persia, Macedonia, and Rome that caused the demise of the polis. A broader process of spiritual detachment had loosened the cohesion of the town civilization of the whole Mediterranean area. Yet the movement toward universality had not differentiated a universal community beyond the order of the political. The impulse of universality had been stillborn because it lacked the full eschatological differentiation of membership in a community of mankind that transcends time. That perspective became evident only with the opening of the full relationship of man with the transcendent God who enters time to redeem and restore it to himself. It was as if the blinders had been removed from the intuited philosophic truth and the structure of existence could be beheld in the clear light of day. To the extent that Christianity is in this sense the culmination of the theophany of philosophy, it is perfectly legitimate to read Plato and Aristotle with Christian eyes, so long as we also remain aware of what we are doing. Justification rests on the degree to which Christianity is the truth of philosophy.

The common core consists in the movement toward spiritual perfection, not as an achievement or a reward, but as an existential reality. It is *areie,* or virtue in the classical sense, the full excellence of a human being. This is the aim of the *Nicomachean Ethics* and the principal source of its appeal. Conformity to law or to convention is left far behind in this testament to the life of the soul formed by love of being in the most comprehensive sense. Discussion of particular virtues always remains secondary to evoking the nobility of soul by which the life of virtue as a whole is ordered. This is why such central importance is placed on certain human types—the *spoudaios* (mature man), the *megalapsychia* (high-minded man), and the *phronimos* (man of practical wisdom). The particular virtues they embody at any given time are of less importance than their constant exemplification of an orientation toward Being. This is why, in the final book, Aristotle declares most clearly what he has hinted at all along: that such a life is divine. It is not necessary to decide whether it is itself divine or the most divine part of us, for what is certain is that it is the highest reality of our experience. We know it as a movement toward the divine. To express this existential increase as an active process, Aristotle coined the term *athanatizein,* or "to immortalize" (*Ethics* X,7). It is the growth beyond the human stature toward Being.

The *Nicomachean Ethics* is the great culminating expression of philosophy as a way of life. In it, we behold the majesty of the philosophic sweep and its fallible limits. The latter are perceptible not because we have attained a superior philosophic vantage point from which to extend a critique, but because, whether Christian or not, we have inherited the further differentiation of virtue manifest within Christ. This is a point considered evident by such religiously suspect a figure as John Locke and even by an avowed anti-theist like John Stuart Mill.[7] The moral superiority of Christianity was and is its radiant center, not because of the merit of greater respectability, but because it constitutes the fullest realization of that transcendent life for which we thirst. Beginning in this life, Christianity deepens the Aristotelian immortalizing. It is already the taste of eternal life. Christianity extends the philosophic enlargement because it is primarily an advance in participation in Being.

This is most evident in the degree of awareness of our incapacity in light of the fullness of Being. We can do nothing of our own efforts to merit the grace of Being, which would remain forever beyond were it not for the divine outpouring that draws us up in love of itself. Christianity is the fullest account of the movement toward Being because it is the one most forthcoming about the necessary structure involved. Transcendent reality is out of the reach of our finite efforts; it can only be entered as the pure fruit of grace from the divine side. Besides rendering the relationship transparent, this illumination has the additional consequence of eradicating the last vestiges of pride within the human soul. It is not coincidental that humility plays a more prominent role in Christian than in Greek experience. Humility is the fundamental attitude of a human being before the transcendent presence, once he or she becomes aware that everything, even the searching openness in love of the divine grace, is itself the result of grace. We have nothing of our own. We bring nothing to the encounter but our nakedness, and even its discovery has been given to us. Such an orientation is more transcendent because it has uprooted even the last vestigial remains of selfishness.

More aware of the hidden recesses of evil within itself, the Christian soul has more fully differentiated its reliance on transcendent goodness as its only refuge. As a result, it is better equipped for the struggle against evil, both within and outside of itself, as well as with the vicissitudes of historical existence as a whole. What is its response? Nothing less than uniting itself with the transcendent self-sacrifice of Being itself. Christ's overcoming of sin and death is achieved through utterly uniting himself with the Father, an outpouring of self that absolutely rejects any hint of rebellious self-reservation. It is a sacrifice of transcendent perfection that was only possible for Being itself. The divinity of Christ, it has long been recognized by the Church, is established less by the miracles than by the supreme silent dignity of the passion narrative. At the heart of the Christian revelation is the recognition of transcendent love as the means by which evil is overcome within each human soul and within the cosmos as a whole.

Again, it is a separate issue whether one recognizes Christ as the one in whom transcendent Love is incarnate. What cannot be disputed is that this is the claim of Christianity and that it has shed its radiance on the direction implicitly present in Greek philosophy as well as in the other revelatory traditions. The recalcitrance of the human material composing society was the central problematic of philosophers and prophets. How could this intractable humanity be reconciled with the order of Being irresistibly present within their experience? They struggled in different ways with the contradiction between a divinely willed order and an impossible human material. The clash that occurred within souls formed by transcendence was unfolded in various directions, from Plato's efforts to reform the polis to Aristotle's detached analysis of the polis straining against its nature, from the apocalyptic judgments of Jeremiah to the visionary reconciliations of Isaiah's Suffering Servant. Only in the latter do we get a glimpse of the Christian solution. It is man's participation in the divine suffering of evil, but not yet God's participation in the human suffering. The advent of Christ is the illumination that they are one.

From then on, it is apparent that the transformation of this recalcitrant reality is the work of the mysterious suffering of evil by transcendent reality itself. Not only does this provide the best practical prospect of evoking change in hardened human hearts, but it is already one with the redemptive transfiguration of the cosmos as a whole. The former element is well recognized. We have the Socratic refusal to participate in lawbreaking as the means of effecting good in the polis (*Crito*). He is as close as it was possible for a philosopher to come to the figure of the Suffering Servant. Moreover, it was a role self-consciously chosen in the realization that his individual suffering would constitute a transformative force within the sensitive souls of the next generation. There is a faith in the underlying order of justice of the cosmos whose emergence is best guaranteed by resolute abstention from injustice. But this is still not the recognition that the suffering of the philosopher is already the means of effecting that transformation. The dimension of redemption has not yet been differentiated, because it is still seen largely in its human context. Human suffering is not yet comprehended as the gift of participation in transcendent suffering. When that occurs, we obtain the assurance of its transfigurative effect, irrespective of the paucity of historical consequences. The light of eschatological transformation irradiates the historical process.

It is this conviction that sustains the heroic endurance of disorder, which is the most effective means of overcoming it. Reason would lead us to recognize the power of the Socratic witness, but the recognition of its redemptive effect raises it to a new level of conviction. No longer burdened by the anxiety of consequences, we are confirmed in the patient endurance of suffering in the face of failure. Once the eschatological perspective is opened, we can behold the full stature of finite actions. They are not measured in relation to mundane success or failure, to the efficacy of efforts to realize the transcendent truth of existence. Rather, they are recognized in their true character, *sub specie aeternitatis*. In the most crucial dimensions, they are not actions within time at all, but points of intersection with the timeless Being that has already accomplished its conclusive effect. The continuing resistance of temporal reality is not threatened with violence or apocalypse, but is disclosed in its true significance. It is the chrysalis of time that scarcely suspects the reality emerging from its dissolution. Discovery of the full transcendent character of temporal action occurs only when the full participation of God in temporal existence is disclosed.

Undoubtedly, this differentiation contains a danger of even greater imbalance. It is no accident that apocalyptic, gnostic, and revolutionary movements have swirled around Christianity and the other transcendent faiths of Judaism and Islam since their beginning. However, before addressing the peculiar challenges arising from the maximal differentiation of transcendence, it is essential to become clear about the gain in rationality that it represents. Otherwise, we will be tempted to trade a reduction in rationality for a reduction in tension. There are no such third alternatives. We cannot be fully rational if we have withdrawn from the full acknowledgement of our humanity. The secret is to recognize the self-sustaining attraction of the more expansive participation in Being. A heightening of the tension of the mystery of existence may be the cost, but it is more than compensated by the greater attunement to divine life that has become possible. What had previously only been glimpsed beyond the cosmos now invites us to full participation. A deepening of mystery coincides with a vastly more substantive assurance of Love. Besides, we have no alternative.

We cannot revert to a diminished conception of reason, no matter how difficult we may find the burden. In many respects, this might be considered the core of the modern problematic. We cannot abandon the achievement of rationality, but we find it difficult to sustain the Christian tension of existence that supports it. The irresolvability of the situation creates the modern dynamic in which a rich succession of substitute spiritualizations fail to meet the criteria of reason. They fall short of the full amplitude of reason differentiated within the Christian context, which is nothing less than the elevation of human action to the realization of its transcendent significance. No longer confined to its intramundane setting, human action, within the perspective of Christianity, takes its ultimate reference from beyond space and time. Each individual action derives its significance not from the scale of historical achievements, but from the extent to which it has remained faithful as the vessel of transcendent goodness. It is the perspective of the one just man through whom the whole city is saved.[8] Of course, pragmatic efficacy still remains important—no common order could be created without it—but the measure of consequences ultimately remains the degree to which an order of transcendent truth has been created within its members. No other measure counts because we recognize human beings as transcendent in their dignity. Through the actions of each one, the world is lost or saved. What they do outweighs history itself. In this sense, it is within the Christian differentiation that tragedy is supremely possible. We behold the possibility of the incalculable gain or loss of a soul. Christ is the one in whom the openness toward Being becomes fully transparent, just as he is the one in whom the condition for its realization has occurred.

In other words, the drama enacted through our lives is a transaction beyond all worldly considerations. Our capacity to order the world, from morality to manipulation, derives from our location beyond it. We can detach ourselves from every mundane content. This is the realization forgotten in an age of technology that, as Heidegger so constantly reminds us, must be remembered as the condition that makes the prowess of technology possible.[9] But it is the recognition of its spiritual precondition that gives this axiological detachment its existential solidity. Intellectual detachment is possible because our being is constituted by the openness to Being. We are free from any and all world content because we take our stand in the relation to transcendent Being. Our actions are in this sense not wholly our own because they are ultimately the refraction of Being itself moving through us. This is why we are engaged in a drama of which we are not the source, and we sense the importance of responding rightly to the pull of Being. What is at stake far transcends any immanent good. It is nothing less than the loss of our participation in Being. The soul of man is, as Dostoevsky noted, a battlefield in which God and the devil are contending. Our decisions are of surpassing significance because they carry a dimension that endures beyond the universe itself. This is the drama of existence that is glimpsed by the Greek discovery of Being, but that reaches its full transparence only in Christ. Not only do we participate in the divine drama of existence, but now it is disclosed that the divine submits to participation in ours as well.

Dissociation of Reason from Revelation

The limits of differentiation have been reached. Reason has emerged in its full stature once it has secured its transcendent standpoint on all reality. But immediately a new danger manifests itself. Having asserted its independence vis-à-vis beings, there is an abiding tendency to expand the attitude toward Being itself. We forget the experiences in which reason discovered itself, and therefore we lose touch with its own deepest reality. Forgetting that *nous* is not ours but that of *Nous* itself, we begin to act as if all might be comprehended from our finite perspective. This is a possibility inherent to the emergence from the start. So long as the constitutive reality of reason is derived from certain illuminative experiences of Being, there is a perennial danger that the result will be separated from the discovery itself. We might even regard it as the permanent temptation of the process of differentiation. What can be more natural than to focus on the instrument of rationality and allow the mystery of its origins to recede into the background? The tendency is almost irresistible when one considers the peculiarly episodic nature of the illuminative experiences and the more solidly definable dimensions of the unfolding of *Logos*.

The pattern is well established at the very inception of philosophy. Among the mystic philosophers—Parmenides, Heraclitus, and Xenophanes—there is a self-consciousness about the tendency of the experience to dissociate from the speculative results. It is noteworthy that they hit upon one of the solutions that has recurred all the way up to the present. They discovered the importance of aphorisms. It is largely because of this style of communication that we can reconstruct their thought so well on the basis of the few pages of fragments that have survived. But that was not the intention. Aphorisms, they quickly discovered, served two purposes. Their surface impenetrability put the listener immediately on notice that the thought would not yield its meaning without effort. It eliminated the inevitable demand for easy access. Secondly, the aphoristic style preserves as much as possible of the immediacy of the experience itself. At the very least, it is capable of drawing us directly into the heart of the existential events. This is a pattern paralleled by the Zen koans, whose purpose is identical. We should also not overlook the modern practitioners, especially Nietzsche, whose efforts are directed along the same road.

Literary cautions can of course only mitigate, not solve, the problem. The mystic philosophers were followed by a much larger group of sophists and others who reduced their speculative conclusions to premises for debate. Only a small trickle of the originating experiences made their way to form the classic philosophy of Socrates, Plato, and Aristotle. Despite their self-definition of philosophy in opposition to the sophists, the classic philosophers exemplified the same tendency to elide experiences and results. Socrates was so insistent on the living character of philosophy that he refused to write anything. Plato undertook the presentation of philosophic truth in the form of dialogues, all the while accompanying them with warnings not to mistake their content for the most important truth. Aristotle elaborated the philosophic meditations discursively and, in the process, established the mode of analysis of problems that has characterized most of its history. Only fitfully does philosophy in the postclassical period pull against the character of topical speculations to recall its genesis in illuminative experiences of Being. Were it not for the heightening of transcendent participation in Christianity, the connection might have been lost altogether.

From its beginning, Christianity stood a much better chance of preserving the relation to its experiential source. On the one hand, it was rooted in a more explicitly spiritual movement of response to the divine call; on the other, its definitive differentiation of transcendent Being had rendered a more inescapable consciousness of the relationship. It is no accident that Christianity formed Western and now modern civilization. While drawing the differentiations of Greek philosophy into itself, Christian culture could exercise its formative role because it had definitively distinguished the realms of being. No competition was possible once differentiation had reached its limits. The full flowering of rationality in its various directions had become possible, whether one contemplates the attitude toward politics, toward personal life, or toward nature. We cannot conceive of an approach to politics that would burden it with the impossible task of effecting the spiritual perfection of human beings. Nor can we regard as rational an expectation of happiness that refuses to countenance the finiteness and imperfection of all we experience. Nature, too, becomes a realm of detached investigation only when we have separated it out from the enchantment of a cosmos that is full of gods. The full operation of reason as we know it presupposes a differentiation of the realms of being that becomes possible only when the openness to transcendent participation has rendered them wholly distinct. The stability of this differentiation is attested by its durability even in a modern context largely shorn of its theological supports, although the strains are evident as the connection becomes ever more attenuated.

Struggle to Maintain Differentiation

Preservation of a culture of reason depends, as ever, on retaining the link to the differentiation of Being that has made it possible. Under the Christian impetus, this had its own special problems. The first was that the transcendent orientation of Christianity drew attention away from the creation of order in this life. Secondly, Christianity had emerged in a context far removed from the governing elites of the ancient world. Third, it took a considerable amount of time for the penetration of Christianity to become socially effective. Fourth, the world for which Christianity then became responsible was under irreversible forces of decline. As a consequence, it was a considerable period of time before the growth of a Christian society became a viable possibility. The necessary civilizational developments had to occur before the issue became explicit. An important turning point was in the papacy of Gregory the Great (590–604) when the project of forming a Christian society was first undertaken by the Church.[10] The coronation of Charlemagne on Christmas Day 800 was another pivotal moment. But the momentum in each case was retarded by the slow rate of civilizational growth and the recurrent collapses into disorder. It was not until the tenth century that one could discern the steady emergence of a fully Christian civilization. The process was considerably smoother in the East, where the transfer of the Empire had ensured a more continuous pursuit of the same ideal.

However, once Christianity had assumed this formative role, it quickly became apparent that the balance between transcendence and immanence was difficult to effect in practice. It was not just a matter of ensuring that the political leadership was in the hands of orthodox rulers. This was merely the starting point, which was well reflected in the emergence of two orthodox empires in the East and

West. These empires arose in marked contrast to the independence of the Roman Empire, which had always sought to subordinate Christianity to its own necessities. But the difficulties went deeper than institutional relationships. Even the periods of most harmonious cooperation between popes and emperors could not be viewed as providing a solution to the civilizational problem. The latter was nothing less than finding a balance between a transcendent differentiation of the order of being and its communication as the form of an immanent order of a civilization. Is a Christian commonwealth possible? On the surface, the answer would seem to be no.[11] Christianity is concerned with the movement toward eternal salvation; what interest it has in this world is very much subordinate to that principal focus. Yet it cannot afford to neglect the order of civilization, not only because it is the arena in which fidelity to the divine will is worked out, but also because it has been charged with the responsibility of differentiating the order of existence. Having advanced the movement of civilization to the point where it has become transparent for its transcendent goal, Christianity cannot turn its back on the process from which it itself has emerged and within which it continues to exist. Having absorbed the earlier shapers of civilization, the task has become its own.

In this regard, it has fared better than the evanescent success of the philosophic order or the hollow brilliance of the Roman world. Christian civilization became a durable form, with reserves of flexibility that have enabled it to weather the metamorphoses up to the present. Key to its durability has been its capacity to sharply define and transmit the originating experiences. Nowadays we think of the formation of canons and the formulation of dogmas as controlling devices by which institutions consolidate their power. No doubt that is a component, but it is by no means the most important aspect. Of far greater significance has been their role in preventing the substance of transcendent experiences from draining away in a profusion of different directions. The Church organized itself as the authoritative transmitter of revelation. Whatever the disputes at the margins, no one could be in doubt about the content of revelation, and as a consequence, a consensual community of believers could endure with impressive cohesion. Dogmas arise out of the devotional life of the Christian community, but they also play a role in preserving that life against confusion and distortion.[12] A stream of responsive participation in the revelatory experiences is carried forward. In this way, the authoritative core of order in transcendent Being exercises a formative influence within the life of reason in its manifold realizations. The protective role of faith eventually allowed the flowering of reason we recognize as the twelfth century renaissance.[13]

It was only as the success of this spiritual stabilization began to grow that the limits of the medieval synthesis began to become apparent. The Church began to experience increasing difficulties retaining the burgeoning devotional movements within the bounds of orthodoxy. It was no longer clear that they could be fitted within the model of a Christian commonwealth that included spiritual and temporal as cooperative powers of one order. Just the same pattern is evident in the Sacrum Imperium, which could no longer contain the rising forces of the new town civilization and the nation-states. Even the efforts that seemed most deeply attuned to the medieval ideal, such as the building of the great cathedrals, bordered on the shift into the construction of an intramundane spirituality. The medieval construction of heaven on earth could easily become so preoccupied with the terrestrial reflection that concern for the eternal became distinctly secondary.[14] That discernible tendency is why we recognize, in the High Middle Ages and its aftermath, the outlines of the modern world.

Why the evident stability of the structure of revelation could not be transferred to an enduring civilizational evocation is among the most central questions we still face. The instability points to the fluidity of all historical constructions that eventually renders every effort at congealment obsolete. But it also alerts us to a deeper realization. It is the character of all evocations of order rooted in experiences of transcendent Being to be unstable. No variation of balance between the transcendent absence

and its mundane presence can ever eliminate the eventual awareness of dissatisfaction. Balance is not a permanent achievement.
It is ever the fruit of struggle against imbalance. This applies
preeminently to the attempt to find a balance between the transcendent source and fulfillment of order as well as the necessity
of embodying its formative impact on life in the present. A transcendent civilization is inherently unstable. The medieval evocation of a sacred empire or Christendom is only one of the possible
variants. Our own modern secular silence about transcendence
might be viewed as an alternative and by no means a less worthy
articulation. So long as secular civilization avoids the dogmatic
assertion of its own completeness, it retains the lively possibility
of embodying most respectfully that which is most present by
its absence.

We will return to such suggestions later in the book. For now,
we need to understand more clearly why medieval Christian civilization proved so inflexible in face of the historical pressures that
seemed to be moving in such a mystical direction. Why were its
institutional expressions modified only through the violence of
rupture? Many factors clearly determine the limits of civilizational
flexibility, including the nature of the demands for modification
themselves. However, if we limit our concern to the spiritual
dimensions, we will be closer to an understanding of the intrinsic
forces at work. For what is most striking is that even the greatest
minds of the period, despite a multiplicity of attempts, failed to
generate the kind of reorientation that would have been needed to
accommodate the very different world emerging. Saint Thomas is
clearly the preeminent example. As the creator of the greatest
medieval synthesis, he is the one in whom the expectation of
elaborating the relationship between reason and revelation runs
highest. Certainly, no one can fault the magnitude of the effort
undertaken in his vast *Summa Theologiae*. But the results fell short
of the transformation of Christian reason that might have occurred. It was the last great synthetic expression of the medieval
age, not the opening of the modern.

What makes both the Thomasic incompleteness and the failure of any subsequent efforts to extend it all the more disappointing is that it contained the promise of such fulfillment. Saint Thomas's organizing principle—that grace does not abolish nature, but brings it to perfection (*Summa Theologiae* I Q.1, a.8)—is capable of elaboration in the direction that discloses its continuity. His conception of nature as a separate, but not a closed, realm is susceptible of such unfolding. It would have been possible to reveal the extent to which nature is constituted by this openness toward grace and to depict the impossibility of ultimately conceiving of nature outside of that context. The conception of nature on its own terms is certainly one of the central consequences of the Christian revelation, and Saint Thomas is notable in his fidelity to the recognition of autonomous natural finalities. But he fails to enter more deeply into the natural openness toward grace, except to note the impossibility of concluding that it is destined for ultimate frustration. We never apprehend the longing for grace from the natural side; it is always read into the situation from the supernatural perspective. As a result, Saint Thomas is lauded as the defender of natural autonomous reason, which, we later realize, is only connected by a slender thread to its revelatory context. We have not succeeded in establishing that the natural order flourishes only in continuity with its revelatory source.

The problems are evident in Saint Thomas's meticulous analysis of natural virtue. Is grace necessary, he asks, for the attainment of natural virtue (*Summa Theologiae* I-II Q. 109, a.2)? The response must obviously be no; otherwise, the idea of an autonomous order of nature falls apart. Grace cannot be necessary for the ordinary operation of nature. But Thomas goes on to distinguish between nature prior and subsequent to the Fall. While virtue could be acquired through our natural efforts before the Fall, afterwards it functioned only imperfectly. Thus, while there was no hindrance in principle to the performance of virtuous acts and the consequent acquisition of a virtuous habit, in practice the fallen condition of nature meant that failure would be a recurrent unavoidable feature. After the Fall, grace became necessary, not for the exercise of any specific virtue, but for the realization of the life of virtue as a whole. It was a subtle and equanimous analysis. But it left shrouded in mystery the process by which the advent of grace permeates and transforms the natural order without suspending it. What is missing in Saint Thomas's magnificent elaboration is a vision of nature transparent for the divinity toward which it points. The accent is inclined to fall on its separability from the divine and, despite the awareness of incompleteness and failure on its own, we are inclined to take our chances on a more clearly autonomous mode of operation. Reassured of its ultimate reliability, we opt to rely on nature as it is.

The reason for the relatively external perspective proffered by Saint Thomas lies in the dogmatic encrustations with which revelation itself had been surrounded. Necessary as this protection was, and vital to the secure transmission of the transcendent order of Christianity, a price was paid in limiting the openness to experiential movements from the natural side of existence. The content of revelation had congealed in its definitive structure. Not only was it increasingly difficult to reconstruct the dynamics of experience through which it had emerged, but it was no longer possible to discover the bridge by which the openness of the natural order for its supernatural fulfillment might be apprehended. St. Thomas's assurance of their reciprocal openness still fell short of the concrete disclosure of their mutuality. Mystical theology was increasingly separating from dogmatic theology. The best that a theological mystic like Saint Thomas could do was elaborate the content of his vision in the conceptual language of distinctions. He could not find the way of drawing us directly into the living unfolding of the meditative movement itself. As a result, his brilliance was expressed in a fragile synthesis that quickly fell apart after his death.

The danger of the equitably distributed balance of nature and grace was sensed even in his own day. It was the possibility that the sphere of autonomously guaranteed reason would assert its independence of all revelatory tradition. The bestowal of even

conditional independence on reason ran the extreme risk of promoting the demand for its complete liberation. This was the danger lurking in the background of condemnations and controversies
ever since the arrival of Aristotle on the medieval scene. In his
largely naturalistic philosophy, Aristotle represented the greatest
threat to the hegemony of Christian revelation as the controlling
horizon of meaning. Thomas was virtually alone in his heroic
effort to absorb and demonstrate the compatibility of Aristotelian
reason with the Christian *ratio*. Indeed, it is hard to see how the
integration of Aristotle could have been regarded without suspicion given that Thomas had not broken through to the revelatory
derivation of *nous*. For all its careful placement within a summa
of Christian theology, natural reason still remained unabsorbed in
its separateness. Ironically, it was the very success of Thomas's
domestication of Aristotle as "natural reason" that proved the
limits of his absorption within a Christian framework.

All of this was dimly sensed in the dismissal of the Thomasic
synthesis of the succeeding generation. The fourteenth century was
dominated by the *devotio moderna,* in which Christian piety underwent a striking intensification, and the *via moderna,* in which
reason was set free to embark on the empirical investigation of the
world. The nexus between the two is the emergence of nominalism, which can only properly be understood in light of its theological motives. Nominalism was not just a chastening of the ambition
of reason in relation to the problem of universals. It was a recognition of the inability of the Christian revelation to absorb the
burgeoning rational energies and the sense that their endowment
with a coequal stature with revelation ultimately threatened the
latter. Philosophical disputes could readily become disruptive of
the coherence of Christian theology. In case of a conflict between
the two, one must always opt for revelation as the superior source
of authority. The serene confidence of Saint Thomas, in the unity
of truth that rendered incompatibility between the two impossible,
had disappeared. Now a willingness to surrender the authority of
reason seemed the most reliable means of securing the unques-

tioned truth of revelation. It was in this context that the self-contraction of reason to the investigator of empirical relations was readily accepted. Gone was the prospect of reason as a mode of wisdom guiding us toward the ultimate truth of reality and even to the very threshold of revelation itself. However, the more modest role of investigating individual beings could gladly be accepted because it went together with a flowering of devotional experience and a consolidation of ecclesiastical organization. Theology alone possessed the authoritative divine guidance, and truncated reason could no longer prove a hindrance or a help.

We recognize the outline of our own world in the fideistic nominalism of the late Middle Ages. Socially, economically, politically, and culturally, it was a period of bursting vitality. Its energies were by no means confined to the mundane sphere, but were extensively translated into new spiritual movements that the Church proved increasingly incapable of absorbing. One has only to contemplate the parochial Christianity of *Piers Plowman* to observe the disintegration of the universal Church at the experiential level. It was the century of the great mystics—Suso, Tauler, Ruysbroeck, the *Theologia Germanica,* and *The Cloud of Unknowing.* The displaced classes of the new towns proved a ripe breeding ground for the appeal of millennarian and mystical anarchists, and peasant rebellions were fed from the same expectations of a universal spiritual renovation. Control of the spiritual initiative slipped away from the Church, despite its formidable organizational achievements, and was free to be captured by figures with the requisite skill and daring, whether saintly monks, itinerant preachers, or the national monarchs. It is the strange combination of rigor and submissivism we recognize from our own naive technicism. Revelation had established its unquestioned primacy as the only medium of authoritative knowledge about reality, but it had lost the capacity for a rational unfolding of the mysteries it preserved. The stage had been set for the increasingly subjective expressions of faith by which it eventually erodes its title to any publicly accessible claim to knowledge. Like so many of the triumphs of the time, it proved hollow. Exclusive preeminence for revelation ultimately pointed toward its alienation from the world of verifiability. Severance of the connection with the world of rational elaboration meant that revelation could eventually be discarded as authoritative knowledge. The only tenuous connection remaining was the fideistic leap of faith, which was tantamount to the admission of absolute subjectivity. On the other hand, the liberation of reason from its revelatory context proved equally illusory. No longer restrained by the pressure of a revelatory tradition, it was certainly free to explore the empirical factuality at will. But without a mooring in transcendent Being, the analyses of science aggregated to no higher meaning. Only with the later expansion of technology did the hollowness of the situation become apparent. It was possible to become equipped with a formidable control over the domain of nature, but, without an ultimate point of reference for the whole, we radically lack a sense of direction. Science could no longer deliver on its implicit promise of wisdom, and religion had ossified into the dogmatic boundaries incapable of reflective engagement with the world.

Nominalism, whose deepest impulse lay in the urge to protect the content of revelation from the unravelling effects of rationalism, had severed the connection so vital to each of them. Of course, the nature of the civilizational schism does not become apparent until much later. This is why it is necessary to introduce the extrapolations toward the present in order to appreciate the full character of the nominalist rupture. To the contemporaries, and even to later historians, the combination of nominalism and mysticism appears almost as a more viable form of the medieval synthesis. Having abandoned the riskier enterprise of reconciling Aristotle and Christianity, the nominalists could claim to have reached a more stable evocation of the relationship between reason and revelation. What could be clearer than the acknowledgement of their strictly separate spheres? The absence of a classic philosophic inquiry, with all of the dangers of the meditative opening toward Being, could hardly be missed. It was enough that philosophy had been domesticated to the level of a technical analysis of problems. No pressing need suggested its expansion to the level of a comprehensive meditation on the order of reality. Revelation had already occupied that space, and it could be more securely held so long as it no longer faced the prospect of competition from rival sources of inquiry. Not only did the arrangement have the virtue of simplicity, but it also promised the incalculable benefit of stability. The tension between these millennial symbolisms and, more importantly, the tension within each of them between illuminative experiences and the articulation of meaning had been resolved.

Testament to its stability is the degree to which this nominalist arrangement still constitutes our world. It is the unexamined background for all our discussions. Faith is one realm, and science is another. Their heteronomous horizons may touch on one another, but there can be no substantial involvement between them. This is how modern science works, confident in its absolute autonomy and self-confident in the defense of its legitimacy. It knows it does not have to provide answers to the ultimate questions of the meaning of existence and is therefore released to roam as it will over the empirical details of reality. By contrast, religion occupies the space that is beyond science. Its connection with reason is increasingly tenuous, as it knows it does not have to answer for the relationship to rational inquiry. Instead, the dimension of feeling is elevated to the highest degree. Experience alone is fraught with the danger of emptiness and, in order to draw back from the abyss, religion gravitates toward fundamentalism and authoritarianism. The arrangement endures because it is so stable. All parties see their concerns best addressed. All, that is, but one.

Omitted is man the questioner. We cannot so readily shelve the movement of reason toward Being, nor can the meaning of revelation be so easily abandoned to declamations of texts or authorities. The separation between reason and revelation cannot be achieved so simply. The origin of reason in the theophanic illumination of *nous* and the unfolding of revelation in the direction of noetic order prevent their easy disjunction. They cannot be separated because that would be to go exactly counter to their reality. No matter how much the untidiness of their interaction might be relieved by such a move, reality cannot be ignored for long. To accept the severance of reason from revelation would be tantamount to their destruction, as has been suggested by the extrapolative sketch above. The crisis of the modern world is at once a crisis of the place of reason *and* of revelation in the order of things. Apart, they cannot determine their place in the world. Therefore, it is not surprising to discover that the nominalist and all subsequent disjunctions of reason and revelation were more apparent than real. The deeper reality of the nominalist bifurcation was that it enabled a synthesis to be sustained at a less contestable level. We are so accustomed to think of the age of nominalism as the great collapse of the more ambitious Thomasic synthesis that we fail to notice the extent to which it represented itself a new evocation of the rational-revelatory order of the West.

A similar oversight afflicts our portrait of the modern world that emerges from it. We all too readily assume that the virtually absolute separation of faith and science we know in our own day was a necessity inexorably present from the start. As a result, we fail to recognize the degree to which the modern world was constituted by its movement through a succession of ever less overt evocations of the continuity of reason and revelation. Even today, we hardly live in a secular civilization. It is rather a secular civilization whose sustaining impulses all derive from a region beyond the limits of mundane calculation. It is only when we contemplate the animating wonder behind our vast scientific enterprise, reflect on the unattainable longing that drives our whole technological development, or focus on the conviction that each human being is a center of the universe and more valuable than the whole in him or herself that we realize the extent to which we still live in a world structured by the opening toward transcendence. Then we gain a perspective on our connection with the medieval aspiration to create a transcendentally derived civilization within time, as well as all the successor attempts in between.

We see the modern world and its nominalist predecessor not so much as a disruption of this project, but as its continuation under different conditions and with different means. They are successive attempts at sustaining the spiritual consensus on which the possibility of the life of reason always rests. We have less difficulty understanding the dabbling of the Renaissance scientists and artists in Neoplatonic and Hermetic speculations or considering their Erasmian hope for a humanist renewal of Christianity all that far-fetched. We can look upon the Reformation, which splintered the medieval Church, as at root the return to a pristine Christianity whose truth would be transparent to all. This continues to be the animating conviction behind the great search for political consensus that found its most evocative formulation in the Latitudinarian Christianity of John Locke. There is no need to regard the various revivals of natural law, whether by the Thomists of the sixteenth century or the Calvinists of the seventeenth, as being in any way disingenuous. They were all deeply felt propulsions toward the core of the revelatory illumination that could command unquestioned response in an increasingly centrifugal world. Can we conclude they were wrong? Can we lightly dismiss their achievement of heightening and expanding the notion of human rights as the indispensable core of an acceptable political order? Reservations are clearly in order regarding the late modern period. But it is difficult to deny that the singular achievements of the emergence of mathematical natural science and the universalization of natural rights remain linked to the transcendent arc defined by the Christian revelation.

Even in the later phase of modernity, we might, despite the horrors reaped in our own century, more fruitfully regard the outcome as tragic rather than wholly evil. If we consider the aspiration for contact with the revivifying spiritual sources as the core of the romantic project, it is difficult not to regard it as the expression of a Christian longing in a context in which the Christian symbolizations have become opaque. That the longing is pursued in a direction that is no longer Christian is not the essential component.

What matters is that it is guided by the same impulse toward transcendent Being. Hegel was perhaps the last great thinker to try to unite the impulse with its Christian differentiation, but in his hands the synthesis fell apart under the pressure to overreach the limits of the Christian experience. Only the Promethean drive toward absolute knowledge remained, becoming the motivating center of the Marxian, Comtian, Bakunian, and Freudian projections of universal emancipation. In the hands of the secular messiahs, the spiritual covering has become threadbare. It awaited only the forthrightness of a Nietzsche to pronounce its mendacity. The twentieth century has provided the practical confirmation of his philosophical insights. When the impulse toward transcendent Being has become utterly disconnected from its Christian moorings, the result is not the attainment of secular transfiguration. It is the unlimited cruelty of idealism without mercy.

The totalitarian convulsion of the twentieth century stands as the most dramatic evidence of the connection between reason and its ordering revelation. In its absence, we become aware of the indispensability of the link. Reason is no longer reason when it is divorced from its source in relation to transcendent Being. Far from being an option of spiritual preference or a matter of largely historical interest, we begin to suspect that reason can never quite function as it should when it has lost contact with the theophanic events. We still harbor some illusion that we might be able to get along without confronting the full implications of the situation. Such illusions often die hard, especially if one considers they have been nurtured in one way or another for over two millennia. The medieval world sought to bring the revelatory events and the rational unfolding into conjunction, but without fully confronting the revelatory character of reason itself. It might be viewed as an incomplete correlation. The modern period has been marked, on the one hand, by a reduction in the demand for synthesis to what can be publicly intuited and, on the other, by a much more grandiose attempt to evoke a new intramundane source of revelation that would abolish the tension with reason altogether. We still live by virtue of the residue of the less ambitious latitudinarian approach, while the later ideological messianism has self-destructed. But we lack a fully self-conscious awareness of our predicament. We continue to generate a multiplicity of attempts at establishing an intramundane order without transcendence and are mildly surprised to discover our way blocked by a series of dead ends. This curiously poignant fixation is what defines the postmodern era. We know enough to recognize that modernity in its most militant inspiration is over, but not enough to find our way through to a wholly transparent evocation of our situation.

The resumption of that meditation is clearly the burden of a book that has the presumption to direct itself toward the meaning of the third millennium. In such a setting, we can perhaps cling to a certain hope that the scale of the moment might lift our horizons beyond the conventional. In place of the received fixities, we might venture to address the central civilizational question, whose full dimensions have not been confronted since the ancient world. Two millennia of Christianity have grappled with it—not unsuccessfully, but variably. There is no expectation that this attempt will yield anything like a definitive or even adequate account of it. A suggestion of a "solution" to the relationship between reason and revelation is suspect in principle. This was the overreaching of the Hegelian expedition. To adequately comprehend the relationship between them would be to transcend the perspective available through them. It would be to step outside of the human condition. There are, in other words, good reasons for considering the inter-relation between theophany and *Logos* inexhaustible as a problem. But we also have good reasons for expecting that our present circumstances and perspective contain the possibility of a profound rethinking of the relationship that is at the heart of our civilization.

This is not in any sense a historiographic enterprise. Familiar as such approaches are and useful in their own way, they do not bring us into the nature of the reality itself. They presuppose that everything worth knowing can be obtained by standing outside of the material of study. It is the conceit that we can dispense with the perspectives offered by the subject itself. The result is, of course, that we are left only with our own external viewpoint on what we are studying. We do not learn anything from it. Here, our interest is quite different. We cannot afford to withhold ourselves from the illumination that may be cast by revelation and reason. That is our concern as we consider them anew at the dawn of the third millennium and recognize the degree to which we are still structured by the interaction between them. Our perspective may be historical, but our interest is contemporary. We want to discover the sources of ourselves. That is why we should enter upon the more unconventional attempt to think through the relations that form the unexamined parameters of our thought world. In the end, we cannot avoid availing ourselves of the opening toward Being, which, even in a reflected mode, is all that is available to a more historiographic account of the thoughts about Being. The reason-revelation tension must finally be examined because it is our own.

No higher perspective is available to us. We cannot dispense with theophanic experiences, because they are finally the source of our own reason. Reason leads us toward the experience of Being, although it cannot disclose it, and is guided by the order flowing from the relationship. What we call reason is reason only to the extent that it is rooted in that which is beyond itself. All other senses are derivative and dependent on that connection. Instrumental reason lacks any ultimate means of guidance; in the blankness of nihilism, it is incapable of seeing. The essence of reason is its orientation toward Being. The great difficulty is that Being cannot be reached through ratiocination. Reason may be drawn in that direction by the intuitive sense of transcendence, but that falls far short of the disclosure of Being. Only the revelatory opening of Being itself can draw us into the opening. This is the differentiation of Christianity in which the revelation can no longer be mediated by a divine man, but only by a human God. Only the fullness of transcendent Being can reveal Being within time.

The civilizational significance of Christianity is that it secures the source of rationality, on which all order depends. Christ is the one in whom the transcendent order is effected within immanence. He is therefore the way by which all others have access to the order of Being within time. Not only is he the center through which transcendent order is transmitted to this world, but he differentiates the unsurpassable structure of reason in which all men share. In this sense, all men are Christians to the extent to which they recognize that their reason is not their own, but derives from its participation in divine *Nous*. Christ is the point at which the full meaning of that relationship is revealed—that is, that the attunement of reason toward eternal goodness, which appears to be the fruit of our efforts, is really the work of transcendent Love that pours itself out for finite creatures. Without the outpouring of transcendent Love, there would be no access to the guiding illumination by which reason is constituted. The Greeks understood the role of eros in unfolding the pursuit of the divine ground. What they did not differentiate is that the pursuit of transcendent Being would not be possible unless Being had already given itself to us. The Christian differentiation continues the Greek and other discoveries of transcendence to reveal the fullness of the mystery available to us. A civilization of reason is made possible only by a civilization of Love.

Notes

1. The story of the "birth" of reason has been told many times, yet its philosophic significance remains to be absorbed. See Bruno Snell, *The Discovery of the Mind in Greek Philosophy and Literature* (New York: Dover, 1982; original 1946); Werner Jaeger, *Paideia* trans. Gilbert Highet (New York: Oxford University Press, 1965); and *The Theology of the Early Greek Philosophers* (Oxford: Oxford University Press, 1947); Eric Voegelin, *The World of the Polis* (Baton Rouge: Louisiana State University Press, 1957). The fragments from the pre-Socratic philosophers are available in Diels-Kranz, *Fragmente der Vorsokratiker* (Berlin, 1954) and an English translation in

Kathleen Freeman, *Ancilla to the Pre-Socratic Philosophers* (Oxford: Oxford University Press, 1948).

2. Heidegger is the preeminent example. See his *Early Greek Thinking: The Dawn of Western Philosophy,* trans. David F. Krell and Frank A. Capuzzi (San Francisco: HarperSanFrancisco, 1975).

3. For a good account of the tensions, see Voegelin, *Plato and Aristotle* (Baton Rouge: Louisiana State University Press, 1957), Ch. 9.

4. Etiennne Gilson presented a now classic articulation of this insight in *The Spirit of Medieval Philosophy* (New York: Scribners, 1936).

5. Particularly useful in the vast literature on the relationship between Christianity and the Greco-Roman world are E.R. Dodds, *Pagan and Christian in an Age of Anxiety* (New York: Norton, 1965); Werner Jaeger, *Early Christianity and Greek Paideia* (Cambridge, MA: Belknap Press, reprint 1985); Charles Cochrane, *Christianity and Classical Culture* (New York: Oxford, 1957); Jaroslav Pelikan, *Christianity and Classical Culture* (New Haven: Yale, 1993); and Christopher Stead, *Philosophy in Christian Antiquity* (New York: Cambridge University Press, 1994).

6. The symbol "Son of God" goes all the way back to the Pharaoh, who is pronounced the firstborn of God, and in turn is replaced by Israel as the beloved firstborn under the new dispensation. See Voegelin, *Israel and Revelation* (Baton Rouge: Louisiana State University Press, 1956). For the broader Christological debates, see William Thompson, *The Struggle For Theology's Soul: Contesting Scripture in Christology* (New York: Crossroads, 1996).

7. Locke, *The Reasonableness of Christianity,* ed. George W. Ewing (Washington: Regnery, 1965); Mill, "On the Utility of Religion" in *Essays on Ethics, Religion and Society* in *Collected Works* vol. 10, ed. J.M. Robson (Toronto: University of Toronto Press, 1969).

8. For a modern expression of this biblical perspective, see Alexander Solzhenitsyn's luminous story, "Matryona's House" in *Stories and Prose Poems,* trans. Michael Glenny (Harmondsworth: Penguin, 1973), 9–47.

9. Heidegger, *The Question Concerning Technology and Other Essays,* trans. William Lovitt (New York: Harper, 1977); and *The Principle of Reason,* trans. Reginald Lilly (Bloomington: Indiana University Press, 1996).

10. Robert Markus, *The End of Ancient Christianity* (New York: Cambridge University Press, 1990).

11. "But there is absolutely no such thing under the Gospel as a Christian commonwealth." John Locke, *A Letter Concerning Toleration* (Indianapolis: Bobbs-Merrill, 1955), 43.

12. The process is masterfully recounted in Jaroslav Pelikan's *The Christian Tradition: A History of the Development of Doctrine,* especially vols. 1–3 (Chicago: University of Chicago Press, 1971–78).

13. R. W. Southern, *Scholastic Humanism and the Unification of Europe* vol. 1 (Oxford: Blackwell, 1995).

14. In general, see Norman Cantor, *The Civilization of the Middle Ages* (New York: Harper Collins, 1984), and Eric Voegelin, *History of Political Ideas,* vols. II and III, *The Middle Ages to Aquinas,* ed. Peter von Sivers, and *The Later Middle Ages,* ed. David Walsh (Columbia: University of Missouri Press, 1997–98). A striking example of the shift of emphasis toward the intramundane is the transference of trinitarian speculation toward history by Joachim of Flora, in which the age of Christ is to be replaced by a future age of the Spirit. Even such an orthodox thinker as Dante felt compelled to introduce the notion of progress toward a terrestrial paradise to complement and supplement the aspiration toward the eternal one.

2

The Schizophrenia of the Modern World

ALMOST FROM THE BEGINNING, the modern world has been a problem to itself. The self-consciousness of its designation as "modern" seems to invite speculation and uncertainty. By contrast, the medieval world had no such concern about its own meaning. "Middle ages" meant quite simply the period between the advent of Christ and the end of the world. It had nothing to do with our perception of the medieval as the period sandwiched between the ancient and the modern. Nor was it assimilated to the "dark ages," a conceit invented to reassure the enlightenment of its modernity. Secure in its status as the age between the definitive opening of revelation and its final consummation at the end of time, the medieval world could turn its attention to the task of living out its transcendent faith within the pilgrimage of time. It is only with modernity that the problem of the meaning of an age surfaces. A break has occurred that constitutes a new era within time, and attention naturally focuses on the meaning of this novel development. The question becomes so pervasive that we might regard the search for the meaning of modernity as its defining characteristic.

There is nothing unusual about our contemporary discussions of the nature of the modern or the postmodern world. Consciousness of epoch is a permanent preoccupation of modernity. What renders the debates interminable is the absence of any defining transcendent event by which the meaning of the age is constituted. Instead, we have a succession of immanent protagonists and events that rival one another in the unending struggle to define the meaning of the age. In place of a pivotal transcendent irruption, we have an endless stream of mundane irruptions that seek vainly to imprint their stamp on an age that ceaselessly flows away from them. There is a comic quality to the futile effort to command the tide of reality, but it is also susceptible to more deadly connotations. The impossibility of constituting an epoch of meaning from any mundane perspective has even today scarcely been recognized. The reason, however, is obvious. As soon as a fulcrum for the lever of meaning is located, the point from which control is to be exercised recedes away from us. Only what is outside of time can continuously provide the meaning of time without diminution. This is why, despite the intense consciousness of modernity as an epoch, it fails to identify any stable event from which its meaning can be derived. It is perpetually reviewing itself in search of the key that will unlock its meaning. Neither Renaissance nor Reformation, Enlightenment nor Revolution, have been capable of persisting as the overarching definition. Modernity, which began with the intense consciousness of epoch, seems fated to see itself evaporate in the flow of time itself. Nothing we do can save the modern self-understandings from their successive dissolution.[1]

All that remains as its defining feature is the consciousness of break. It is different from the medieval. The curious consequence of this structure is that the very effort to establish the distance of the modern world from its predecessor leans all the more heavily on the latter for its self-definition. Is it possible to be modern without consciousness of the medieval past? The contrast is indispensable. By establishing its independence from the framing context of revelation that constitutes the medieval order, the modern world fixes its contours. Modernity is rooted in the claim to the self-sufficiency of reason, outside of a revelatory context, as the source from which order can be created in the world. Revelation does of course continue, but now it is reached from the perspective of the individual subject whose assent of faith becomes the exclusive focus of attention. The perspective of finite subjectivity is primary. All evocations of an overarching meaning, whether spiritual or political, must first receive the assent of free individual judgment. Institutional carriers of meaning, including even the Church, have their authority mediated through the exercise of free subjective assent. In a world whose comprehending meaning has shattered, the only irreducible bedrock is the consensus emergent from individual rational inquiry.

The Subjective Turn

Despite the enormous complexity and extent of the modern world, the overriding pattern is clear. It is confidence in the capacity of intellectual freedom to operate independently of any theological supports, even when it is engaged in the movement toward theological affirmation. The Reformation is not its most obvious illustration, but it is its most revealing because it occurs in a context of ostensible spiritual openness. What is remarkable about the Reformation is not that it splintered the universal Church, but that it installed the perspective of subjectivity at the core of the modern understanding of faith. Of course, faith always involves a moment of individual assent. It is crucially rooted in such a confession. But Luther went further in insisting on the exclusivity of the individual perspective. Any suggestion that the individual might only have a partial apprehension of the reality in which he or she participated was wiped away. The authority of private conscience became irrevocable, and not merely because of Luther's own heroic "Here I stand."[2]

The deeper reason lay in the question from which his whole theology began. How can I be certain, he worried, of how I stand in the sight of God? Emphasis was almost wholly directed toward the personal assurance of salvation, under the pressure of an anxiety about divine judgment that was widely shared. The need for a personal guarantee had been heightened by the prominence of a nominalist God whose impenetrable will lay far beyond the reach of any illumination of reason. Standing alone before God, the soul felt the full weight of impervious divine judgment and longed for the word of justification that would fill up the abyss of condemnation within itself. The realization that the miracle of righteousness was to be apprehended through faith in Christ had a transformative effect. It released Luther from the staggering impossibility of pleasing God. But it also reduced the bond between man and God to the tenuous link of individual faith in the promises of Christ contained in Scripture. The weight of judgment may have been lifted, but an even greater responsibility was placed on the movement of private faith. Nothing could mediate or sustain that movement. The soul stood naked before God.

Not only is the perspective individualist because of the absence of an ecclesial community of interpretation, it is also ultimately subjectivist because the soul is finally the judge of the divine gift of righteousness received by faith. The nobility of the Lutheran self-reflection in the presence of God should not distract us from the enhanced role of the self in this process. Luther's intention was certainly to view himself through the eyes of God, but he could not escape the admission that this was still reducible to the human side of the equation. It is the eyes of God as perceived through our eyes. The difficulty could have been overcome by unfolding the mystical intersection of the two perspectives in the momentary glimpse of illumination. But that was not Luther's direction. Even mysticism might draw too much away from the absoluteness of God. Ironically, the consequence was to make the transcendence of God depend more heavily on its apprehension by finite subjectivity. Only the theological systematization of Calvin saved the Reformation from imminent collapse, although nothing could be done about the centralization of judgment in individuals cut off from wider intimations.

The connection between the Reformation and individualism is well understood in relation to scriptural interpretation. Absent an authoritative church, there is no alternative. What is less widely appreciated is the extent to which the roots of this attitude lie deep within Reformation theology. The break with the universal Church was the effect, not the cause, of the Reformation. What makes the initiative of Luther paradigmatic for the modern world is that it grounds at the deepest level the perspective from which all meaning is constituted. The isolated modern self goes through progressive states of dissociation from the matrix of reality, but its most profound expression is surely the Lutheran anxiety of judgment experienced by the soul from which God is absent. Whether the divine justification has been received or not must then be judged by the soul alone, as the ensuing preoccupation with predestination made abundantly clear. It is not too much further to reach the point where the presence of God and his inexorable judgment is subjected to examination. From the finite individual perspective, the temptation becomes strong to conclude that, even if he is present, a God who would place such impossible demands on human beings is hardly deserving of our moral respect. Indeed, it is striking how close to the surface in Luther's reflections the resonances of revolt against God lie.

There can be no doubt that human judgment has been installed at the center. The forgetfulness of Being consists precisely in the misperception that the center of *our world* is not the same as the center of *the world*. That amnesia, as we have seen in the ideological movements, was capable of giving rise to the most grandiose schemes of self-perfection. Fueled by the outbreak of revolt against God, the nineteenth-century messiahs and their epigones sought to assume the role themselves of creating the world anew. Despite their Promethean will, reality itself has eventually exhausted their drive to master it. At the end of the age of ideological militancy, we are left with the more moderate (and therefore more enduring) expressions of the modern spirit. It is not the ideological revolutionaries that shape our world, but the more rational and more pervasive voices of technological science and individual rights. Apocalyptic dimensions are not for that reason irrelevant. They bring the theoretical character of modernity into focus with unparalleled power and thereby make plain the depth of reorientation required of our world. However, they do not touch the constructive achievements of the modern spirit or do so only indirectly. The revolutionary convulsions of our age have been a powerful expression of the spirit of destruction and a lesson we cannot forget. The task of reconstruction, however, demands another spirit, and this is still best found in the dimensions of modernity that held themselves apart from the ideological madness.

To the extent that there is a center of meaning in the modern world, it revolves around free rational subjectivity as it is elaborated in a variety of fields and modes. For the sake of convenience, we may identify its representative expressions as the enterprise of technological science and the promotion of universal human rights. Science and rights are not the only carriers of the modern spirit by any means, but they are among the most authoritative. It would be hard to deny, not only that they define the modern ethos, but that their demonstrable power is constitutive of the achievements of the modern world. The vast technological enterprise that has sustained global development has its roots in the advances of modern science. Technical accomplishments alone could not distribute their benefits in the absence of a tolerable political environment in which human life could flourish. This political achievement is the fruit of an order of liberty that is rooted in respect for universal dignity and rights and elaborated in the institutions of self-government by which they are sustained. All other modern accomplishments, especially of a cultural nature, are contestable to a greater or lesser extent. Only the stature of modern science and the indubitability of human rights stand unassailable. It is possible to pose as a critic of modern art or literature and not be regarded too strangely. But no one can suggest a serious critique of the validity of science or the legitimacy of rights and expect to be considered rational.

Science and rights enjoy an unquestioned authority because they embody the sense of an advance in rationality as distinctive of the modern world. They sustain the sense of modernity as meaningful because of the tangible increase in meaning they represent. A halo effect extends from their respective achievements to underpin the broader myth of progress with modernity as its culminating expression. Moreover, they are reflective of the modern self-understanding of separation from the revelatory context of medieval civilization. Science and rights have earned their authority by cutting the connection with any putative theological horizon. In this self-grounding authority, they demonstrate their independence from all extraneous points of reference. Historically, they have no difficulty in acknowledging their derivation from a Christian and philosophical context, but insist that that has no intrinsic bearing on the methodological exigences that define their validity today. Irrespective of personal faith, one can follow and acknowledge the power of experimental science and acknowledge the indispensability of universal rights. In short, science and rights seem to have made their case as independent sources of truth.[3] Their secret is not hostility to religion but the calm demonstration of the advance in rationality attained by following the rigors of scientific method and conceding the primacy of human dignity within the moral universe. Even God, we now seem to acknowledge, must be measured in relation to such criteria of reason.

Independence from Revelation

The picture that emerges is that the civilizational advance of modernity is accomplished by sloughing off the outmoded authority of revelation. No doubt a strongly Promethean element of self-reliance is embedded in this sentiment. But, unlike the messianic expressions of the militant ideological movements, prideful indomitability is not allowed to eclipse a humbler submission to the order of reality. Science and rights are still a rational elaboration. They owe their success to their capacity to conform to a rational ordering of existence. But whence derives this astonishing spirit of self-restraint? The stoic willingness to discipline one's longings is out of all proportion to the tangible benefits that result. We are entitled to wonder about the source of this noble self-limitation. Certainly, the accomplishments of the modern world are impressive in the aggregate, but for any individual it involves the disciplined dedication to a specialized task from which greatness is largely excluded. How has it been possible to harness this collective energy toward the construction of the vast interdependent modern civilization we enjoy today? The spirit of titanic striving is less the explanation than the principal obstacle to be avoided.

Can it indeed be that the disconnection from all transcendent reference is the key to the discipline of reason? From this perspective, the ideological convulsions are merely regressive expressions of such residual religious influences, not emblematic of the modern spirit as a whole.[4] The broader movement of modernity is more properly reflected in the intellectual asceticism of science and the political self-discipline of rights. As such, they stand for nothing more than themselves. In each case, it is sufficient that they uncover what is true and acknowledge what is right, irrespective of whether the cumulative implications coalesce around some grand idea or meaning. Having abandoned the revelatory horizon, the modern world is constituted by its willingness to live within a structure devoid of any ultimate meaning. The aggregation of provisional and transitory meanings is sufficient for the day. An admirable intellectual resignation permeates the activities of the scientist and the rights advocate at every turn. They are engaged in pursuits that are of value irrespective of any ultimate frame of reference. It is enough that we understand more fully the reality in which we live and respect more faithfully the inviolable dignity of each human being. No one can provide an incontrovertible justification for such endeavors, and the attempt to do so is even a little distracting. Certainly, no one can serve a higher calling than the search for understanding and the promotion of mutual respect.

The crucial question is, of course, whether this impressive modern rationality has been gained because of the severance from revelation or despite it. Already, an outline of the answer can be discerned from the preceding reflections. The attitude of unwavering submission to the truth, wherever it may lead, is itself a tacit expression of a transcendent orientation. It is an unconditional affirmation of trust in an order of reality whose mystery may not be fully disclosed, but whose validity cannot be seriously doubted. Higher than any gain we may obtain, higher even than any confirmation of our significance in the order of things, is fidelity to the imperious demand of truth. It was not for nothing that Nietzsche recognized that he too worshipped at the same altar as Plato had.[5] Truth remains the beacon beyond all values even for a world in which nihilism has befallen its meaning. There is an affirmation beyond the inconclusiveness and provisionality of all that we know and do. Even if the sum of our endeavors in science and economy, the arts and communications, do not reach a comprehending account of it all, there is still a lodestar of honesty by which we are guided. It is enough to have lived as a human being without dissembling. A life without illusion is its own reward. Can we not recognize in this noble self-abnegation of the modern mind at its best a faint glimmer of that transcendent luminosity that stands at the source of our civilization?

We live not so much in a secular world as in a world from which the divine has withdrawn behind a veil. Mystery is still present—indeed, it is constitutive of the horizon within which our finite rationality continues to operate. There would be no painstaking collaborative unfolding of science, nor a persevering commitment to the defense of human dignity, if there were not embedded within such movements the sense of contact with a depth of endless fascination. To behold the increments of scientific discovery or the finite character of all political achievements as all there is is to rob them of their sustaining momentum. They are of value in themselves, but not because they are all that we have. It is because they are all that we have now. By remaining faithful to their exigences, we are drawn toward a more expansive horizon whose presence can scarcely be glimpsed from where we are now. This is the vitality of life that was so important to Nietzsche and

Dostoevsky, for it was not life as such that drew them, but the growth of the soul toward an indefinable fulfillment that life itself seemed to promise. Our paradigmatic modern endeavors of rational inquiry and individual dignity occupy the most prominent role because they are the most visible medium through which that enlargement of the soul takes place today. There are, of course, many other such vehicles in human life, from the intimacy of love to the ecstasy of faith, that follow the same path. It is merely that science and rights are the most publicly authoritative expressions of our sustaining momentum.

The problem is that our commentary on this dynamic has involved a departure from the modern secular self-understanding. While the modern world may have found a variety of vehicles through which the intuitive participation in transcendent Being can take place, that realization cannot become transparent to modern self-consciousness itself. We fail to recognize the extent to which our most apparently secular pursuits are profoundly constituted by the horizon of transcendent mystery. As a consequence, we are perpetually in search of an interpretation of ourselves, but persistently failing in the task of identifying who we are. Despite a proliferation of philosophical perspectives, none of them seem capable of capturing what we are about, although none of them fail completely to hit on some of the relevant dimensions. The result is the peculiar character of the modern world, which Charles Taylor has described as split between powerful moral sources of inspiration and a powerful incapacity to adequately articulate them.[6] Without the language of transcendent revelation, the modern world is unperceiving of its own deepest resonances. Its schizophrenia consists of the dissociation between its reality and its self-understanding.

The disorientation of the modern world is generated by the disconnection between its transcendent commitments and its studiously mundane frame of reference. There is nothing unstable about an implicitly transcendent orientation as such. It is only when its character is misunderstood and mistaken for a utilitarian construction that confusion occurs. Then we encounter the perennial modern misconceptions about the nature of science and rights. Frustration and irritation arise from the failure to convince the incomprehending that such pursuits are not adequately captured by any calculus of immanent benefits. They are self-justifying orientations that, even if they rendered nothing in return, would still be deserving of our utmost support as the noblest attainments of which we are capable. But the problem is more than terminological. The inability to articulate the sources of the modern self leads toward a deeper confusion. Absent a transcendent frame of reference, we are not simply without a "sacred canopy"; we become incapable of distinguishing between the immanent and transcendent dimensions of what we do. The differentiation collapses, and the mundane reality is made to bear the mystery of it all. An implicity present transcendent dimension is not problematic so long as its character is understood. It is when the inner tension is forgotten that we are launched on a path of distortion in which the investigation of nature or the protection of rights are pressed to yield an illumination higher than that of which they are capable.

Endangered Science

The schizophrenia of the modern world is not a harmless idiosyncrasy of interpretation. It is a systemic source of distortion that perennially threatens the achievement of rationality as a whole. In other words, the modern pursuit of science labors under a considerable burden. It must continually resist the temptation to extrapolate from its partial and provisional perspectives on reality to a comprehensive theory of the whole. No matter how frequently science reminds itself and us that such definitive penetration of reality is not what it is about, the lesson rarely sinks in or lasts longer than the latest infatuation. The excitement of scientific discovery seems almost to promote the sense of momentum toward a qualitatively higher viewpoint. It always seems only a matter of making that final, tantalizing leap toward the highest of all viewpoints. The holy grail of absolute knowledge seems to move ever closer. What we are unable to comprehend is that it is, in principle, incapable of rational apprehension. The closer we seem to approach it, the more unattainable it becomes. But the dream is so beguiling that we fail to notice the greater expanse that emerges before us. So enthralled by the vision, we forget that its attainment would constitute the end of science as a mode of inquiry forever. Once final knowledge is reached, investigation and its loving pursuit of understanding must come to a rest.

To the extent that we have distanced ourselves from the differentiation of transcendent Being, science has had to struggle with more distorting expectations. This is a paradoxical observation because we are accustomed to the progressive model of the history of science as an inexorable march of rationality. A more accurate perception would suggest that the progress of science has occurred despite a decrease in the rationality of the framework surrounding it. The only way in which this is possible is through the successive compartmentalization of science from its surrounding context. This is a feature with which we are familiar through the fragmentation of specialties as well as the increasing separation of science from the common sense understanding of the world. Science is increasingly isolated within its own frame of reference. It is impenetrable to the larger social world because its rational presuppositions cannot be apprehended by the world. Science is like an island of rationality within a sea of superstition. The rationality of science has been won at the cost of successively shedding the penumbra of distorting expectations with which it began.

Foremost among these is the anticipation of science as a window into the order of being as a whole. One has only to consider the contrast between medieval and Renaissance science to perceive this pattern. Medieval scientists were by and large nominalists, very often Franciscans or influenced by them. For them, nature was a discrete realm, open to empirical investigation, but in no sense an avenue into the inner working of divine reason. God ruled the universe through his will, which remained inaccessible to rational speculation. Only through his self-revelation in Scripture was access provided into the divinely willed order of things. Nature by itself could not disclose its ultimate structure. There might not be a rational necessity to be apprehended within it. Ultimately, whatever rational order was to be discovered empirically fell under the shadow of the impenetrable divine will. Scripture alone allowed us entry into as much of the mystery as God was willing to disclose. The result was that science could proceed without external pressure as an unfettered empirical examination of nature.[7]

No doubt there were serious problems with the truncated conception of reason as well as with the capricious understanding of nature within this nominalist outlook. But, from the perspective of empirical science, the burden was relatively light. Free from the pressure to find a mode of integration with revelation, we might even regard the nominalist reason as the epitome of free scientific inquiry. Where it led was a matter of supreme indifference, since nothing of ultimate significance rested on the outcome. All that mattered had already been settled through the fideistic response of faith to the divine word of Scripture. Perhaps at no time since has science been so free to pursue its unfolding without glancing at the larger picture of reality it is constructing. No one looked to science to provide definitive guidance in existence. It was free simply to be itself, pursuing only its own intimations and obedient only to its own canons. Without the burden of ultimacy, the rationality of science was unleashed.

Contrast this with the much more central role of science in the Renaissance. It is no accident that a veritable explosion of scientific interest occurs at precisely the moment when the authoritative force of revelation begins to decline. The Renaissance is marked by a raw hunger for new ways to God. Nature and the cosmos as a whole are probed tirelessly to discover the secret by which more direct access might be attained. Late medieval devotional fervor had lost much of its impetus, and Christianity had increasingly devolved into acrimonious dogmatic disputes, a pattern that only seemed to be extended with the Reformation aftermath. The spiritually attuned began to look elsewhere for the opening toward divinity. What could be more appealing than the project of reading the mind of God expressed directly in the natural order? The Bible of nature was available to all. Beyond the reach of theologians and prelates, it seemed to promise revivifying contact with the ancient theology from which all religion had originated. The result was the pervasive turn toward nature we recognize as the proximate source of the scientific revolution that culminates in the seventeenth century. Modernity itself seems to have its birth in this new found preoccupation with the empirical order of the world.[8]

The only difficulty is that the early scientists were curiously unscientific, not only by our standards, but also by medieval standards. Renaissance science is enveloped in the rediscovery of the esoteric spiritual traditions that had continued a subterranean existence since the ancient world. Now the syncretistic myths of the *Corpus Hermeticum* and the Kaballah, together with a rejuvenation of alchemical techniques and the rich speculative framework of Neoplatonic mysticism, burst on the public scene. The sixteenth century is astonishing for the extent to which priests and scholars, kings and popes, embrace the new learning that emanates from these exotic mytho-speculative sources. It is not until the end of the century that their divergence from Christian theology becomes abundantly apparent. A moment of such recognition can no doubt be dated with the burning of Giordano Bruno, a paradigmatic instance of the Renaissance magus, by the Italian inquisition in 1601. Shattered by the ever firmer drawing of dogmatic boundaries in the seventeenth century was the dream that had sustained the flowering Neoplatonic-Hermetic spirituality: that here at last had been found the opening toward the ancient theology, the pure original divine revelation to mankind in nature.

The connection between this inspiration and the proliferation of empirical investigations and speculations has long been understood as the moving force behind the scientific revolution. What has been less clearly understood is why the pursuit of God in nature should also entail a veritable explosion of magical and mystical practices. Renaissance science presents this extraordinary picture of an expanding interest in natural magic as perhaps its deepest inspiration. Marsilio Ficino and the Neoplatonic Academy of Florence were firmly insistent on the difference between their concern and the traditionally and properly excoriated interest in dark or Satanic magic. They sought only to make contact with the sympathetic bonds of harmony that unite all the layers of the cosmos. Far from appealing to Satan, their goal was to enter more fully into the web of occult influences by which God governs all things. In this way, they could regain more direct contact with the divine will and enter more fully into man's role of co-governor of the material world. The divinely willed plan to restore and perfect all things could proceed more effectively once man became a fully self-conscious partner in the work. Man was to become a magus again, rediscovering the original divine powers of transformation that he had enjoyed before the fall. The means was to penetrate to the inner sympathetic relationships that would allow man to ascend and descend through the order of the cosmos. Talismans, incantations, music, foods, memory systems, gammatria, alchemical operations, and manipulations of all kinds were employed ceaselessly to render the connections transparent. When successful, man would emerge as the perfected microcosmos who could proceed with the reordering of the larger cosmos in the same direction.

It was no accident that the writing of utopias coincided with this eruption of unlimited expectations. The term was coined by Thomas More in his *Utopia* (1517), literally "no place," which was written some time after his visit to the Neoplatonic circle in Florence. From then on, the writing of utopias became a prolific genre under the impetus of the same inspiration. It was now permissible to indulge the dream of perfection, for the access to it had been glimpsed in the Hermetic-Alchemical-Kaballistic figuration of the divinized man. Behind the grandiose schemes for universal reformation stood the supremely self-confident magus. The reordering of his soul in line with the cosmological pattern of divine influences had provided him with a ladder up to the heights of divinity itself. Under God, man had been restored to his original miraculous condition of knowing and moving through all things. It was even possible for him to contemplate the supreme test of his creative powers in the Kabbalistic operations for creating a homunculus, a little man.[9] The note of rivalry between man and God was barely contained, and its realization occasionally spilled over into consciousness. Indeed, the schemes for cosmic transformation underwent such megalomaniacal elaboration that reason was in danger of being eclipsed entirely.

In short, it is a problem to recognize in Renaissance Hermerticism and its offshoots the background for modern natural science. Yet it is there and not only in Bruno and Kepler and Paracelsus; it even persists long after the Hermetic texts have been correctly dated and lost some of their pristine lustre. As central a figure as Isaac Newton is still engaged in alchemical investigations, as well as numerological speculations relating to the Book of Revelation, well into the seventeenth century.[10] It is a puzzle to behold the father of modern science, the discoverer of the comprehensive laws of motion, simultaneously pursuing the esoteric connections and meanings that will lead to a higher illumination of all reality. What the connection between the two sides of Newton's work is remains to be investigated. It is only in recent times that scholars have felt comfortable enough with even acknowledging the alchemical and speculative dimensions. The intellectual confusion in regard to Newton is reflective of the broader uncertainty about the origination of modern science in what can only be described as a widespread decline of rational differentiation. Certainly, the empirical investigation of nature continued apace, but it was pressed into service in the great Hermetic project of ascending and descending through the hierarchy of being. Compared to this aspiration, any medieval conceptions of hierarchy appear overwhelmingly static and tame. Enthusiasm for the occult influences of nature accounts for the motivation of the empirical turn, but it simultaneously seems to deflect it away from any open disclosure of the factual relationships involved. Everything is immediately absorbed within a preconceived frame of reference—exactly the opposite of our model of empirical science in its norm.

How was it possible for the explosion of Hermetic enthusiasm to give rise to the scientific revolution? The answer is probably best given by the example of Newton himself. He kept the spiritual and empirical-mathematical dimensions separate, assigning them to different books. The *Principia* (1687) would hardly stand as the great model of the scientific mind at work, mathematizing the phenomena of motion throughout the universe, if it had been embedded in schemes of alchemical and apocalyptic transfiguration. But it was Newton's capacity for keeping these two modes of thought separate in his mind that was the real cause of his scientific success. Gradually, the mystico-speculative side had been stripped away and Newton could stand as the culminating figure in a line of early physicists meticulously mapping the various types of motion. His genius was to reduce them all to one system that was capable of explaining motion, from the smallest terrestrial to the broadest celestial levels. It was a staggering achievement and stands even today as a model of the scientific method. What accounts for its extraordinary success as a mode of investigating reality is the rigorous elimination of all elements of an anthropocentric nature. All of the interest in man's access to the occult harmonies of the universe must be utterly set aside. Scientific reason consists in the abnegation of human interests before the disclosure of reality as it is.

The difficulty of sustaining this commitment is considerable. Popularly, science is conceived of as being a methodology of verification whereby knowledge advances incrementally. Discovery and development of hypotheses for falsification are commonly acknowledged to be its most creative moments. But what of the even greater creativity required in transforming the broadest theoretical frameworks within which hypotheses are elaborated? These are the great paradigm shifts that are neither easy nor frequent. Scientists are human too. They are incapable of pursuing a line of investigation that runs directly contrary to their own enframing worldview. For them too, reality as a whole must make sense; it cannot be too egregiously riven by cognitive dissonance. We continue to live with some sense of reality as a whole, and that context defines the limits of what can be hypothesized and questioned. This is why the "scientific revolutions" so famously identified by Thomas Kuhn are the great seismic events of the scientific world.[11] Few minds have the temerity to contemplate them, and a steady accumulation of pressure is required to detonate them, but when that does occur it constitutes the shift to a whole other way of thinking of reality. Scientists are as susceptible as the rest of us to the containing and constraining influence of worldviews. For, much of the time, we would rather retain a flawed reality model than undergo the kind of massive upheaval in which everything we have known undergoes reexamination.

Newton's achievement was to have created the modern scientific paradigm—the conception of reality as matter in motion—that endured up to the quantum and relativity shifts of the twentieth century. But even he could not eliminate the need for an extrascientific worldview that would extend and elaborate the picture only partially conceived within science as such. He could separate out these distinct phases by assigning them to different books, publishing the scientific treatises while withholding the esoteric. He could demonstrate the imperative of maintaining a clear line of separation between physics and theology. Yet he could finally not eliminate the pull toward spiritual elaboration.[12] The speculative side of his work is eloquent testament to the ineliminability of the framing philosophical questions from science. At some level, they remain the irreducible residue that persists as the great source of motivation and distortion in science. Success in the scientific enterprise turns on our capacity to remain within the more modest expectations of phenomenal relationships. Straying into the speculative construction of a worldview invites the loss of scientific reason. The preservation of science consists of remaining on the right side of this tension, which can neither be abolished nor resolved.

The bounded rationality of science is a raft floating in a sea of uncertainty. As Newton exemplifies, everything depends on recognizing the line of the boundary so that the speculative extrapolations are never confused with the more modest empirical justifications. The model of the scientist disinterestedly working away on laboratory experiments, unaffected by broader spiritual ramifications, is only slowly beginning to fade. Historiography of science still has a good deal of work to do in exploring the connection between spiritual worldviews and the range of what can be empirically acknowledged in science. Kuhn's work has been particularly innovative in this regard, suggesting a whole avenue of approaching the history of science. It has made us more aware of the dependence of the empirical methodology on what the worldview renders permissible. Even calling attention to this bounded rationality of science has generated its own controversy and discomfort. It was immediately seized upon as an assault on the objectivity of science. Were we reducing the scientific enterprise, the last bastion of modern rationality, to an inconclusive flow of variable paradigms that amount to no higher claim than the relativity of all knowledge? Despite the initial plausibility of the suggestion, the anxiety was misplaced. The very existence of paradigm shifts presupposes an advance in rationality and therefore confirms the degree to which a shared sense of objectivity underpins the process. Why shift at all if there is nothing to be gained? But the overcoming of this most obvious objection does not affect the deeper implication of Kuhn's work: the recognition of the bounded rationality of science. The tension between science and the extra-scientific worldview sanctioning it is ineliminable, and the rationality of science consists of resisting the pull to overstep its limits.

The reason why this problem remains so central to early modern and later science is that it exists within a world without authoritative revelation. Absent a transcendent perspective, the partial perspectives must struggle to elaborate the order of the whole. As the most successful mode of knowledge in the modern world, science is inevitably surrounded by an aura of expectation of a higher illumination. Much of what sustained the momentum of the vast scientific enterprise on which we collaborate is the fascination with piercing the mystery of it all. That was the impulse of esoteric penetration at the start of modern science, and it continues as the great imbalancing pressure against which it must resist. What science knows, it knows at the cost of foregoing the greater illumination. But the outcome is not always so successful. The more modest piecemeal process of investigation is increasingly overburdened as the subject rises in the scale of significance. It is not simply that the methodology of the hard sciences yields more certain results, but that they are capable of remaining more faithful to their methodology than the biological and human sciences. Living and human reality is not just more complex, it is also more intimately bound up with the illusory expectations of the investigators themselves. After all, one's humanity is a more integral dimension of oneself than the mere physical or chemical substratum shared with all other entities. As a consequence, the need to extrapolate toward the meaning of the whole becomes all the more intense. The need to occupy the space vacated by the revelation of transcendent reality is virtually irresistible, even though the inclination defines the loss of rational science.[13]

No doubt the best known example is the theory of biological evolution emanating from Charles Darwin. It is always a warning indicator when a scientific theory plays a greater role outside its field of application than within it. Fascinating as Darwin's account of *The Origin of Species* (1859) was, its real contribution lay beyond the explicit reference of the study. More important than understanding the stratification of the emergence of species and even than the evolutionary mechanism propounded to explain the emergence was the function of Darwin's theory in constituting a worldview. It was welcomed and repulsed for the exact same reason. Darwin had shown how creation could dispense with a creator. A world of chance developments could, over a sufficiently long period of time, evolve into a world of order. It was not the suggestion that men were descended from apes that was the most shattering realization, but that everything had originated through the survival of the best adapted random mutations. The most compelling natural indication of a supreme intelligence—the argument from design—had been decisively undermined. With such large theological reverberations, it was no wonder that Darwin's theory of biological evolution should receive scant attention on its own merits. It is a situation that prevails virtually up to the present.

Darwinian evolutionism functions to such an extent as the overarching worldview of modernity that even its subjection to scientific analysis is treated with deep misgivings. Everyone is more comfortable if its examination is reduced to the stylized opposition between evolutionism and creationism. That way, no one has to pay serious attention to the minor consideration that neither of them can be taken seriously as scientific theories. They cannot be disproved because the theories are designed to accommodate all contrary or missing evidence against them. This would be no more than a harmless intellectual idiosyncrasy if it did not have such disastrous consequences for science. Like counterfeit, the problem is that bad science drives out the good. Even today it is virtually impossible for conscientious biologists to admit that the evidence for evolution is extraordinarily thin. We simply have little tangible proof that one species evolves into another. As Darwin recognized, the fossil record, which is ultimately the only conclusive indication, is the weakest source of support. We have neither experience nor evidence of intermediate forms. It is clear that different species emerged and disappeared at different times, just as it is clear that chemical and genetic continuities are present across species. But the incubus of evolutionism hangs as such a dead weight on the scientific mind that even the best efforts to consider its revision encounter levels of resistance out of all proportion to their content. No one dares to attempt the removal of the ideological carcass for fear of the consequences of universal disapproval. More often than not, the voices of dissent come from outside the biological community.[14] One wonders what force holds such regressive formalism in place. The only suggestion is that the ani-theological significance of evolutionism as a worldview continues to outweigh its scientific value. By calling into question the Darwinian universe, we would at the same time be restoring the openness to the transcendent creator. It is in other words the fear of God that prevents the biological community from too openly discarding a theory they have long ceased to honor in practice.

The physical sciences, notably astrophysics, have much less difficulty in recognizing the limits of their competence. There is far less hesitation in reaching conclusions that seem to point toward the openness toward transcendent Being. Probably the most obvious example is the Big Bang theory of the origin of the universe, a theory that is by no means settled, but that has endured the vicissitudes of examination to represent something like a consensus so far. What is significant is not whether cosmology can demonstrate the origin of the universe at a moment of creation, but that such an implication causes it no inherent disturbance either way. Without taking a stand for or against transcendent Being, science is free to work its autonomous dynamic. Problems arise only when science conceives itself as supplanting the knowledge of ultimate reality. Then it finds itself in the unenviable position of attempting to comprehend the whole from its position as a part. The temptation is inseparable from the human condition, but the success of science depends on maintaining the balance of a perspective that resists its illegitimate expansion. Ultimately, the rationality of science is dependent on the differentiation of the order of being. If the distinction between Being and beings is forgotten, then it is almost inevitable that the investigation of beings will assume to itself the task of drawing us toward Being. Even the attitude of spiritual openness that characterizes much contemporary physics, with its talk of an anthropic principle, the role of beauty, and so on, runs the risk of promoting both bad science and bad spirituality.

But whatever the dangers that confront the physical and life sciences, they are surely nothing compared to the disarray of the human sciences. Having begun with an outburst of grandiose expectations—very often convinced that they were on the verge of discovering the basic laws of human behavior that would allow a systematic reorientation of society toward peace and happiness—reality has repeatedly disabused their messianic self-confidence. It was no accident that the social reformers and revolutionaries of the past two hundred years have been associated with the social sciences. Whether it is Marx or Mill in economics, Dewey or Laski in political science, Freud or Skinner in psychology, or Comte or Marcuse in sociology, the emancipatory impetus remained the same. These were disciplines profoundly shaped by the assurance that the rationality of science could be applied to the resolution of the most enduring problems of man and society. Crime and misery could be eliminated; world peace could be inaugurated; and the social injustice endemic to history could finally be overcome. Nothing stood in the way except the expenditure of effort required to develop the appropriate theoretical instruments by which a new golden age could be guaranteed. The brightest minds were drawn to the task of realizing the enlightenment conviction of progress by applying the power of science to the study of man himself. What obstacle could prove resistant to the penetration of science?

The short answer is human nature. A century of systematic human cruelty has definitively exploded the myth of historical progress. No one can any longer take seriously the suggestion that we are on the verge of an age of universal benevolence. In many respects, the brutality and narrowness of human self-interest seem to be more in evidence than ever. But what has shredded the human sciences has less to do with the failure of the progressivist expectations they shared with the age than with the substantive inability of their methodology to yield any meaningful knowledge about the human condition. Despite more than a century of work, little in the way of valuable insight has been generated about the central problems of social and political order. Not only have the problems proved resistant to solution, they have even proved resistant to comprehension. No one knows why crime occurs, why marriages break down, why war occurs, why economies fall into depressions, or why governments cannot eradicate corruption. The problems turn out to be far more complex and their sources more profound than we had anticipated. It is therefore not surprising that the human and social sciences present a sharp contrast to their naturalist cousins. In place of the steady accumulation of results and their coalescence into ever more coherent wholes, the social sciences exhibit increasing fragmentation of data and their dispersion into ever-narrower frames of reference. It is no wonder that there are no press reports or celebrity prizes for achievements in the social sciences. The hard truth is that the results of all their labor is depressingly thin.[15]

What happens to disciplines that dissipate into triviality is, of course, that they become the preserve of small minds. There are no great thinkers in the social sciences because bright people quickly recognize their futility. In place of an interest in problems—the great questions of existence and the pressing problems of society—the social sciences have narrowed their focus to those issues that can be investigated through an approximately rigorous application of the scientific method. Even if the method cannot yield fruitful results, its transformation into a fetish can still manage to sustain the appearance of rigor. In this way individuals, whose own work does not amount to anything very significant, can still comfort themselves with the assurance that they are generating useful results that might eventually be comprehended within some meaningful theory. The problem is that the promise of theoretical elaboration is never fulfilled. No one raises seriously the question of why, in principle, human and social reality might never be susceptible to such theoretical comprehension. Instead, the deepest minds depart and the lesser minds churn away on piecemeal studies that, unlike the natural sciences, are never absorbed into some larger understanding of things. One might view contemporary social science as an illustration of what happens when the experimental side of science is utterly dissociated from its theoretical collaborator. It produces a plethora of isolated, meaningless studies. This is why they are never referred to or utilized by the broader society of which they are a part.

However, the point is not to critique the social sciences. It is to understand why they are such an abysmal failure, for such consistency cannot be the fault of any personal inability. Rather, the cause lies in the nature of the project itself. Human beings are not, in their most decisive aspects, illuminated by the methodology of natural science. However elementary it may seem, there is a decisive difference in reality between a human being and a rock. Both may be intelligible, but only the human being is intelligent. That means that human behavior is to be understood primarily in terms of the reasons adduced by each of us for what we do. Intelligent self-enactment and self-disclosure, as Michael Oakeshott suggests, is not an unvarying achievement.[16] Often, we fail to live up to the high calling of intelligent self-government. But, even when we fall short of the full exercise of our intelligence, it is precisely as a failure of intelligent self-reflection that our actions are to be understood. Relatively little can be gained from viewing them as a set of external phenomena unrelated to the more or less intelligent self-direction that stands behind them. Indeed, it is almost impossible even to describe human actions as phenomena except by some elementary reference to what they mean for their respective agents. Meaning remains the gaping hole at the core of the human sciences. It is still possible for some of their better practitioners to intuitively assess the meaning of the phenomena they investigate, but this is achieved despite the myopia of the methodology that virtually deprives them of the power of sight. Flying blind, it is not surprising that the social sciences provide so little useful information and prove so inept at prediction.

Why, we are forced to ask, this dogged persistence in a direction that yields so little rationality? It is not simply the lure of scientific methodology. Positivism, like all of the great ideological illusions, is bound to exhaust its expectations over a long period of disappointment. It becomes increasingly difficult to sustain the confidence that illumination is just around the corner. No—what maintains the human sciences today, besides their achievement of institutional control, is the absence of any conceivable alternative. Any approach outside of the phenomenal would entail the assumption of a stand within the world of meaning to be investigated. It is impossible to interpret the meaning of human actions and expressions without taking a position on its meaningfulness. The submergence in the plurality of social meanings with their conflicts and convergences would embroil the scientist in the controversies of the investigated material itself. He or she could no longer preserve the distance from which objectivity and science are possible. It is the inconceivability of a science of order that renders a science of human life and society impossible. It is far better to stick with the truncated science that is at least defensible from the perspective of blind externality.

The source of this attitude is the refusal to acknowledge what is inescapable in the project of a science constituted by meaning: the observer is included. Marriage, the family, sexuality, markets, religion, and government are not really phenomena. They have a phenomenal or external dimension, but their reality is inner, as the bearer of the lives of the human beings engaged in them. Scientists and scholars who study them do not suddenly acquire a wholly other mode of existence; rather, they are part of the world of social meaning that is already there and extends beyond, after their brief interlude of scientific investigation has passed. Social science is not just about society; it also occurs within a social whole that sustains and limits it. Rather than conceiving of the subject matter of the human sciences as a set of phenomena, it is preferable to regard them as lines of meaning. They constitute a field of meaning that includes the observer. What objectivity is possible depends on the scientist's capacity to identify the most objective perspective that has differentiated within the social world of which he or she is a part. It is from that vantage point alone that we can approach the truth. All other viewpoints, including the pseudo-objectivity of externality, merely subscribe to prevailing prejudices that cannot even compare to the best objectivity of the society itself.[17]

The distance we are from a rational social science can be gauged from the degree to which even the efforts in such a direction are derailed by talk of "normative perspectives," "values," and "participant observation." Such terminology is intended to suggest that the evaluation of meaning can be patched on to a fundamentally unchanged externality. "Values" and "norms" are of necessity ad hoc additions because they represent merely subjective viewpoints. Nothing, it appears, can dislodge even the claims of pseudo-science because nothing else has even the vestige of objectivity about it. This is the problem of a genuinely scientific study of man, as Max Weber contemplated most profoundly. Is there any perspective that is not itself merely one of the perspectives under investigation? Can any viewpoint maintain the primacy of its claim to truth? The only one that can, as the classical philosophers discovered, is the one that is rooted in the pull toward transcendent Being. It alone can lay claim to an objectivity or truth that transcends the partiality of all merely historical perspectives. Being is the only thing that escapes the passing reality of all finite existence and thereby provides a measure by which to judge all that comes into and goes out of existence. The admission that it is a perspective beyond the human level is not relevant. If it is what constitutes wisdom, then human wisdom consists of recognizing it. We are wise only through the love of wisdom that is divine. A science of man and society is possible only when we admit with Plato that God, not man, is the measure (*Protagoras*).

The dependence of a science of order on the revelation of transcendent Being does not solve all the problems. It renders the task of science more complicated and far less convenient, but we cannot change the situation in which we find ourselves. To the extent that the life of reason, as we have seen, is made possible through such differentiation of Being, then the elaboration of a rational perspective on humanity is correspondingly tied to such experiences. The unavailability of any perspective outside of human experience itself means that science must always take its stand on the most differentiated viewpoint that has emerged within history. That is the task of the human sciences and the reason why they remain implicitly Christian. To the extent to which the human sciences retain a rational model of human nature as the intuitive background from which to explore human life, it is imprinted with the lineaments of a Christian perspective. Addiction, for example, is viewed in wholly negative terms as a form of escape from the more rigorous demands of self-responsibility. But why should we care about the higher goals of self-realization unless there is a higher self to be realized? The problem with contemporary social science is that its own hold on rationality can scarcely maintain its superiority to that of the addict. It may indeed be more rational to escape into the temporary relief of oblivion than to struggle futilely for equally evanescent satisfactions of careers, fame, and achievements. What contemporary social science remains incapable of explicating is the root causes of addiction that lie in the unfillable transcendent longing of the human heart. In other words, the rationality of social science is hampered by its inability to follow out the full implications of its own viewpoint. Like all science, social science derives its rationality from the recognition of the order that emanates from transcendent Being. Its uniqueness is that this relationship is equally constitutive for the rational self-ordering of the object of its study.

Forgetfulness of the boundary of Being is therefore a source of greater distortion in the human sciences than in the natural sciences. In the former, it deforms our capacity to view the reality before us; in the latter, it merely affects our background presuppositions. For it makes a substantive difference whether one conceives of the radical inexhaustibility of each human being or not. Without the constitution through the glance of transcendent openness, human history could become a finite realm in which progress can reach its culmination, evil be eradicated, and happiness achieved. Human beings could be rendered in terms of the aggregation of their attributes, influences, and contributions. Rights would be susceptible of limits, and a definitive order might be imposed as the guaranteed attainment of universal fulfillment. The logic of the social sciences as an analysis of phenomenal relationships between human beings might finally reach its conclusion in a science of the techniques of universal rational control. Only the questions "for what?" or "for whom?" cause a hesitation in this smooth unfolding. When man too has been subsumed into science, then we seem to be left without an ostensible beneficiary of such useful knowledge.

The crisis of a manipulative social science draws us deeper into the problematic of a bounded science as such. This is a problem shared across the disciplines. Sciences that operate without reference to anything beyond themselves inevitably run into difficulties in defining the reality of their study. As sciences, they cannot do more than begin with the reality that is given, but then they cannot use their instruments of analysis to probe the givenness of what has been given. To do so, they would have to leap outside of their own area of competence, since they cannot utilize the principles derived from the given reality to elucidate what lies behind the givenness. Any empirical discipline develops its analysis in relation to what is there; it can never legitimately extend those analyses into the derivation of that order of reality from another. This is the whole set of problems that arise under the heading of reductionism. They run the gamut from the consciousness-physiology problems to the search for the secret of life and the origin of the universe. Strictly speaking, they are nonproblems because they are incapable of explication in terms of the sciences involved. But they are not nonproblems in terms of human curiosity. They are irresistible in that sense, because our minds are inevitably drawn toward what lies beyond the limits of any field of investigation. We can scarcely avoid peering over from one realm into another, nor assuming that methods proven successful in one area can fruitfully be extended elsewhere.

But they cannot. Despite the liveliness of current controversies, successful scientists recognize that the rationality of their disciplines is dependent on the restraint of their ambitions to the modest purview of what is given. The illegitimate extrapolation beyond such boundaries—a temptation that is reinforced through the ubiquitous extension of technological control—is an abyss from which nothing returns. Not only is it impossible to penetrate beyond the givenness of a reality stratified from conceptual thought to subatomic particles, but the attempt to do so is tantamount to the destruction of science itself. Without a relatively stable realm of reality for investigation, there would be no science. If all is reduced to a promiscuous fluidity of levels and dimensions where chemicals can become alive and neutrons can bear thoughts and stars have feelings, then the lines of demarcation within which science can explore relationships would disappear. Analysis of phenomenal relationships and the identification of the laws of their regularity cannot proceed unless the levels of reality remain constant. At the very minimum, the phenomena themselves must be susceptible of an identification that does not prove to be evanescent. If all reality was to be explained in terms of the laws of physics, then our understanding would be poorer, not richer, and we might have good reason for suspecting that the physical constancies were themselves merely provisional for something else. The rationality of the sciences is crucially dependent on the recognition of the richly multilayered character of the reality within which they move.

It is, of course, an inevitable side effect of the detachment of scientific objectivity and of the technological tools generated by it that we would be inclined to imagine a point at which we could stand outside of reality as a whole. If one can exercise partial detachment, why not total? The answer is that our partial detachment presupposes a whole within which it occurs. This is the response to the widespread suggestion that modern science ultimately undermines an order of nature, both conceptually and practically. This was the problem that so obsessed Heidegger and is at the heart of the modern world. He saw what most of contemporary science has yet to glimpse—that science itself would become impossible if an order of givenness is eliminated. Science explores the relations within the givenness of reality, but, if everything is now to be derived from the manipulations of scientific technology, then there is no longer a realm for investigation. All is open to construction. The postmodern understanding of meaning, where nothing refers and everything is constructed, would extend to the so-called hard sciences as well. We would live within a reality that is available for comprehensive reconstruction at our will. But we know that even our technology—the sphere in which this constructivist impulse is most advanced—cannot live up to its grandiose self-image. Rhetoric aside, we do not create life any more than we can engineer human beings. Our technology consists of manipulating what is there and crucially presupposes an order that is given and disclosed through the investigation of science. We may extrapolate toward the dispensability of nature, but we cannot reach it without eliminating the possibility of our extension of control.

Even such extrapolation is only possible for a being who is capable of adopting the perspective of transcendent Being, just as the empirical exploration of nature is itself made possible by the very same viewpoint of differentiation. It must surely rank as one of the supreme ironies of the self-assertive control of nature made possible by modern science that it ultimately rests on the gift of Being, which remains beyond our control. The illusion of self-creation is as fatal in science as it has proved to be in politics. By chasing such dreams, man can only provoke the nightmare loss of all that is possible for him. Destruction is the fruit of the decline into irrationality that has become so imbalanced at its own self-prospect that it no longer recognizes the limits that enable it to exercise its direction. The paradoxical extension of man's control over the whole world turns out to entail the destruction of the world that makes control possible. Split between the spiritual openness toward Being that makes modern rationality possible and the megalomaniacal enthusiasm to subsume the whole of reality into itself, the modern world is imperilled at the deepest level of its existence. The schizophrenia that renders it incapable of accounting for the source of its own rationality is no mere incidental failing. It strikes at the heart of the possibility of science and increasingly accounts for the irrational rationality of a technological world bereft of any ultimate order.

Erosion of Rights

An understanding of the bounded rationality of reason goes a long way toward unravelling the confusion that also afflicts the central modern evocations of order. Human rights is the distillation of the moral and political substance of the modern world. It is the articulation of fundamental human dignity, whose differentiation is regarded as the principal moral advance of modernity. Not that such a conception was absent from the Greco-Roman or medieval worlds; indeed, there is a common recognition of the derivation from premodern sources, but there is also a unique prominence afforded the equal rights of all as the distinguishing achievement. Everything about our political order—from the disappearance of aristocratic privilege to the resistance against all collectivist ideologies—bespeaks the centrality of individual rights. The inviolable dignity of each human being is the coin of common moral discourse the world over. A heightened sensitivity to the inviolable freedom and dignity of each human being is the evocative center from which the requirement for public and private self-government radiates through the world. Respect for individual rights is the touchstone of moral rectitude. Whatever other aspirations may define a community, they cannot be purchased at the price of any diminution of the preciousness of each human life.

This is an intensification of such power that it may rightly be regarded as the great moral-political achievement of the modern world. It is the central articulation of liberty, whose elaboration has supplanted all other moral languages and whose political expression has displaced all competing models of legitimacy. The triumph of liberal democracy is no paper victory. Like modern science, it has a staying power that has endured in the face of virulent opposition. However, like science, it too has often been suspected of concealing a hollowness at its core. The schizophrenia of the modern mind seems even more in evidence when a language of rights simultaneously exalts the transcendent worth of each individual while denigrating every authoritative spiritual tradition that would provide its claim with justification. Increasingly, the contrast between rhetoric and rationale works to dramatize the virtual impossibility of the liberal high-wire act. Not only is the gap between justification and principle a difficult tension to sustain, but even liberals have latterly come to admit that they cannot conceive of any articulation by which it might be closed. The wire has thinned to the point of invisibility.

Yet the movement continues. No one can afford to ignore the most palpable dimension of the impossible actuality of the liberal order of rights. It works. Like science, its prestige is derived in no small measure from the fact of its experiential success. To some extent, the theoretical shortcomings are a matter of irrelevance because it seems to endure despite them. But the qualification is important because the failure of justification has a cumulative debilitating effect. The lack of a rationale does not immediately spell the demise of liberal rights, but it does strain their credibility. However, despite all of this, we recognize that when moral pluralism renders agreement impossible, we can always shift the argument to the higher ground of individual rights. As an existential disposition, the conviction still flourishes that the language of rights is capable of illuminating the most intractable debates. Whether it is abortion or euthanasia, genetic engineering or affirmative action, the central issues still revolve around the question of equity in rights. No greater testament is possible for the durability of the liberal rights tradition than that it is the global reserve currency of moral debate. Its practical demonstration is still its greatest strength.[18]

What is missing is an appreciation of the fundamental nature of rights as a mode of discourse. We urgently need to understand the paradoxical character of our rights vocabulary, which seems to advance and undermine its own convictions at the same time. The pattern is reminiscent of the self-generated abyss at the heart of science that is tempted to extrapolate to the point at which the givenness of nature has been wholly absorbed within itself, thereby rendering a science of nature impossible. A similar proclivity to push the demand for rights beyond the boundaries on which they depend is evident in the moral sphere. If human dignity entails the right to live our lives in our own way, the argument goes, then why not extend it to include the conditions of life as well? Thus we arrive at such strange formulations as the right to die, the right not to be born, the right to radical alterations in endowments, and so on. What is striking about such extensions of the fundamental right to choose is that the choice no longer functions within any presupposed limits. We are not talking about choosing options that are more or less given. We are contemplating the limits of what is given itself. An inexorable pressure seems to urge us forward to regard any social or natural boundaries as questionable. If human beings have the right to choose their own way of life, should not they be free to choose their own genetic endowments, their own moral values, and their own conditions for existence? At the end of it all, there is something fundamentally "illiberal" about a natural or moral order that constricts the range of liberty available to us. Why not simply extend the freedom to choose to include the choice of our own natures? What could be a more exalted definition of human dignity than the comprehensive choice of who we are to be, when we are to exist, and when we are no longer to be? The project of liberty shades into the project of self-creation.[19]

The allure of liberal overreaching quickly encounters the reality that now rights have lost all meaning. In place of a well-defined understanding of human dignity, we are left with a blank slate on which anything we wish may be written. Having removed all limits within which rights are to be applied, we have lost all boundaries that might define their meaning. Contrary to the expectation of an enlargement of liberty, we have seen it rendered powerless before the most comprehensive exercise of despotism. What can be a more extensive intrusion of control than the mapping of all the genetic material that constitutes a human being? How will such knowledge be used? How can we ensure that its use will be confined to the elimination of disease and not extend toward the optimum possibilities? We not only have the scientific problem of how health is to be defined in this limitless context, but the more fundamental question of how such a human being is to be regarded as the possessor of rights. If we have a right to be born as optimum babies, then there is surely no limit to the degree of intervention that can be justified on our behalf. Indeed, it is impossible to conceive of any limits, since there is no entity before the engineering process has gotten underway. Not only is the human being entirely subsumed into the process of manufacture, but it is meaningless to talk about the rights of an entity that does not exist before we have created it. Only what exists has rights, what is in process cannot transcend the movement of which it is a part. There is nothing there we have not placed into it ourselves. It was the vague presentiment of this abyss that provoked the widespread revulsion at the suggestion of cloning human beings. Everyone knew that, once we had exercised such total control over our offspring, we would never be able to regard them as more than functional subordinates to our interests and will. Choice can lead us into the nightmare landscape in which all human beings are radically shorn of transcendence.

At the other end of human life, the demand for euthanasia commits a parallel breach of the boundaries. How can one have a right to die—and thereby a right to assistance in suicide—if one is not going to survive the right? All conceptions of benefit presuppose one's continued existence; otherwise, there is no one to be served by the action. Again, this is no merely theoretical problem. Its practical consequence is that the disappearance of a putative beneficiary robs the action of any criterion of guidance or limitation. How will we decide when a patient is benefited or injured by such an intervention? They are no longer around to provide the irreplaceable response. It is up to us to decide, and, in such determination, we cannot avoid the necessity of deciding who will live and who will die. Which life is not worth living? Again, by stepping outside of the boundary of what is given, we find ourselves in the trackless desert in which all landmarks are merely our own temporary impositions. It will prove impossible to sustain the sense of transcendent respect for another human being, absolutely equal to ourselves, when we have sat in judgment over the worth of their continued existence. The danger of callous pressure toward suicide is the least of our concerns. In principle, we have already reached the point at which we can no longer contemplate the other as an other self. How else is it possible to conclude a life is not worth living unless we have weighed it in relation to some functional purpose, never as an end-in-itself?

The self-destruction of rights may be dramatized in the extreme instances of controlling birth and death, but the pattern originates in the tendency of rights assertions to undermine any authoritative moral order. We demand the freedom to choose our own values, never realizing that it is this very overreaching that robs our liberty of any meaning. What is it that makes the exercise of self-determination so precious? It is surely that by this means we are capable of apprehending the morally good. Liberty is the ladder by which we participate in that which is transcendent in goodness and reality. Apart from that capacity, liberty is a useless and frequently mischievous appendage to human life. But what if there is nothing inherently and absolutely good that is worthy of our choice? Then liberty reduces to a futile frittering of time that might be better expended satiating our appetites. It is no accident that this is how liberty is most often perceived: as the unlimited gratification of whim. Once the fatal step has been taken—of extending liberty to the determination of good and evil itself—then nothing stands in the way of the endless abyss of choice without purpose.

Everything hinges on the preservation of the givenness of reality within which liberty can exercise its right. By losing contact with the bounding framework, liberty is not extended but exhausts itself in a wasteland from which not even the value of liberty itself can be retained. The schizophrenia of our world can be more exactly characterized as the inability to sustain the framework that is presupposed by our most animating convictions. Instead, we find ourselves drawn unthinkingly toward the overreaching of our principles, which renders them moot. Much philosophical reflection has been expended on the apparent groundlessness of the modern world. It is variously attributed to an excessive literalism of principles, to the ubiquitous relativism of a social setting in which institutional authorities have lost their primacy, or to the incoherence of the presuppositions from which a larger philosophical explication has sought to be extracted. No doubt all of these considerations, and more, play a role. But none have quite the centrality of the loss of the relationship to transcendent Being. The disorientation of our world derives directly from our incapacity to deal with the boundary problems, and the latter is rendered inaccessible because the sense of what constitutes the boundary has drained away. Differentiation of the boundary is crucially dependent on the revelation of transcendent Being. Forgetfulness of that openness toward what is beyond does not render the foreground of immanent reality more visible. Rather, disorientation is the consequence when mundane reality is made to support the tension toward the Being that is forgotten but not omitted. Rationality in our moral-political discourse, just as much as in science, turns on our capacity to preserve the differentiation between reality and its transcendence.

Fidelity to the intimations of an order of rights confirms this necessity. One does not have to wait for Being to reveal itself, for the self-revelation occurs in every moment we are capable of receiving it. It may be true that reverence for the irreplaceable depth of each human being presupposes the relationship to transcendent Being, but it is also the case that an unwavering commitment to human rights discloses the boundary of transcendence that renders them meaningful.[20] The encroachment of liberal rights on the boundaries they presuppose can be resisted most effectively through the enlargement of the awareness of what is at stake in each case. It is nothing less than the recognition of each human being as a depth of mystery beyond all telling. By blithely ignoring the limits that cannot be breached, we do not catapult into a paradise of fulfillment. Rather, we find ourselves in a shapeless desert in which everything has been reduced to its functional value. Thinking we have leaped into a realm of greater control, we find we are bereft in a condition in which everything is measured in terms of its return, including ourselves. We cannot dominate reality without subjecting ourselves to an order of domination. Such a line of reflection makes blindingly plain that it is the treasure of finitude that makes it possible for us to be drawn by the grace of Being into our full transcendence. An order of rights is not only dependent on the revelation of God; it is also a revelation of that relationship as well.

The success of science and rights is attributable to their insistence on separation from the whole of which they are a part. Their authority in the modern world is derived from this independence of their theological background. However, there are limits to that assertion, and their transgression undermines the rationality they have achieved. Science and rights constitute a realm of modernity because they concentrated the transcendent energies of the human soul on achievements within this world. But their viability depends on not severing the connection with their transcendent source too completely; otherwise, they cease to be capable of maintaining the differentiation of being so indispensable to the life of reason. It is noteworthy that the manifestations of modernity that moved furthest from Being—the militant ideological movements—were also the ones that most thoroughly exhausted themselves in irrational self-destruction. The slender balance on which reason in the modern world is based depends on living within immanent existence while never becoming wholly of it. Narrowing the focus to the essentials of empirical science and the order of liberal rights must never be allowed to generate amnesia about the source of the rationality thereby so powerfully applied.

Extrapolations of the capacity of science and extensions of the liberty of rights inevitably give rise to expectations beyond their capacity to deliver. Science cannot transform the order of nature because it takes its bearings from within the givenness of an order it can manipulate, not create. Rights cannot be extended beyond the limits of the human condition because their meaningfulness is premised on the givenness of life itself. Not only can the exaggerated expectations not be delivered, but even the attempt to reach them will dissolve the slender hold on reason we have gained so far. Everything depends on moderating the anticipations within the boundaries demarcated by a transcendent reality no longer clearly discernible. In other words, all the assistance must come from the side of the partial perspectives provided by science and rights themselves. The self-limitation to the givenness of an order of reality not only preserves reason from impossible imbalancing expectations, but also renders the presence of the boundary transparent for the order of transcendent Being that constitutes it. In this way, fidelity to the modest attainments of reason become the means of securing the sense of order by which reason itself is sustained. The result, as we will suggest below, is not only that openness toward Being is recovered, but that mundane rationality is liberated to work its fullest within the realm of its real possibility. Without the burden of supporting the impossible, reason can effect the transformation of the possible.

The recognition of the truncated character of instrumental reason is so widespread that it may well be regarded as the defining problematic of modernity. Enlightenment science was perceived as excessively constrained to phenomenal analysis and therefore deficient in illumination of any higher meaning by the whole Romantic generation. Their response not only took the form of the poetic celebration of nature as the path toward its deeper mystery, but also the serious intellectual effort to elaborate a philosophy of nature begun by Goethe and continued by the Idealists. Hegel went furthest in explaining why modern science fell short of the nature of science of necessity, since it fell short of the character of absolute knowledge. His own subsequently exaggerated claim to have reached absolute knowledge in no way negates the validity of his critique, nor of the inescapability of his conclusion that human science is constituted by the participation in divine science. It is a formulation that is strikingly close to the Greek conception of philosophy, as Heidegger reminds us in his impressive effort to regain the fount of Western differentiation. The inconclusiveness of such efforts, widely shared across the past two centuries, does not in any way vitiate the truth of the aspiration. It was not so much that they failed as that they failed to complete a trajectory clearly demarcated before them. In this sense, the modern world remains what it has always been—a world fundamentally incomplete. It is a world constituted by the differentiation of Being that renders a rational elaboration of order possible, but its development has consisted of the unfolding of reason outside of reference to the differentiating movement in which it began. The possibility of order depends, as always, on regaining contact with the lost source. Our arrival at the dawn of the third millennium of our history suggests a more expansive consideration of the possibility—that a world from which transcendent Being has been forgotten might not prove so inhospitable to the representation of transcendence as precisely that which cannot be fully symbolized as present.

Notes

1. An illustrative survey of the successive periodizations linking them to one of the earliest is Henri de Lubac, *La posterité spirituelle de Joachim de Fiore*, vol. 1 *De Joachim à Schelling*, vol. 2, *De Saint-simon à nos jours* (Paris: Lethielleux, 1979, 1982).

2. See Harold Bainton, *Here I Stand: A Life of Martin Luther* (New York: Mentor, 1950) and Gerhard Ebeling, *Luther: An introduction to his thought* (Philadelphia: Fortress, 1970) as well as Heiko Oberman, *Luther: Man Between God and the Devil,* trans. Eileen Walliser-Schwarzbart (New Haven: Yale University Press, 1990).

3. A recent example of the self-confidence of science vis-à-vis religion is Edward O. Wilson, *Consilience: The Unity of Knowledge* (New York: Knopf, 1998), and the same spirit declaims in Stephen Hawk-

ing, *A Brief History of Time* (New York: Bantam, 1990). On the self-sufficiency of the rights perspective, see the century's most theoretical elaboration in John Rawls, *A Theory of Justice* (Cambridge: Harvard University Press, 1971) and the later disregard of its incoherence in Richard Rorty, *Contingency, Irony and Solidarity* (New York: Cambridge University Press, 1989).

4. This is precisely the argument advanced by Hans Blumenberg, *The Legitimacy of the Modern Age,* trans. Robert Wallace (Cambridge: Massachusetts Institute of Technology, 1983). See the discussion in Stephen McKnight, *The Modern Age and the Recovery of Ancient Wisdom* (Columbia: University of Missouri Press, 1991), Ch. 1, "Blumenberg and Modernity."

5. "But you will have gathered what I am driving at, namely, that it is still a *metaphysical faith* upon which our science rests—that even we seekers after knowledge today, we godless anti-metaphysicians still take our fire, too, from the flame lit by a faith that is thousands of years old, that Christian faith which was also the faith of Plato, that God is the truth, that truth is divine." *The Gay Science,* trans. Walter Kaufmann (New York: Vintage, 1974), par. 344.

6. Charles Taylor, *Sources of the Self* (Cambridge: Harvard University Press, 1989).

7. The case has been well made by Stanley Jaki over the years in such works as *The Road of Science and the Ways of God* (Edinburgh: Scottish Academic Press, 1978) and *The Savior of Science* (Washington: Regnery, 1988). Jaki's work builds on the great earlier study of Pierre Duhem, *La système du monde: Histoire des dotrines cosmoligiques de Platon à Copernique* 10 vols. (Paris: Hermann, 1954–59). Jaki, *Uneasy Genius: The Life and Work of Pierre Duhem* (The Hague: Nijhof, 1984). See also David C. Lindberg, *Beginnings of Western Science: The European Scientific Tradition in Philosophical, Religious, and Institutional Context, 600 B.C. to A.D. 1450* (Chicago: University of Chicago Press, 1992) and Edward Grant, *Foundations of Science in the Middle Ages* (New York: Cambridge University Press, 1996), as well as R.K. French and Andrew Cunningham, *Before Science: The Invention of the Friars' Natural Philosophy* (Atlanta: Scholars Press, 1996). A profound recognition of the medieval contribution is contained in Alfred North White-

head, *Science and the Modern World* (Cambridge: Cambridge University Press, 1953; originally 1926), Ch. 1, "The Origins of Modern Science."

8. Within the vast literature on Renaissance science, the most relevant for its spiritual context is surely the work of Frances Yates, *Giordano Bruno and the Hermetic Tradition* (Chicago: University of Chicago Press, 1964), *The Art of Memory* (Chicago: University of Chicago Press, 1966), and *The Rosicrucian Enlightenment* (Boston: Routledge, Kegan and Paul, 1972); D.P. Walker, *Spiritual and Demonic Magic: Ficino to Campanella* (London: Warburg, 1958) and *The Ancient Theology* (New York: Cornell University Press, 1972). See also C.S. Singleton, ed. *Art, Science and History in the Renaissance* (Baltimore: Johns Hopkins University Press, 1967), and Allen Debus, *Man and Nature in the Renaissance* (Cambridge: Cambridge University Press, 1978).

9. Gershom Scholem, *On the Kaballah and Its Symbolism,* trans. Ralph Mannheim (New York: Schocken, 1965) and *Major Trends in Jewish Mysticism* (New York: Schocken, rev. ed. 1946).

10. Betty J.T. Dobbs *Foundations of Newton's Alchemy* (Cambridge: Cambridge University Press, 1975) and Paolo Rossi, *Francis Bacon: From Magic to Science,* trans. S. Rabinovitch (Chicago: University of Chicago Press, 1968).

11. Thomas Kuhn, *The Structure of Scientific Revolutions* (Chicago: University of Chicago Press, sec. ed. 1970). See also *Science, Pseudo-Science and Utopianism in Early Modern Thought*, ed. Stephen McKnight (Columbia: University of Missouri Press, 1992).

12. The pull is a persistent feature of the scientific enterprise in one way or another all the way up to the present. Interesting illustrations are Goethe's work on the theory of light, the idealist search for a *naturphilosophie*, the generalization of Darwin to account for creation as a whole, Einstein's longing for a comprehensive field theory, Teilhard de Chardin's evolutionist vision of reality, and such more recent dabblings in the mystical penumbras of science, such as those of Fritjof Capra and Carl Sagan.

13. This argument forms the often overlooked core of John Henry Newman's classic discussion of a liberal education in *The Idea of a University,* first published in 1858.

14. Recent examples are Phillip Johnson, *Darwin On Trial* (Washington: Regnery, 1991); Michael Behe, *Darwin's Black Box* (New York: Free Press, 1996); and William Dembski, *The Design Inference: Eliminating Chance Through Small Probabilities* (New York: Cambridge University Press, 1998). For the debate within the biology community, see Stephen Jay Gould, "Darwinian Fundamentalism," *New York Review of Books* 12/6/97: 34–37; Niles Eldredge, *Reinventing Darwin: The Great Evolutionary Debate* (London: Phoenix, 1995); Michael Denton, *Evolution: A Theory in Crisis* (London: Burnett, 1985).

15. A good, brief account is contained in Alasdair MacIntyre, "The Character of Generalization in the Social Sciences and their Lack of Predictive Power," *After Virtue* (Notre Dame: University of Notre Dame Press, sec. ed. 1984), Ch. 8. The glaring failure of social science to intimate the possibility of the collapse of the Soviet Union is reviewed in Martin Mahalia, *The Soviet Tragedy: A History of Socialism* (New York: Free Press, 1994).

16. "On the theoretical understanding of human conduct," in *On Human Conduct* (New York: Oxford University Press, 1975).

17. The impossibility of stepping absolutely outside of the social setting is well explored by Michel Foucault and may well be regarded as his principal theoretical achievement. But he utterly fails to arrive at a science of order, either in relation to the sustaining order of society or in relation to the implicit perspective from which his own critique is launched. The blinkers of passion render Foucault into "Weber with an attitude." See his *The Order of Things: An Archaeology of the Human Sciences* (New York: Vintage, 1973).

18. This is a topic I have explored more extensively in *The Growth of the Liberal Soul* (Columbia: University of Missouri Press, 1997). For recent expositions of the liberal shortcomings, see Mary Ann Glendon, *Rights Talk* (New York: Free Press, 1991); Pierre Manent, *An Intellectual History of Liberalism*, trans. Rebecca Balinski (Princeton: Princeton University Press, 1994); George Grant, *English Speaking Justice* (Notre Dame: University of Notre Dame Press, 1985).

19. A remarkable passage redolent with such suggestions of unlimited self-possibilities appears in the Supreme Court opinion of *Planned Parenthood v. Casey* (1992): "At the heart of liberty is the right to

define one's own concept of existence, of meaning, of the universe, and of the mystery of human life. Beliefs about these matters could not define the attributes of personhood were they formed under compulsion of the State." The prospect of limitless self-creation echoes the words of God to Adam, as envisaged by Pico della Mirandola (1487): "We have made you a creature neither of heaven nor of earth, neither mortal nor immortal, in order that you may, as the free and proud shaper of your being, fashion yourself into the form you may prefer." *Oration on the Dignity of Man,* trans. A. Caponigri (Chicago: Regnery, 1956).

20. This is why individuals like Andrei Sakharov or Elie Wiesel or Martin Luther King, who have dedicated their lives to the cause of human rights, become something more than ordinary public figures. Whatever their own religious affiliations (and Sakharov had none), they function as secular saints of our age.

3

Christianity as the Limit of Differentiation

PART OF OUR DIFFICULTY in conceiving the relationship between Christianity and modernity is the metaphorical nature of language. It is virtually impossible to avoid the impression we are discussing two external entities from a perspective outside of both of them. Our linguistic habits are overwhelmingly derived from a world of objects, and it is difficult to resist their extension into all other realms of discourse. A conscious effort must be made to remind ourselves that there are no such things as "modernity" or "Christianity." They are not objective realities outside of us; rather, we are part of the reality that extends into them. Far from having a vantage point outside of them, we would have no meaning at all, except for what has emerged within them. Modernity is not a world, but the limits of the perspective in which we find ourselves. It is as far as we are presently able to apprehend ourselves and our place in the order of reality. As such, it constitutes a world without being identical with it. The crucial consideration is whether modernity is the limit or is itself subsumable within a larger perspective. Has modernity surpassed Christianity, or is the Christian differentiation the horizon in which modernity has become possible?

On the answer to this question turns the meaning of the third millennium. Is the event no more than a residue of a common

Christian past, or does it recall us to the ineluctable Christian limits of differentiation in the present? Do we live within a modern or a postmodern world, or has it been our fate to forget about the source of the world that still defines us? They are intriguing questions, made all the more so by our arrival at a moment of diminished certainty as to where we are going. If "postmodern" means anything, it signals the collapse of modern self-assurance. But how can we reconceive a link with the vanished Christian past? Does Christianity not itself suffer from the same sense of historical obsolescence as any public symbolism? Modernity began on the presumption of the supersession of the Christian civilization that preceded it. Can we seriously consider rethinking the link between Christianity and civilization at a time when the only public consensus is the acknowledgment of fragmentation? In particular, how is it possible for Christianity, which has accommodated to its role within the modern world, to reconfigure itself as the sustaining horizon of that world?

The burden of this essay is to suggest the far-reaching reorientation of our self-understanding that is required in order to grapple with the challenge of our time. If we wish to do more than bemoan the crisis of meaning, we must be prepared to move away from the externalist metaphor of knowing and admit we are immersed in lines of meaning before we even begin to reflect. Besides the objectivity of the investigation of objects, there is also the reality of the investigator and the world in which he takes his bearings. The latter is constituted by meaning before the inquiry ever begins, and the possibilities of inquiry are very much structured by the differentiations already achieved by that constitutive illumination. Unlike the objects indifferently lying in wait for our encounter and analysis, the boundary constituted by meaning marks the limit of our self-understanding. It can be elaborated, but not easily extended. There is no perspective beyond what has historically been differentiated and appropriated as the working framework of our thinking. Heidegger worked tirelessly to call attention to the opening within which thinking occurs. The differentiations that make thinking about objects possible are not themselves produced by thinking. Only the illumination of Being establishes that space in a not readily surpassable way. The modern world, which began in the self-confidence that it could dispense with such constitutive illuminations, has seen the collapse of its horizon of meaning cast serious doubt about the viability of its indifference. We are compelled to wonder if modernity does not simply presuppose a revelatory opening from which it has become disconnected.

Christianity as Ultimate

The suggestion is borne out by the unavailability of any more differentiated perspective than what has emerged through the Christian tradition. Modernity may be able to separate itself from Christianity by standing apart from it, but the modern self-understanding cannot attain a higher viewpoint that includes the Christian conception of existence. Whether we think of the universal equality of human beings, their fallibility and distance from moral perfection, the mutual need for repentance and forgiveness, their incapability of obtaining the unmerited grace of divine redemption and resurrection, the result is the same. In no other symbolic form is the apex of differentiation reached. Only through Christianity is the height and the depth of human existence fully disclosed in such a way that we are enabled to live profoundly at home in the world without confusing it in the least with our final home. The authority of Christianity derives from its moral truth. Only an advance in the moral imperatives of existence could establish the ground from which a judgment of its validity could be rendered. The so-called anti-Christian critique of the modern ideologues has been, as Nietzsche understood, parasitical on the very Christianity they sought to displace.

This was the problem that preoccupied Nietzsche most profoundly. He had grasped the incompatibility of the Christian virtues within a secular age, yet understood that their removal could only be in the name of higher virtues beyond the Christian. It was an impossibility that disclosed itself the deeper it was contemplated. Objection to Christianity ultimately must become a challenge, not just to the finitude of human virtue, but to its divine completion. How can the critique extend to the One whose infinite perfection redeemed all human defects? This is why Nietzsche was compelled to admit, "There was only one true Christian, and he died on the cross" (*The Anti-Christ*, par.39). How could a Christian disagree with this sentiment? Christ is indeed the measure by which we are all seen to fall short, but he is also the means by which the incapacity is completed. His perfection reveals the extent to which the deficiencies of human virtue are absorbed and transcended by the divine redemptive suffering in which we participate. A careful reading of the modern critics reveals a similar pattern. The critique of Christianity can ultimately not be extended to the figure of Christ, who escapes the strictures levelled against his disciples and, we are inclined to conclude, disarms even those who sought to oppose him. A higher viewpoint beyond Christ seems morally impossible.[1]

We have no perspective beyond what has differentiated in the course of history. To the extent that Christ constitutes the limits of the differentiation of order, then his is the illumination in terms of which reality must be seen. To adopt anything less would be to settle for a less differentiated and thus less rational viewpoint. We are not free to select or develop an alternative orientation because we are embedded in the historical process. Only what has emerged historically is available to us, and it is our responsibility to immerse ourselves in its ordering light. We do not enjoy the standpoint of absolute reality capable of embracing the whole, viewing it from whatever angle we choose. Our vantage point is from within reality and, to the extent we can attune ourselves to the absolute perspective of Being, then we will see things more clearly. But we must pursue the trail of revelation in order to grasp that fluttering glimpse. We do not possess it. Submission to the gift of revelation as it has differentiated order over history is the only means available to us. The epiphany of Christ represents a unique moment in this perennial human odyssey of illumination.

The aptness of the millennial calculation from the birth of Christ is not merely a holdover from a Christian civilization. It is still expressive of a fundamental structure. Christ is the turning point of history because he marks the limit, the fullness, of the perspective of revelation.[2] No more definitive opening toward transcendent Being is possible. The perspective of order illumined by the participation of God in human existence identifies the boundary of illumination. No higher viewpoint can be attained within time. It is noteworthy that Hegel alone, of all the great modern thinkers, recognized this. A measure of the opaqueness of the Christian revelation is the degree to which it has not only been rejected by the ideologues, but marginalized in the broader universe of discourse. Therefore, Hegel's affirmation of the centrality is all the more striking and is a mark of his stature as a thinker. He understood that philosophy cannot simply dispense with revelation and continue as if it had never happened. However it is handled, revelation cannot be ignored because it constitutes an advance in differentiation beyond the perspective emergent in philosophy. One cannot simply neglect what the revelation of Christ says about human nature, its participation in the divine, the redemptive and transfigurative finality of history, as well as the definitive separation of mundane from transcendent Being. No doubt, the task of philosophy would be greatly simplified in the absence of revelation, but we do not create the mystery in which we find ourselves and are called to make our way. Revelation, once it has occurred, is inescapable. A decisive break within time has occurred when the limit of revelation itself has been reached.

The fullness of revelation constitutes a limit to the perspective of philosophy as well. It is not that philosophy loses its independence once it acknowledges the authoritative truth of revelation. Rather, the completion of revelation is the fulfillment of philosophy as such—an enlargement to the limits of what can be conceived. But it is, in no sense, a stepping beyond the limits of philosophy. The truth of revelation is apprehended because it is recognized as an extension of the truth revealed within the philosophic movement of the soul. What, for the philosopher, had to be extrapolated as a myth, enlarging the surroundings of his experience, is now encountered as a living reality within existence. Christ displaces much of what the philosopher must symbolize by means of the likely story, although he does not remove myth entirely, since even he cannot reveal the whole of reality from within the perspective of participation. Creation and eschatology as events outside of time cannot be symbolized in any way other than mythically. However, the saving presence within time does not itself have to be mythicized; it is encountered as the living presence of Being incarnate. Divine presence in the cosmos does not have to be mediated in terms of a story from the beginning; now it is apprehended as an event within the order of creation itself. No other occurrence can have quite the same radiance as the illuminative center of history, casting its light back toward the beginning and forward toward its end. An absolute reference point within time has emerged because it is the perfect conjunction with the absolute Being beyond all time. The enlargement of the philosophic perspective that results means that philosophy too must now take its bearings from the fullness of divine self-revelation in Christ.

Science as Absolute Knowledge

Intuitively, we recognize that the philosophic universe has been expanded through the influence of Christianity, but it remains to be seen whether the theoretical means of acknowledging that dependence will be forthcoming. Two millennia of struggle with the problem have not generated a stable resolution, if such is possible. In the modern period, separation, indifference, and hostility have most often characterized the relationship. Hegel appears as a lonely, flawed voice in grappling with the continuity of philosophy and revelation. The failure of his project through the deformation of philosophy and revelation within the system does not diminish the significance of the aspiration. Just as much can be learned from Hegel's great errors as from his undoubted achievements. Foremost among the latter is his understanding of the theoretical shift required to ensure any possibility of bringing the movements of philosophy and revelation into conjunction. On our capacity to resume the Hegelian problematic depends the coherence of the modern world that has emerged from their intersection, yet has so far proved incapable of bringing them into any transparent correlation.

The sidelining of the attempted reconciliation in the Hegelian system is not the last word. Of even greater significance is his apprehension of the problem and of what its resolution entails. He understood more clearly than most of his contemporaries the requirement for the realization of science. It was not enough to invoke a methodology and undertake an investigation of phenomenal relationships. One had also to place such an inquiry into a context of significance, and no such horizon was adequate until one had reached the viewpoint of the absolute. All other viewpoints were partial. Empirical science sought objectivity, but it was an objectivity that was itself in need of a grounding. At best, it could attain the laws of phenomenal regularity, but it could provide no penetration of their meaning or necessity. The self-contained world of science was a conditioned signification, which seemed to presuppose a larger world of meaning it could never attain. Critical history was capable of ever more minutely dissecting the facts, but could never pierce their ultimate meaning. The recognition of what is going on presupposes the attainment of a perspective on the whole. Only absolute Being can provide this glimpse.[3]

Hegel went too far in his expectation that the attainment of the absolute perspective would provide a comprehensive apprehension of all reality, to wit in the System of Science. But the fundamental insight remains. Human science falls short of science in the true sense, as the Greeks understood in calling themselves philosophers rather than sophists. This realization is the anchor for science. Its claim to science depends on the awareness of its distance from science in the full sense. We know about it, not through the rendering of objective analysis, but through the whole within which all analysis must take place. Hegel's great theoretical achievement was in calling attention to the neglected perspective of participation. Reality and its transcendent ground are not to be known through dogmas or concepts, but through the illumination that expands from the perspective of participation. Hegel overcame the isolated autonomy of Kantian reason by returning to the whole within which awareness of separation arises. Even the consciousness of difference is already an apprehension of unity. The boundary of empirical knowledge, so rigorously defined by the Kantian critiques, is simultaneously a knowledge of what constitutes the boundary. In some sense, however limited, the boundary is overstepped.[4] Hegel's error was in insisting that such a glimpse could become tantamount to knowledge in the full sense and not merely remain the measure by which we estimate the shortfall in our understanding. The famous dialectic asserted that the apprehension of difference was its sublation.

Necessity of Revelation

Despite the derailments, however, Hegel's meditation brings us into the depths of the matter. He understood that the apprehension of transcendent Being as constitutive of the boundary of human consciousness could not occur except through the advent of revelation. As a result, the drama must be understood as unfolding primarily from the divine side. Human response remains integral, but its decisive interventions occur through the participation of transcendence in immanence. Structure, whether in science or in the unfolding of history, is established at the point of such irruptions. The revelation of Being constitutes order. As a consequence, for Hegel the history of the world is intelligible only as the history of God's self-revelation. It is a theme that is taken up in a more orthodox fashion by the older Schelling. Regrettably, Hegel's and Schelling's example was not resumed in the subsequent history of thought, with the possible exception of the work of Eric Voegelin. Most successors have perhaps been discouraged through the misimpression that Hegel's absolute perspective claims a comprehensive penetration of the empirical materials. Voegelin's great enterprise, by contrast, was to combine empirical respect with the amplitude of revelatory openness. Heidegger turned his considerable profundity to the establishment of the opening itself in the midst of an intramundane civilization.

We can do no more than take up their suggestions. Despite all appearances, our world may not be as self-sufficient, as secular, or as rational as it asserts. The schizophrenia that insists it can dispense with the very foundations that sustain it need not be viewed in a wholly negative perspective. Contradiction provides the opening into which our meditation may enter, as we begin to explore the extent to which a rational secular order might become capable of acknowledging its constitution through the definitive self-revelation of God in history. What is needed is the confidence that the rationality of the modern world will lead us back to the differentiation of Being from whence it is derived. A faithful unfolding of reason itself eventually makes plain its dependence on an order of Being from which it takes its bearings. Far from a conflict with revelation, the deepest reality of reason is that it exists in continuity with the self-disclosure of transcendent divinity. A secular world as such can hardly even be identified, except through the dedivinization of the cosmos in the full transcendence of revelation. Our problem is to retain or rediscover the enchantment of its tension toward the ground that can no longer be identified with it. A beginning is to be found in the operation of reason itself. The reenchantment of our world can most effectively begin with the instrument that is most transparent for its constitutive relationship to Being. Indeed, nowhere is the movement from the Beyond so available to us as it is through the opening of the soul. Having rediscovered the subjective pathway, we can then appreciate more fully the source of the great symbolic forms that marked the earlier eras of enchantment.

Reason has always been the illuminative center of human exist-ence. Only its discovery is a novelty, and that particular moment is tied, as we saw in chapter 1, to the revelation of transcendent Being that can be apprehended by no other means. The memory of that derivation may have receded, but it is never closed up. It awaits, as Heidegger understood, as a destiny ready to seize us when we least expect it and therefore remains available for the meditative recovery we seek to obtain. Reason is embedded in the revelatory opening, and it can never finally cut itself off from that source without turning its back on reason. Our confidence is therefore well founded that reason, faithfully pursued, will lead us back to the full amplitude of differentiation. To stop at anything less than the definitive attainment of differentiation would be to settle for a lesser hold on rationality. This is impossible for reason, without turning away from itself. To settle for a reduced standard of rationality is to choose what is irrational. Reason cannot be itself if it fails to live up to its own exigences. Left free from preconceived restrictions and released from the ideological incu-bus, reason enlarges itself freely until it reaches the limiting hori-zon of differentiation. To be rational means to live within the differentiated horizon of the ultimate revelation.

The modern world is not only historically Christian; in a deeper sense, with implications for the relation to other world religions we will explore in the next chapter, it is essentially Christian. Its rationality is not only derived historically from a Christian orbit; it is structurally related to the maximal differentiation of being achieved there as well. Christianity defines the limits of rationality. To the extent that we submit to the norms of rationality, we are drawn inexorably toward their fullest expression within Christian-ity. Resistance at any point along the way involves a diminution of rationality. Of course, it is not necessary to begin at the end point of fulfillment. Anyone who undertakes the rational opening to-ward truth is implicitly within its orbit. All that is needed is faithfulness to the imperatives of reason itself for the amplification within the full Christian differentiation of Being to disclose itself.

It matters little where we begin. Ineluctably, we are drawn toward the discovery of the presumptions of our worldview and toward the recognition of their beginning. The differentiations on which we ground our rationality do not arise ready-made. They depend on an illumination of Being that demarcates the main lines of their reality. It has long been understood that the conception of divinity, the organizing framework of religion, provides the ultimate horizon of meaning for any society. We are accustomed to applying this perspective when studying other societies and civilizations. It is the theological that furnishes the most comprehensive principles of reality and, therefore, the constitutive self-understanding of a social whole. But we rarely apply the same insight to ourselves. Curiously, only the postmodernists have begun to compel a reexamination of the perspective from which our own scientific study of the world and society derives its validity.[5] The problem is that such critics themselves share too much of the modernity they critique. They take the objectivity of modern science at its face value as rooted in the claim to have detached itself from all premises and presuppositions. As a viewpoint utterly detached from any interest in the organizing framework of reality, modern science and liberal rights can assert their superiority. But it does not take much to deconstruct the myth of neutrality. Even modern science cannot escape the acknowledgment of its assumptions about the nature of reality, man's place within it, the purpose of human life, and the expectations of good and bad. The problem of the deconstructionists is that they themselves share the bankruptcy of foundations. They cannot conceive of any grounding of rationality. It must therefore be, they conclude, irreducibly relative, culture bound, and interest driven.

The difficulty is not inconsiderable. How is it possible for a contingently located human being to arrive at any perspective on reality or any conception of the good that itself escapes the condition of contingency? Can we assert more than the idea that truth is what appears true from our point of view? On what basis can we claim to have reached a privileged viewpoint? Is our view of causality anything more than a rival means of organizing phenomena than that found among animists? Are they not ultimately different and incommensurable ways of seeing the world? We are more than familiar with such conundrums in the moral and political arena. Public life seems to reduce to the obsession with never asserting the authority of a normative judgment, lest we too aggressively undermine the relativist equality of all cultures. The notion of culture as itself normative has long disappeared to be replaced by an irreducible plurality of cultures whose commonality cannot even be explored. Increasingly, the same tolerationist sensitivity has come to invade the realm of science, beginning with the social sciences, but not excluding contact with the natural sciences. "All reality is socially constructed" is taken as the last word. Missing is any serious consideration that this observation, like all such espousals of skepticism, cannot have any reflexive reference. Toleration itself escapes the delimitation of culture boundedness. It stands as a profession of unquestioned truth.

However, inconsistency is not the definitive verdict on the modern world. The reason why this world succeeds is that it finally triumphs over its own schizophrenia. When a conflict arises between its espoused principles and the imperatives of rationality and fairness, the latter generally win the day. A world driven by a sense of rationality and of rightness is not about to set aside its deepest convictions merely because of its own intellectual incoherence. But what it desperately needs is to discover a means of enlarging its innermost convictions so that the grounding integrally present within them can become transparent. The self-discovery can take place once the weight is shifted toward existential reality and away from the conventional strictures obscuring it. Science and rights arise not from our human attainment of a position of universal objectivity within time, but because they are integral to the stance of human beings in every time. We are capable of seeing things objectively because we are never simply the sum total of our temporal attributes. No matter how exhaustive the inventory, we ultimately escape encapsulation.[6] Finite reality cannot absorb us because there is a dimension of the infinite in us. It is this ineluctability that provides the possibility of distancing ourselves from any and all contexts, and therefore provides the possibility of objectivity in our apprehension of truth. Nothing requires us to bow to prejudice.

Of course actualization of the possibility is its fullest revelation. What is it that draws us toward truth, that refuses to settle for anything less than reality in all its rigor, that compels us even to accept the incoherence of our worldview rather than impose any undue limitations on what can be known? Whence originates this unquenchable drive toward reality, a drive that heads inexorably toward the whole without limit? It is none other than the participation in transcendent Being toward which we are ultimately directed. The end is present in the beginning. This is not merely the meditative structure of reflection. It is the sustaining movement of human existence. What appears to be a chaotic manifold of desires is ultimately shot through with the defining orientation toward Being. We can do without many things and are prepared to accept counterfeits of all kinds, but we are not capable of doing with less reality. The compulsion to submit to the strict requirements of scientific objectivity or to persist immovably in the conviction of the equal rights of all is not only a stance made possible by transcendent openness. It is its prime actualization.

The classic philosophers discovered that justice is not simply an aspiration. At its deepest level, it is a reality that is constitutive of human existence. The pull toward the transcendent Good was not realized through abstract reflection, but through the existential struggle to live in accordance with its reality. The growth of the soul is itself a distinctly expanded reality of the human condition. Aristotle coined the verb *athanatizein* (immortalize) to convey a sense of the enlargement of reality it entailed. Striking too is the extent to which Nietzsche recognizes his own forlorn dedication to truth as deriving from the same source. It is with some discomfort that he acknowledges that his own critique of truth is derived from the same altar at which Plato worshipped. Nietzsche was not only the most pious of the godless, but the most self-perceptive. Even the nihilistic will to transcend all values drew its strength from the love of transcendent Being. How else can we identify the will to go beyond all limits? The modern impulse, whether exemplified by Nietzsche's unresolved honesty or the truncated objectivity of science and rights, is rooted not so much in a turn away from transcendent Being as in its inconclusive realization. A tragic incapacity to recognize the source of its own deepest inspiration is the defining feature of our world.

Yet, as Heidegger reminds us, opening toward Being remains the ineluctable condition no matter how much its attraction may be forgotten. Millennial neglect does not obviate the constitutive self-revelation of Being. It remains not only as the condition, but as available for rediscovery in its constitutive role. All we have to do is reflect on our own longing driven propulsion. Behind it all is the desire—dimly sensed but irrepressible—to settle for nothing less than reality without limit. How can such a transcendent compulsion have arisen if it was not through the self-revelation of its fullness? At this point, we begin to step beyond the Greek parameters, within which the question of whence the revelation comes is scarcely broached. Nevertheless, even there the awareness of the revelatory character of the event is preserved. The Beyond cannot be known in any other way. Nothing else can disclose it except its self-disclosure. The dynamics of the experience make this structure plain, for it is evident that the encounters are irruptions of transcendent Being we are powerless to command or repeat, no matter how profound its impact may be. Plato, in particular, comments (in the *Seventh Letter*) on the difficulties for a science of order on such an uncertainly transmittable basis. This is not yet an understanding of the character of revelation itself, but it is headed inescapably toward the realization that only the transcendent God can reveal himself.

Christ as the Limit of Revelation

The advent of Christ is the event that brings the structure of revelation into focus and, with it, the differentiated order of being compactly expounded in philosophy and the other world religions. This is not to say that Christianity renders its predecessors and their successor developments obsolete. Even within Christianity, it is noteworthy that it found its immediate predecessor, Judaism, of such continuing relevance that it absorbed it as its own Old Testament. We will explore the subject more fully in the next chapter, but it is still necessary to observe that the less differentiated articulations remain of continuing interest, both for their own sake and for their irreplaceable evocations of the modes of participation in Being. The fecundity of the drama of man's encounter with Being not only enriches the comparative perspective, but also attests the inexhaustibility of the intersection of transcendent Being with time. Their continuing conversation is among the most notable opportunities of the third millennium. Christianity, while it invites and in an important sense contextualizes the exchange, does not in any sense preempt the content of what will be said. Holding the position of the most differentiated revelation does not in any way imply a monopoly on the means of expressing its unfathomable truth. In many respects, the fulfillment of revelation requires the openness to the full range of its equivalent pre- and post-figurations.

It is primarily the limits of differentiation that Christ reveals. He is the one through whom the One is manifest because he is identical with the divine Being itself. In the limiting case of revelation, the transcendent God can be revealed only through himself, since all other mediators fall radically short of the reality that is beyond everything finite. The world and our own longing may point us toward God, but we cannot know his being unless he makes us participants within it. Not only is the capacity to know God strictly beyond our nature, as St. Thomas emphasized, but it is beyond the reality of everything we know. The being of the "I AM" is so inexpressibly other than the being of everything else in existence that the predicate can only be employed analogically (*Summa Theologiae* I, Q.13, a.5). We would have no sense of what the Being of God is, apart from his self-disclosure. He would remain a wholly hidden divinity, an unknown God, were it not for the free gift of himself as the God who is "I am with you." Just as his presence is an unmerited self-donation, there is no necessity for transcendent divinity to enter incarnately into time. Yet, once it has happened, a definitive clarification takes place concerning our relationship to divine Being.

We recognize that the inner revelation of God in the human heart—a flow of gracious divine presence throughout history—can never fully disclose the openness of human being for Being itself. The incarnation of divine order within reality can never be adequately manifested by the imperfect, creaturely struggle for realization. Only God himself can reveal the meaning of his order within time. Nature can scarcely evoke the transparence for what lies beyond it, and the fitful human stirrings in response to the gift of revelation are never more than glimpses through a glass darkly (1 Cor. 12:12). The resplendent fullness of transfiguration through the light of transcendent divinity can occur in no other way than through the incarnation of God himself. Then we begin to see the finality of all creaturely opening toward God, but beforehand this transcendent illumination had been no more than a dim possibility. It is almost as if there is enough of a trickle of transcendent revelation emerging through history to enable us to recognize the one in whom its transfiguring fulfillment is present.

The advent of Christ marks a qualitative turning point, although it does not mark a palpable transformation of the conditions of existence. Accounts in the Gospels oscillate between moments when the luminosity of Christ is beheld and the inevitable return to the mundane present in which the faith must be lived out. Christ himself is the central embodiment of this pattern. The Gospels are built around his relationship with the Father, which erupts into transparence at pivotal moments. His last supper discourse in Saint John is the most articulate reflection of the mutuality of trinitarian self-consciousness, but it is apparent in all of the pivotal moments of Christ's temptation, prayer, mission, and submission. From the perspective of the apostles, the episode of the transfiguration is the most telling. The imagery of resplendence is intended to suggest the experiential event of beholding for a moment the fullness of divine presence in Jesus. However, contemplation even of the fullness of revelation cannot endure without terminating the conditions of existence within this world. The return down the mountain, as well as the reduction of the relationship with Christ to the bond of faith, is accepted as the ineluctable mystery in which such illuminative events occur. Disclosure of the fullness of revelation does not abolish time. It only renders its meaning in principle.

The epiphany of transcendent Being incarnate introduces a qualitative change in the understanding of existence, although not in its diurnal reality. Nothing can be understood in quite the same way any longer when we behold the openness of creaturely existence for the Being that lies beyond it. But the apprehension of that illumination remains tied to the same conditions of episodic luminosity. Essential eschatology, as the Church came to conceive it, is different from realized eschatology.[7] In other words, the fulfillment of revelation can be missed, and its recognition depends on the same conditions of responsiveness to the promptings of grace. Again, the Gospels provide a faithful narrative of the failure of human beings, including the apostles, to recognize Jesus as the Son of God. As with all revelation, circularity is its fundamental structure. Revelation can only be apprehended by those who have faith, and the faith can only be sustained by the revelation. The mystery of the interpenetration of grace and freedom remains inaccessible at every point short of the eschaton. Emergence of the fullness of revelation does not alter the conditions for its reception. Flesh and blood do not reveal who Jesus is, as he remarks at Peter's confession of faith, but the Father who is in heaven (Matthew 16:17). Jesus is recognized by those whose hearts are open to the pull of the inner revelation of the divine Beyond.

The situation is filled with intangibles and imponderables. Many do not hear of him because they lived before Christ or the word never reaches them. Of those that do, they hear of him in a context in which his divinity can only remain opaque. Much of the modern world, as well as those in other religions, are surely in this category. The others who do receive the message, but fail to respond, cannot be judged either because, as Jesus himself reminds us, judgment is accessible to the Father alone. Only those who open themselves toward his presence provide an insight into the structure of the event. Nothing compels a response to the humble guise in which the Son of God walks among us—nothing except the discernible promptings deep within ourselves by which we are enabled to recognize who he is. Miracles do not prove the divinity of Christ as the Gospel writers well understood, since they are never performed for those who do not already have faith. It is faith that enables us to recognize the source of the miracles, of which the greatest is faith itself. Whence then does faith come? It flows from the same mysterious source of the Father from whom the Son also is derived. In the absence of faith, miracles are superfluous; they cannot even be seen as miracles. The great mistake in modern rationalist readings of the Scripture is this failure to understand the genre of experience they entail. As moments in the drama of the soul encountering God, their components cannot be separated out from the movement of faith as a whole.

The definitive fulfillment of revelation does not mean the definitive transformation of existence. In the absence of the latter, the transmission of the former remains bound by the same conditions of uncertainty and rejection that characterize all movements of illumination. But even if a qualitative change has not yet taken place, its imminence has been announced. The transfiguration in principle is itself decisive. From its retrospective radiance, the openness of all reality toward its transcendent ground is recognized, but the prefigurative structure would never have become visible without the further opening of transcendent Being. Intimations dimly sensed in the intracosmic order are clarified in their full extracosmic radiance. The limiting self-revelation of God establishes a definitive differentiation of the order of being. It is not inconsistent with the prior intimations; rather, like every self-disclosure of transcendent Being, it emerges as a pure gift beyond all possibility of anticipation. Created reality may be constituted by transparence for the source whence it came, but the irruption of Being always occurs as a radical novelty within it. When the revelatory outburst reaches the limiting case, the intervention of transcendent Being is definitive in structure. No further possibility of revelation is possible when God has made himself fully present in a human being. Divine being cannot be disclosed more fully to us than the manifestation of the man in whom its fullness is present. All of the differentiating finality of the Christian vision derives from its definitive revelatory structure.

Christ as the Limit of Reason

The reason why we live in a Christian worldview, despite all appearances to the contrary, is that it has become impossible to think beyond the limits of its differentiation. Nothing remains untouched by the illumination emanating from the discovery of the transcendent openness of being for Being. The tensional pull is already there before the limiting outburst, but the radiance could not reach as far or as clearly in the absence of the epiphany of Christ. However strange it may be to confess that reason is thus dependent on such irruptions of transcendent luminosity, the limiting revelation of Christ makes the structure unmistakable. Illumination can only come from the Beyond. Once it occurs, we recognize the degree to which all being is constituted by its receptivity toward a Love that is far beyond its immanent capacity. Since the revelation of Christ marks the limit of that openness—the fullness of divine reality present within time—the differentiation of reality has correspondingly reached its limit. The fullness of God's self-disclosure is simultaneously the limiting illumination of finite reality. This is why the Christian differentiation of the order of being exercises its authority even over those who do not explicitly subscribe to its source. Irrespective of personal inclinations or faith, it is impossible to think outside of the categories defined by the revelation of Christ. Departure from them can only be made by becoming less rational. They are the spiritual equivalents of the laws of identity and noncontradiction.

Foremost among such parameters is the recognition of this world as a world. It is only the light of transcendent perfection glimpsed momentarily that reveals the finitude and imperfection of everything else. We see reality as it is, without illusion or false expectation. This is why Christians can be the most hard-bitten realists. No one, for example, is more unblinking in his contemplation of the shortcomings of this world and life within it than St. Augustine[8]. Through the heightened participation in the higher transcendent life, existence in this world is beheld in all its vicissitudes and inconclusiveness. Without the burden of supporting the unlimited aspirations of the human heart, the mundane order is free to disclose itself as it is, without construction or addition. The degree to which we suffer from illusory anticipations in the modern era is a barometer of the decline of Christian experience. It is only with difficulty that we can exert the will to strip away the illusions with which we are inclined to gild our view of reality. The harshness and unsatisfactoriness of all finite reality are inescapable dimensions of the existence we know, yet we pull away from the full rational acknowledgment of the consequences. How is it possible to live in a world without illusion? The possibility has been opened up by the Christian differentiation, but we sense our grasp of it slipping as the illuminative experience recedes.

Only Christians, it seems, can be fully secure in their acceptance of the unsatisfactoriness of existence. St. Augustine even approaches cynicism in his realism. But cynicism is, rather, what is left when the transcendent light has withdrawn. Instead, Augustine's attitude is more rational still; it is without the tone of resentment that attaches to the cynic. The Christian acceptance of finitude and death remains the most positive because it views this immanent reality in its highest possibility. The world is the temporary vehicle for the transcendent presence. As such, its incompleteness can be fully acknowledged without disvaluing it in the slightest. By pointing toward the higher fulfillment it is incapable of attaining, this world achieves its highest purpose. We begin to see finite existence as it is and in relation to its highest possibility. The Incarnation is the deepest affirmation of the mystery of created reality and at the same time, the unmistakable identification of its provisionality. Without bearing the significance of ultimate reality, immanent being nevertheless plays its role in the larger drama of transcendent Being entering time to redeem it for itself. Paradoxical as it may appear, it is only the differentiation that recognizes the full finitude of existence that can affirm most profoundly its full transcendence of itself.[9]

This is the point of greatest divergence with the Greek world that preceded Christianity. The Incarnation, with its drama of suffering, death, and resurrection, was the major stumbling block. How can we accept a God who takes on the grossness of material flesh and blood to undergo the most degrading death that was conceivable? It seemed to fly in the face of all that we knew about the gods, who were characterized by their elevation above the contingency and mortality of our condition of existence. If anything was true of the gods, it was their ascent to the higher regions of the cosmos. The highest One dwelt beyond the cosmos itself in utterly detached, immovable perfection. Purified souls of men might aspire to travel toward that realm and ultimately could reach the highest possibility of standing on the rim of the cosmos, whence they could contemplate the eternal One (*Phaedrus* 247c-d). But why would anyone wish to reverse the direction, least of all the transcendent God? Why should God wish to leave his realm of perfection? The Greeks had finally not broken through to the full transcendence of God. He was still too closely tied to the cosmos, whose ascending ranks defined his perfection. They had not yet recognized that transcendent Being is utterly different from the cosmos, which would itself have no relation to him apart from his gift of self-disclosure. The accent still fell on their own experience of ascent rather than on the irruption of transcendent illumination from Beyond. They did not yet see that they would not even know about Being had it not made itself present within existence.

Unable to recognize the degree to which the transcendent is always radically beyond the capacity of finite apprehension, they could not fully apprehend grace or the receptivity for it.

By hewing more closely to the reality of the cosmos, the Greeks devalued this world. Despite the apparently more worldly character of Greek thought, it is ironically the full contingency of existence that is missed. In retrospect, the consequence is not surprising, given the preeminence attached to the being of the cosmos itself. As the perfect manifestation of the One, the divine icon, it provided the paradigmatic measure toward which all other reality must be directed. Without sharply differentiating between the transcendent Beyond and immanent existence incapable of its manifestation, it was inevitable that the latter would never be seen for what it is. Contingency and mortality are accorded only the negative tonality of what must be pulled against in the movement toward the higher cosmological actualization. The dynamics of the struggle for attunement to the higher attraction of the Good is well differentiated, but it falls far short of our understanding of a science of nature or of society. Greek science was bound to the model of cosmic perfection, therefore, its function was conceived to be the elaboration of the laws of rational necessity governing all things. This generated an elegant mathematical conception of nature, but not its empirical investigation. Precisely, the contingently factual relationships were considered not worth studying. It is only if nature is differentiated as a realm of its own that it can become a subject of empirical exploration. Contingency can be apprehended and its investigation considered a value only where the radical transcendence of Being has differentiated its openness and its worth. Nature, despite our translation of *physis*, does not mean the same thing.[10]

Christ as the Limit of Virtue

Nowhere is our distance from the Greeks more evident than in relation to human nature. Aristotle, as we have seen, struggles manfully to hold together the hylomorphic model of the organism with the transcendent openness of the soul. The results are the notorious tensions between books I and III of the *Politics,* as well as the enduring inability to break the hold of the polis as the community of fulfillment even in the midst of its swan song. The historical openness of humanity as an eschatological community could not become visible so long as the hold of the cosmic embodiment of reason could not be broken. A universal human nature incapable of any finite fulfillment (and therefore constituted by the history of its movement toward the Beyond) remained on the boundary of Greek consciousness. They could not penetrate to the rational reorientation required because the irruption of transcendent Being had not reached its limits. Reason in the Greek world was bounded by the twin convictions that the cosmos is itself the perfection of order and that the human telos must be achievable within it. Within those parameters, the achievements are remarkable and definitive, but we recognize that the boundaries themselves are impositions of arrested rationality.

Such restrictions do not permit us to come to grips with the deepest problems of existence. Among these are the realization that life, even for the most fortunate, falls far below what could be counted as complete fulfillment and, for the vast majority, is far less than even their natural expectations would lead them to hope. A determination to expend every effort on the acquisition of the only excellence within our power—virtue—ultimately fares no better. Prolonged attention to the problem of virtue brings two things to the forefront. First, as Aristotle discovered, is that the source of virtue is ultimately impenetrable and must be ascribed to a kind of gift of nature. We know how to make men good once they have decided to become good, but we are helpless to bring about the prior movement of decision to seek after goodness. Second, the advance in virtue eventually generates the awareness of how far we still have to go. Plato betrays a fleeting awareness of the problem in his analysis of the parallel, if not proximity, between the philosopher and the tyrant. Do we ever reach a point at which virtue has become a secure and expanding attainment, or is there not lurking always the inclination to transform the very achievement of virtue into a means of domination? The abyss of evil within the human heart may become more evident in light of the transcendent grace required to overcome it, but it is there all along and its rational assessment necessitates its acknowledgement. Nowhere is the closeness of the relationship between reason and revelation more evident than in the necessity of confronting the problem of evil.

This is the core of what Christianity is all about. It is not primarily a movement of salvation from this world or of reconciliation with the divine judge above it. Christianity is, first of all, a liberation from the evil that destroys us. Everything else follows from this. We recognize the depth of the evil that held us in light of the divine gift of self required to overcome it. The predicament in which we had been fastened becomes blindingly clear. Our condition had been one of fallenness, the immovability of souls barely able to sense the direction they should go, but utterly powerless to move a muscle toward it. It was not only that our gaze was limited to the range of finite reality and therefore was incapable of drawing us toward our transcendent fulfillment; the darkness within ourselves went deeper than the absence of light. It was infected with the spirit of revolt. Not only did we recurrently fall into evil and consistently fall short of our aspirations. There was a distinct component of wilfulness to it. Evil was not merely an affliction; it is also an inescapable fatality of our souls. We choose evil for no other reason than that it *is* evil. Irrational and surdic as it may be, we are prone to overstepping the limits for no other reason than that they are there. We want to be the center of our own existence even when we know we are not. Fallenness is not a mythic extrapolation to the beginning; it is primarily the mystery of iniquity that we recognize as holding us in its grip. The good that I seek is not the good that I will; rather, it is the evil I do not wish (Romans 7:13–25). It is the realization finally that nothing separates us from the evil we wish to avoid—the abyss we are powerless to close within us—that opens us up to recognition of the transcendent fullness that can alone close the emptiness.

What Plato intimated in the proximity of the philosopher/tyrant, we recognize as the universal condition of human hearts. Our capacity for evil is the mirror image of our unlimited openness to good. Evil is not merely a fall away from goodness. It is its inversion, and nothing can ensure against its irruption. The very unattainability of transcendent fulfillment can be redirected toward its opposite and prove equally insatiable. Our life is balanced in every moment on that knife edge of possibility where, for no reason, we might yet choose the evil we seek to avoid. Habit can consolidate the practice of virtue at every step of the way, but it can do nothing to secure the innermost orientation of the soul toward it. The final temptation is to do the right thing for the wrong reason. Augustine's critique of philosophic virtue lays bare the reserve of pride that can still remain untouched by all its impressive resolution.[11] The twentieth century has presented the shock of limitless gratuitous cruelty to the de-Christianized modern consciousness, but it would have surprised neither Augustine nor Dostoevsky, who both recognized such a possibility within themselves. Once again the rational apprehension of reality seems supportable only by the light of transcendent grace dispensed by Christ. It is because we see in him the transcendent fulfillment of our longing that we are able to acknowledge its abyssal character within us.

Grace is the inner movement of what we outwardly recognize in Jesus. It is the touch of transcendent reality we recognize as our final fulfillment and whose mere brush is enough to bring about the decisive reorientation of our lives. This is the repentance at the heart of the Gospel message. Without it, not only are we unable to move toward our transcendent fulfillment, but even the limited goodness of which we are capable by nature will fail. As Augustine explains, the incompleteness and conditionality of our orientation toward the good, eventually infects even ordinary virtues with its corrosive influence.[12] Thinking we can get by with a merely human effort, we eventually lose the defenses needed to prevent the coop-tation of our efforts in the service of evil. This is why a purely natural order cannot stand long. Virtues of tolerance and kindness ultimately lack the fortitude to resist the more imperious demands for self-interest and survival at any cost. Only Christianity can provide the adequate underpinnings for the realization of natural virtue because Christianity alone has differentiated the constitu-tion of nature from its transcendent source. The capacity to ration-ally analyze the sources of the abyssal disorder that afflicts the natural order is intimately connected with the revelation of the transformative grace of restoration. Repentance generates an order within this life because it is rooted in the order beyond it.

Christ as the Limit of Myth

In Christ, the transparence of this world for its constitution from Beyond is actualized. In him we behold the movement we appre-hend within. As a result, we not only have the limiting differentia-tion of the movement toward order as immediately experienced, but we also receive the definitive symbolization of the mystery of the whole within which the drama unfolds. Previously, the phi-losopher's and other forms of myth were required to extrapolate the order of the whole; now it is encountered in the immediacy of a personal narrative. Moments that are distended in the other symbolizations of order are here brought into conjunction. Instead of distinguishing between the immediate disclosure of the Beyond within the soul and the mediated experience of order within the cosmos from the Beginning, we now have them joined together in the personal encounter with Jesus, who is the redemptive word.[13] The uniqueness of the revelation of Christ is not only the limiting manifestation of transcendent Being; he is also the particular vehi-cle through which the transcendent can become manifest. Tran-scendent reality can disclose no more than its fullness manifesting itself, the variability of mythic possibilities has also shrunk to the unrepeatable particularity of the man who is God. Just as no more revelation is possible, so no more extrapolative elaborations are possible. In the incarnate divine fullness, revelation and myth converge. The meaning of the opening of transcendent Being is identical with the action of Christ.

The relationship is reciprocal. We understand the experienced gift of transcendent Being through the encounter with Christ and vice versa. For this reason, the experience is interpreted in the same terms as the process of the whole. Just as we are redeemed through the touch of divine Being, so the action and passion of Christ is the redemption of the cosmos. Our participation in divine Being is, at the same time, the participation of the divine in human being. All of the movement of human openness to the divine pull throughout history culminates in this unique epiphany of the fullness of divine reality in human nature. In the unrepeatable uniqueness of Christ, the meaning of the mystery of the whole is disclosed. Our responsive opening toward the revelatory pull of the Beyond is always recognized as our participation in the wider drama of the divine redemption of order from disorder. Now it is recognized as the unique event of God's participation in the human drama by which that redemption is effected. Christ illuminates not only the drama of grace and freedom, but the ultimate victory over evil within the cosmos itself. Through Christ, we enter into the redemptive movement, and it is in him that redemption takes effect. Man's participation in the divine suffering of evil in existence is recognized for what it ultimately is: God's participation in the human suffering of evil by which the redemption is achieved.

The experience of the transcendent formation of order is irresistible. God's knowledge and his will are one. It is enough to be brushed by the divine spirit of creation to know the force of that inexorable reality. Nothing is more certain, yet nothing is more invisible from our perspective. The conflict between the two harrowed the Hebrew prophets and, in a parallel sense, tortured the classic philosophers. How was the truth of transcendent Being to become incarnate in a mundane reality that seemed incapable of its reception? How could the people of Israel become the people of

God, or the people of Athens fulfill the nature of the polis? Neither side could be denied. The conflict was inexorable and irresolvable, without abolishing the conditions of existence as we know them. Only the advent of Christ effects the reconciliation. Finite reality becomes wholly subordinate to the divine will in the man provided by God himself because he is identical with God. As such, his actions carry representative significance. The answer to the struggle of millennia is disclosed. Both prophets and philosophers grope toward its outlines, but it is only in Christ that its radiance can be apprehended. Not only is he the illuminative center of divine order within history, he is also its effective point of redemption. The mystery of redemptive suffering stands revealed as the central truth of the whole in which we participate. Transfiguration in the image of the revelation of Being is no longer an aspiration or a frustration. It is the mystery of the transfigurative process already underway within history.

The extrapolation of the theophanic experience is complete. Atonement for the fall into evil has been made when it is accomplished by the self-abnegation of God himself. Only in this way can the sin of revolt against infinite goodness be recompensed. The experiential confrontation with the abyss of sin would make this realization clear, but it is only in the revelation of Christ that it can emerge in its full stature. He is the culmination of the interior movement and the exterior narrative of revelation and myth. They converge in the recognition of Christ as the one from whom both ·the experiential grace of redemption and its eschatological victory emanates. The mystery of redemption stands revealed. It is nothing less than the revelatory gift of transcendent Being that surrenders itself to finite consciousness utterly without the merit or ability to reach it. In Christ we behold the actualization of this inner drama. He is the divine Being poured out for us as the only adequate means of reconciling our sinful nature with his divine goodness. Why there is a world and a fall and the need for redemption and restoration remain questions beyond the range of penetration. But the most central illumination has been assured to us. We know the presence of transcendent Love as the abiding reality because we behold what we glimpse inwardly. God so loved the world that he gave up his own Son so that we might be saved. From this radiant center, a transcendent order of love is created within history.

The definitiveness of the revelation of Christ is exemplified by the degree to which experience and extrapolation intersect. He is not only the point from which the redemptive action radiates throughout history, he is also the fulfillment of the transfiguration toward which he leads all things. Christ is both the escahatological turning point and its completion. The Church—the community formed through faith—now lives in the mystery of the eschatological present in which everything has been accomplished, and yet it awaits its final transfiguration of the world. What is clear is the transfigurative direction. The resurrection of Jesus and his bodily ascension to the Father is continuous with the victory over sin and death. Having submitted himself completely to the will of the Father, Jesus is wholly united with him through the Spirit. Again the vision of the resurrected is the glimpse of eschatological transformation that represents the limits of what can be contemplated within the conditions of this world. The common thread in all the Gospel accounts is that the recognition of the glorified Christ turns on the faith that is capable of apprehending the meaning of the events of his life and death. It was in the breaking of bread, the central expression of his sacrificial offering for all of us, that the disciples on the road to Emmaus recognized their companion (Luke 24). Nothing has changed in the conditions of life and death through which we exist, but their meaning has been shot through with a shaft of eschatological light.

We cannot cling to the risen Lord, as Mary Magdalene sought to do in the garden (John 20:11–18). Even if we attempted to do so, we would find ourselves holding only to the wrappings, a consolation about as reassuring as the endless quest for scientific confirmation of the historical Jesus. Transcendent Being cannot be drawn into immanent reality without abolishing the latter. Even after the resurrection of Christ, our only access remains the inner opening of faith. Only with the eyes of faith can we recognize who it is that stands before us or hear the voice by which we are addressed. Even after the resurrection, it is still the opening of transcendent illumination within us that enables us to recognize what we behold; it is not a rival source of luminosity emergent within immanent being. The resurrection of Jesus is the radiance of transcendent Being. The eschatological glimpse it affords is no more than the definitive extrapolation from the strand of revelatory experiences reaching back in human history. Transfiguration is not accomplished for us yet, but we can catch an unmistakable glance of its realization. A limiting clarity is attained as we see the resurrection of the body as the fruit of its total transfiguration by the fullness of transcendent Being. Eschatological completion does not signify the abolition of immanent being. Rather, the resurrected Christ points toward the transfiguration of all finite reality as the vessel of transcendent presence. Just as the unrepeatable presence of Being in Christ augurs the uniqueness of his personal physical presence, so the openness of all beings to the same transcendent reality makes them irreplaceable recipients of the one divine Love. None are dispensable; all are destined for unique transfiguration.

The luminosity of Christ's resurrection casts its light not only on our movement beyond this world, but also on the significance of earthly existence. Emphasis falls not merely on the liberation from this life; it also raises the value of the material substratum that is moving toward the moment of its subsumption into transcendent glory. Imagery of the world as a tomb or a prison from which escape is regarded as joyful was widespread in the ancient world. However, it generally prevailed in circles dominated by Platonism, Neoplatonism, Gnosticism, and Stoicism. Rarely do we find a Christian hint of denigration of mere earthly existence. On the contrary, this life is more highly valued both as the prelude and preparation for what is to come and as the material whose transformation is assured. No higher value can be attached to finite existence than to regard each individual as a unique irreplaceable vehicle for the radiance of transcendent presence. Nothing can be lost of what the Father has given Jesus because each has been called to enter fully into the divine Love. Each is an unrepeatable refraction of the infinite depth of transcendent Being in finite being. The attachment of that spark of infinity within each one forms a unique being whose whole existence is radiated with the light of the One. Each human being is the whole or the presence of the whole in this finite medium. Everything about him or her is irradiated by the light from the Beyond. Just as it is impossible to conceive of a revelation beyond the fullness of God, so it is equally impossible to move beyond the sanctification of earthly life by this same relationship.

Christ as the Limit of Balance

Christ is the culminating revelation of our movement toward God and of the significance of existence within this world. Eschatology points toward both the beyond and the present. It is because Christ illuminates both simultaneously that he is the great force for order in history. Civilization is perpetually struggling for balance. The aspiration toward transcendent Being—the inexhaustible longing for complete and perfect reality—must be balanced with the realization of its inherent unattainability within time. If we were either to reach our goal or to conclude that it is impossible, then the dynamic unfolding would cease. All that we known as human life—its restless striving and inquiring—would be no more. Our constitution toward an horizon of mysterious fascination that, the more we approach it, the further it recedes, is the permanent condition of our existence. The difficulty of maintaining a balance between the tensional poles of longing and postponement is a source of notorious instability. How is it possible to maintain the constant fidelity of striving without yielding to the false preemption of fulfillment or the dejection of futile disappointment? Balance can only be maintained if we have been able to reach an insight into the mysterious continuity between the two. Postponement is no longer a source of frustration so long as fulfillment is perceived as being already mysteriously present in the process. The balance realized through the mythic elaboration of trust in the whole is crucial to preserving the revelatory truth from distortion.

No one has done more to bring this problematic to light than Eric Voegelin. It is the major theoretical contribution he sought to articulate over a lifetime. He understood that the great imbalancing tendency in illuminative experiences is the tendency to forget that they emerge from reality as a whole. They are movements of exodus toward transcendent Being, but they are not movements out of reality. Despite the luminosity gained, they do not transfigure earthly existence nor accomplish its abolition. Yielding to illegitimate extrapolations not only distorts our perception of reality and undermines the possibility of balance within it; it destroys the revelatory experience itself. Now the illumination is treated as a piece of information on the basis of which we might effect our escape or domination of reality as a whole. Participation in transcendent Being shrinks into insignificance as the imagination is seized by the prospect of identification with the transformative process itself. The extrapolation eclipses the original experience from which it derived. This was the tendency against which the Church had to struggle from the early days in combatting heretical movements. Transfigurative fantasies are not just a source of imbalance in individual and social life; they are lethal to the preservation of the only process of transfiguration available to us. It is no wonder that all the heretical movements are ultimately directed against the Church itself as the embodiment of the provisional eschatological presence. However, it is a great mistake to suggest, as Voegelin does, that the Church is defined by its struggle with the heretical distortions.

The perception is understandable given the occasional intensity of the polemics, but it constitutes a fundamental misreading of the Christian revelation. Christianity is pictured as being endemically afflicted with heretical controversies. The reality is that heretical movements existed at the peripheries of the Church and, from time to time, exercised a degree of influence, but at no point could it be said that they had permeated the Christian worldview. For most

Christians, the attraction was limited. This is why heresies were successfully suppressed. It was the solid bedrock of Christian consensus expressed in the criterion of catholicity, rather than the appeal to repressive political interventions which had only variable success anyway. What needs to be understood is the durability of that common Christian core. It is this that is missed in Voegelin's imbalanced concern with the problem of balance.[14] What his reading fails to recognize is that the heretical distortions could not ultimately threaten Christianity because it was precisely in the acceptance of the mystery of balance that Christianity excelled. Devaluation of material existence is scarcely compatible with the revelation of the transcendent fullness incarnately present within this world. Indeed, the burden of mystery—the impenetrable pull toward eschatological transformation—is made infinitely supportable through the disclosure that it is a condition to which divine Being itself submits. The mystery is still there, but the assurance of its meaning is definitively deepened.

The balance between exodus and fulfillment toward which the philosophers and prophets struggled seems effortlessly accomplished within Christianity. How can we give way to impatience when God himself has provided us the example of its endurance? We have confirmation of the invincibility and the ineliminability of the process of transfiguration. Trust in the order of the whole does not have to depend on the intimation of faith and its elaboration in a myth of the beginning and end. Irrefragable divine demonstration of the validity of the submission to the mysterious process presents us with a formidable affirmation of balance. Why should we rebel against the postponement of a fulfillment that Jesus himself has shown is mysteriously bound up with the order of earthly existence? This life is not something superfluous we should seek to slough off. It is the station through which divine providence intends to prepare us to become receptacles for transcendent fullness. From the Incarnation, the radiance of divine presence has pervaded the whole world. This life is not something to be quit, but to be valued as the precious means by which we open in reception of transfiguring grace. Far from a devaluation, it is in Christianity that a reevaluation of life occurs, as in each instant there is a unique, unrepeatable opening toward the transcendent. Differentiation of Being as accessible only through its incarnational gift of itself raises the earthly condition to the highest possibility of transparence.

For this reason, Christianity is not only the way of salvation beyond this life; it is also the means of living most fully within it. Again, the conventional misconception of Christianity as an otherworldly religion is only partially correct. It is incorrect in discounting the principal route to the greatest deepening of human life available to us. What it fails to understand is that only an otherworldly religion can affirm most fully the value of this world. Everything we do here is not only appraised in finite terms, but is irradiated with transcendent significance. As such, it shatters the scale of mundane measurements. Achievements and renown are not disregarded, but they are seen for their true significance as being less central than the spirit in which they are received. What we accomplish will eventually recede in memory and effectiveness in the obsolescence of time, but the inner disposition in which they are performed touches on what endures. Mysteriously but perceptibly, this is the point at which the openness to transcendent Being occurs. "We are not called to be successful, only to be faithful," as Mother Teresa reminds us. As a consequence, the glory of accomplishment is surpassed by the humility of demeanor, and the valuation of all human life is most universally affirmed. A Christian civilization is a civilization of love in which the radiance of transcendent Being endows all life with its highest possibility.

It is not in any sense an escape from responsibility in this world, since it is precisely through such fidelity that we move toward eternity. Christianity raises the stakes. Failure to fulfill our responsibility is not merely a personal dereliction, a waste of natural endowments and social inheritance. It is a loss of Being, a turning away from the possibility of transcendent life. Yet this heightening of responsibility toward ourselves and our world is kept within a balance that saves it from overreaching or despair. We are not responsible for the transfiguration of all things, for the correction of all injustice and the restoration of all brokenness. That process, we are assured, is already mysteriously underway from its divine source. Our part is only to play our part as fully and faithfully as we can within the drama of redemption. It is a part that can be played by no other, but it is equally not a part impossible for us to sustain. Saved from aggrandizement and resentment, we are free to follow the graceful promptings that make up the sufferings of the body of Christ. Nothing is more important than the fulfillment of our task within this life, and yet nothing is less important than its successful outcome. Life is lived most fully when we cling least to it.

The validity of the Christian disposition to remain most completely in this world while not, in the slightest, becoming of it is intuitively recognized. A balance must be obtained between the energy we pour into our projects and recognition of the finitude of our accomplisments. The modern world seems to demand a limitless dedication of effort, yet it promises no more than intermediate satisfaction. Rationality depends on the preservation of an equilibrium. If we veer too much toward limitless exertions, then the sheer excess spills over into our expectations. If we dwell too long on the inconclusiveness of all our achievements, then we eventually sap the will even to go on living. Life itself seems to call us toward boundlessness, yet provides no more than bounded fulfillment. The problem is crucial in a secular world that cannot find the means of adequately symbolizing its transcendent intimations. We lurch unpredictably from outbursts of mundane enthusiasm, the ideological orgiastic fantasies, to the desuetude of quietist somnolence, the lassitude of postmodern nihilism. Often, a balance can only be obtained by concentrating on the immediacies of family and work in a world from which the big questions have been banished. But it is a difficult orientation to maintain because the great issues inevitably reassert themselves, and devotion to the personal cries out for a larger affirmation of meaning. Everything about our secular seriousness embodies the balance of transcendent dedication in a finite world, yet it is utterly incapable of explaining itself to itself.

Our sanity depends on the possibility of recognizing that the schizophrenia of the modern world is not unique or even mistaken. It accurately mirrors human existence. We are torn between the poles of poverty and fullness, as Plato diagnosed in the *Symposium*. Our modern split becomes schizophrenic because it forgets the partial nature of its perspective. The part is not the whole, yet it is compelled to act as if it is. Either we become incapable of articulating the transcendent significance of our exertions, or their finite achievements are made to carry a transcendent import. Disorientation is the result as we struggle ever more unsuccessfully to maintain a balance within a context in which the poles of reference seem to have disappeared. This is why the limiting differentiation of the order of being through the advent of Christ is so crucial to the preservation of a life of reason. Transcendent Being is recognized in its unattainability, and immanent reality is stripped of all illusory appearance, yet their integral relationship could not be more fully bodied forth. The building up of civilizational progress could not be placed on a firmer basis than the Christian conviction that action in this world is transparent for the redemptive drama of Being. It is the lost center restoring the wholeness of the modern fragmentation. Whereas the finite exertions desperately sought to touch transcendent consequences, now they are revealed as moments in the flow of the timeless within time. The raw hunger for Being is no longer an impenetrable source of disorientation. It becomes luminous from the balance incarnate in Christ between perfection and imperfection.

This has always been the appeal of Christianity. It is not the promise of eternal salvation, since that cannot mean anything to us except in terms of the difference it makes in our lives here and now. Fullness of life is not merely a promise projected beyond time; it is apprehended incipiently within existence as well. Christianity is the heart of civilization because it is the fullest realization of life in human experience. Without turning its back on this world, it directs us to live completely within it without losing ourselves in its false infinity. No higher possibility can be conceived than the life that is lived at the highest attunement to Being while remaining within a world of beings. We would never have penetrated to the possibility had not the transcendent Beyond assumed full material presence among us, since all glimpses of the Beyond come only by way of the revelation of its fullness. But now that the opening of Being has occurred, we cannot return to a more compact mode of existence. The whole modern world, with its focus on the rational development of this world, is premised on the differentiation of Christ.

Recognition of the schizophrenic character of its isolation is the prelude to the rediscovery of the source from whence it has come and by which it is still invisibly sustained. Only through the incarnation of transcendent Being can we see the way by which mundane existence can be raised to its highest possibility without the irrational overreaching that would tempt it to futilely surpass God himself. The temptation is removed, not through the restraint of aspiration, but through its fulfillment in the only way possible. We can become God through God becoming man. Christ stands at the center of our world because he is the one who delivers on its promise. He reveals the unattainability of the longing that animates it because he announces its true transcendent fulfillment. Openness toward rational development is vouchsafed by the recognition of the incapacity of a finite world to adequately contain infinite divinity. But at the same time, the measured and manipulated world of finite intelligibility is saved from becoming a homogeneous desert. It remains transparent for the transcendent fullness it can point toward, but not attain, through its own unfolding.

Notes

1. Even John Stuart Mill, despite his ostensible hostility to Christianity, gives voice to the irreproachable witness of Christ: "And whatever else may be taken away from us by rational criticism, Christ is still left—a unique figure, not more unlike all his precursors than all his followers, even those who had the direct benefit of his personal teach-

ing." *Collected Works,* vol. 10:487. Of course, the most powerful statement of the unsurpassability of Christ comes from the pen of Dostoevsky: "I can tell you about myself that I am a child of this century, a child of doubt and disbelief, I have always been and shall ever be (that I know), until they close the lid of my coffin. What terrible torment this thirst to believe has cost me and is still costing me, and the stronger it becomes in my soul, the stronger are the arguments against it. And, despite all this, God sends me moments of great tranquillity, moments during which I love and find I am loved by others; and it was during such a moment that I formed within myself a symbol of faith in which all is clear and sacred for me. This symbol is very simple, and here is what it is: to believe that there is nothing more beautiful, more profound, more sympathetic, more reasonable, more courageous, and more perfect than Christ; and there not only isn't, but I tell myself with a jealous love, there cannot be. More than that—if someone succeeded in proving to me that Christ was outside the truth, and if, *indeed,* the truth was outside Christ, I would sooner remain with Christ than with the truth." *Selected Letters of Fyodor Dostoevsky,* ed. Joseph Frank and David I. Goldstein, trans. Andrew MacAndrew (New Brunswick: Rutgers University Press, 1987), 68.

2. "In the light of the New Testament, the years of Christ's earthly life truly constitute the *center of time*; this center reaches its apex in the Resurrection." John Paul II, Apostolic Letter, *Keeping the Lord's Day Holy,* par. 74.

3. One of the clearest discussions of the necessity of the perspective of absolute knowledge for the attainment of knowledge is contained in the *Introduction to the Lectures on the Philosophy of History,* trans. H.B. Nisbet (New York: Cambridge University Press, 1975). But, in general, see the *Phenomenology of Spirit,* trans. A.V. Miller (New York: Oxford University Press, 1977).

4. Heidegger's commentary deals with this meditation in the earlier part of the *Phenomenology.* See his *Hegel's Phenomenology of Spirit,* trans. Parvis Emad and Kenneth Maly (Bloomington: Indiana University Press, 1988), and *Hegel's Concept of Experience* (San Francisco: Harper and Row, 1970).

5. A noteworthy example is Jacques Derrida's later work. See Harold Coward and Toby Foshay, eds., *Derrida and Negative Theology* (Al-

bany: State University of New York Press, 1992); and Derrida and Gianni Vattimo, eds., *La Religione* (Rome: Laterza, 1995). Heidegger provides the classic confirmation, both of his own and of Nietzsche's filiation with the negative mystical mode. "What Nietzsche is practicing here with regard to the world totality," he comments on the eternal recurrence, "is a kind of 'negative theology,' which tries to grasp the Absolute as purely as possible by the holding at a distance all 'relative' determinations, that is, all those that relate to beings. Except that Nietzsche's determination of the world as a whole is a negative theology without the Christian God." *Nietzsche* vol. II, trans. David Farrell Krell (San Francisco: HarperSanFrancisco, 1984), 95.

6. The classic literary evocation of this realization is Dostoevsky's *Letters From The Underworld*, trans. C.J. Hogarth (New York: Everyman, 1968). See the recognition of its centrality in the treatment by René Girard, *Resurrection From the Underground: Feodor Dostoevsky*, trans. James G. Williams (New York: Crossroads, 1997).

7. Pelikan, *The Emergence of the Catholic Tradition (100–600)*, Ch. 3.

8. His *Confessions* still furnish as acute an analysis of the dissatisfaction of life as any we encounter in our age of anxiety. "When I am in trouble I long for good fortune, but when I have good fortune I fear to lose it. Is there any middle state between prosperity and adversity, some state in which human life is not a trial? In prosperity as the world knows it there is twofold cause for grief, for there is grief in the fear of adversity and grief in joy that does not last. And in what the world knows as adversity the causes of grief are threefold, for not only is it hard to bear, but it also causes us to long for prosperous times and to fear that our powers of endurance may break. Is not man's life on earth a long, unbroken period of trial?" *Confessions,* trans. R.S. Pine-Coffin (Harmondsworth: Penguin, 1961), Bk. 10, 28.

9. A line from Patrick Kavanagh captures perfectly the correlativity between these moments: "He had the knack of making men feel / As small as they really were / Which meant as great as God had made them / But as males they disliked his air." "If ever you go to Dublin town," *The Complete Poems,* ed. Peter Kavanagh (Newbridge: Goldsmith Press, 1972), 253. A parallel evocation of the dignity of the person in contemplation of the full finitude of existence is surely the core of the music of Shostakovich.

10. Heidegger's whole enterprise is devoted to uncovering this dynamic openness in the meaning of *physis*, precisely as the space in which Being is encountered even if it is not present. See, in particular, *The Principle of Reason*, trans. Reginald Lilly (Bloomington: Indiana University Press, 1991, lectures 9–10), as well as *Early Greek Thinking*.

11. "For if the Law is there with its commands, but the Spirit with its help is absent, the very prohibition of the sin increases the craving to sin, and when that craving wins the day, the guilt of transgression is added to the evil impulses. Not infrequently, to be sure, the obvious vices are overcome by vices so masked that they are reputed virtues; and the king of those is pride, an exalted self-satisfaction which brings a disastrous fall." *City of God*, trans. Henry Bettenson (Harmondsworth: Penguin, 1972), Bk. XXI, Ch. 16.

12. "And yet men must not think to free themselves from this degradation by posing as despisers of glory and paying no heed to the opinions of others, while they esteem themselves as wise men and win their own approval. For their virtue, if it exists, is dependent on the praise of man in another kind of way. For the man who wins his own approval, is still a man. But he who with genuine piety believes in God and hopes in him, is more concerned about what he finds displeasing in himself than what (if anything) is pleasing, not so much to himself as to the Truth." *City of God*, Bk. v, Ch. 21.

13. On this distinction see Voegelin, *The Ecumenic Age* (Baton Rouge: Louisiana State University Press, 1974), Introduction.

14. Commenting on 1 Corinthians 15, Voegelin concludes: "This tale, placing the vision in the perspective of God's way with the cosmos and man, dominates the imagination of Paul so strongly that the perspective of the Metaxy [in-between state of existence] recedes to comparative insignificance. The domination of the tale rather than the tale itself is the cause of the ambiguities which spread from the symbols 'death' and 'time' to the various strata of Paul's exegesis. For the death of the tale is not the death every man has to suffer even if he believes in Christ. The difference could become shadowy to Paul, because he was obsessed with the expectation that the men living in Christ, himself included, would not die at all but, in the wake of the Parousia, be transfigured in their lifetimes." *Ecumenic Age*, 249.

4

Common Center of a Pluralist World

THE OBSERVATION THAT CHRISTIANITY is the sustaining differentiation at the heart of the modern world is a hard saying. It relegates the independence of scientific rigor and the pride of human rights achievements to a subordinate position. They no longer stand on their own, or, if they do, it is with less self-assurance. But what can we say? The reality is that the space of differentiation is unfolded through the revelation of Being and not otherwise. Illuminative experiences are the mode in which reason is discovered and its continued differentiation is sustained. As the limiting differentiation of transcendent Being, Christianity is also the limiting differentiation through which reason becomes what it is. Differentiation arises in no other way, and to turn our back on it would be to choose less rationality, if not unreason. We can even sense the inner resistance of reason against such a possibility, but we cannot provide the illuminative glimpse by which the movement of resistance is sustained and enlarged. Transcendent reality is beyond all access, except through the gift of its self-revelation. Given the increasing incoherence of modern self-referential reason, we have no other option but to acknowledge its transcendence of all foundations in the opening of Being itself.

Reason cannot consistently function in the absence of existential order. Only if we are open to the promptings from the divine side will we be sufficiently attuned to the flash of Being by which we become more fully rational. Uncomfortable as it may be to admit, reason is not an instrument through which we extend our control over being. It is first of all the intimation through which we ourselves are controlled. A responsive unfolding of the invitation that comes toward us from the Beyond is the source of what enables us to live in order. Substantive reason, rather than the iron cage of formal or instrumental rationality, is created only when reason is constituted by the luminosity from what is beyond itself. The sterility of the postmodern debates about foundations is compelling testament to this dynamic. What is sorely lacking is the illuminative glimpse that would render the irretrievable contingency of all possible points of reference transparent. Our postmodern predicament is on the verge of the Christian boredom of the world, but it is incapable of understanding itself as such because the source of the disenchantment is beyond its grasp. It stands in need of the touch of transcendent Being that reveals itself as its own adequate manifestation, but thereby becomes more fully present in all things. The world from which God is absent is the Christian one in which his presence has been fully revealed in Christ. Secular reality is never simply secular. It is a provisional pointer toward what it knows it can never adequately represent; yet through its transparence, it radiates transcendent Being. In other words, the limit of rational differentiation depends more than ever on the recurrent, but unroutinized, encounter with God. The inconvenience of the theophanic structure of reason may have prompted the amnesiac temptations to render it manageable by means of formulas and dogmas for over two millennia, but they have not been able to abolish it.[1]

A large part of our hesitation in contemplating this existential character of reason can be explained by our reluctance to confront the judgmental consequence it suggests. We are uncomfortable with acknowledging the revelatory dependence because we sense that it involves a ranking of the spiritual traditions of the world. Those that propel the movement of differentiation furthest are the ones that represent a higher claim to truth. In particular, the linking of Christianity with the modern secular civilization of scientific method and human rights seems to constitute an undue privileging of the Western religious tradition. Is it not enough that Western science and morality have extended their global reach, without imposing the presumption of spiritual preeminence as well? Discomfort with the suggestion of Christianity as the formative source of the modern world becomes palpable in the recognition of its incompatibility with a plurality of spiritual traditions. How can we sustain mutual toleration and respect among religions if the link between modern civilization and Christianity is more than historical? How can the other traditions survive if the rationality of our world is shown to derive its essential justification from Christianity as well? Spiritual imperialism is suspected as the unspoken agenda behind the modernizing advance, and talk of a clash of civilizations draws its inspiration from such inarticulate murmurings.[2] It is no wonder, therefore, that the secular vanguard of science and rights often deny even more vigorously their Christian lineage in order to assert modernity's independence of all ultimate questions.

Our meditation has proceeded far enough to recognize the bluff entailed, but we have not yet found a way of assuaging the fears that have provoked its necessity. The concerns are legitimate. To the extent that modern civilization becomes global, it carries a set of religious implications whether it wills to or not. We have already seen the protective reaction of religious communities, both in the West and elsewhere, to the perceived secularizing threat. Fundamentalism has been the most defining feature. But what if the threat was to be perceived as religious in nature rather than merely irreligious? Can we expect the Hindu or Islamic or Buddhist traditions to submit before the acknowledged differentiations of Christian revelation? And if we cannot anticipate the Christian conversion of the world, what should our mode of conversation be? How is it possible to sustain a global modern civilization while acknowledging the diversity of spiritual traditions surrounding it? The problem is formidable because even the delineation of the relationship between modernity and its own Christian background has proved challenging enough. What prospect do we have of sorting out the relationship of modernity to the other world religions and then engaging them in dialogue with Christianity and one another? It is not an easy task, but the difficulty is not sufficient reason for avoiding it. The modern world itself puts us more in contact with one another at this millennial moment than at any other time in human history. Our calling is to rise to the occasion, no matter how daunting the challenge may be.[3]

Truth Underpins Dialogue

The first step in the face of forbidding premonitions is to reexamine the source of our unease. It may well be that the fears arise from assumptions that themselves prove insubstantial. In particular, we must subject the underlying objection to the possibility of truth to critical examination. Whatever about the social and political prospects for persuasion, the prior question concerns the possibility of truth in religious traditions. Is it possible to reach a determination as to which is further and which is closer to the reality they intend? Or are we in a realm of irreducible solipsism, in which the validity of Christianity remains confined to its adherents, but cannot make any truth claim on Buddhists or Muslims? Conversely, is there anything of the Hindu or Confucian sense of reality that remains authoritative for Jews, Christians, and philosophers? The difficulty of reaching beyond descriptive familiarity to the juxtaposition of truth claims seems sufficiently daunting that most of the modern world has abandoned the task. Far better to preserve the political peace by lowering the epistemological expectations. Where truth is incommensurable, disputes become irrelevant. Moreover, modernity itself seems to provide us with a comfortable refuge from such unsettling questions, because the independence of secular learning suggests that knowledge of all things can be obtained without taking a position on truth.

The only difficulty is that detached indifference undermines the value of study itself. Why study the religions and civilizations of the world if they are not instructive of who we are and why we are here? Is the aesthetic pleasure of appreciation sufficient? Surely the world religions themselves are the greatest counterpoise to that attitude, since their power and beauty is derived precisely from their claim to truth. It is a curious feature of the scientific study of religion that the matter under examination seems to embody a higher viewpoint than its putative observers. How could it be otherwise when we approach the study of religion with the confidence that we already occupy a perspective above it? Religion can no longer become the road to truth by which we are illumined, once we have determined to enclose it within our ready-made conceptual framework. The superficial glibness of the modern mind that is acquainted with everything except what is most needed is never more in evidence. Impoverishment in the midst of the profusion of knowledge is the inevitable outcome of an attitude that fails to recognize the perspective from which the examination must begin. Convinced that religion is a phenomenon within the world, we cannot but fail to recognize that it is really a field of meaning whose lines include the observer as well. The only perspective on religious truth is from within our participation in it. No independent viewpoint is available outside the relation to truth, by which we not so much judge, as are ourselves judged.

Neutrality is an illusion. We do not possess the luxury of detachment by which we are able to view the whole of reality in relation to its competing symbolizations, nor can we dispense with the need to take seriously the quest for truth about the whole in which we find ourselves. The former attitude gives rise to the phenomenal study of religion, the latter to the secular indifference to all meaning. Neither can be sustained for very long without adopting some alternative, if inarticulate, orientation toward the order of being as a whole. Human beings are inescapably transparent for the question of Being. That means we are embedded in the quest for truth. We cannot turn our backs on it without casting the shadow of doubt over all that we do. Even in the principled agnosticism of our sciences, we know that they nevertheless conceal an unacknowledged metaphysical faith. This was Nietzsche's great insight into the irony of the modern world. It still worshipped truth, and truth cannot be worshipped without drawing us ineluctably toward its source. Even the modern world draws its parsimonious analyses from the inexhaustible well of Being. Once this is admitted, as Heidegger has shown, the game of neutrality has been exposed.[4] Without a refuge, we are thrown back on the only resources available to us—the historical differentiation of meaning in the great spiritual traditions. Not only do they stand before us, evocative of richness beyond our experience, but now we are compelled to acknowledge the unavailability of any perspective outside of them. The juxtaposition of the historically emergent streams of revelation becomes central once they are recognized as being all we have. We cannot study them apart from submission to their luminosity. They are not outside of us; we are outside of them.

Once the conceit of neutrality has been demolished, everything changes. The truth claims of the world religions cease to be an object of curiosity and become an existential pressure. "Who do *you* say that I am?" (Mark 16:15) Just as the Gospels are written to make this central question unavoidable, all the great scriptures are written with the same moment of self-disclosure in mind. This is why they cannot be read properly with the methods of secular literary analysis. As a genre, they do not conform to the external imperiousness of eyewitness reports. The word is a challenge, a promise, and a threat, to be received only in the humility of fear and trembling. There is more at stake than correctness of interpretation, although that is certainly included in the enterprise. At root, it is about the gain or loss of life. What we are to become hangs on our interpretation-response. Are we to move toward Being—the possession of more eminent reality—or are we to fall away into the dissolution of diminished existence? Detachment is needed more than ever to arrive at the truth irrespective of personal inclinations, but indifference can have no role when it is the fate of the student that is being decided. In other words, the true science of religion, does not shrink back from the question that religion poses of us and is therefore the only question that ultimately illuminates the subject of our study. Unlike physics, the intimacy of religion to its student is unavoidable because it encompasses the contemplation itself.

We have no choice but to seek to determine where truth lies in the confluence of world religions. But how are we to decide in the absence of any independent perspective? If we are confined to the viewpoint of participants, are we not irremediably consigned to relativism? Must the conversation amount to no more than an exchange of assertions? Certainly, no outside arbitration is possible, but this does not preclude the mutual recognition of authoritative truth. The irreducibility of the respective spiritual traditions does not mean that movement is not possible within and between them. Indeed, their very character as historical irruptions of meaning confirms their capacity to change. Each of the great spiritual illuminations arose in a specific theological context that was perceived to be insufficiently differentiated. The movement of articulation that each of them carries forward is based on the presumption that the opening from the perspective of compactness is possible. Obstacles and inertia may militate against such spiritual upheavals but they are not in principle impossible, as attested by the very emergence of the world religions themselves. Spiritual traditions, almost by definition, already engage in the conversation by which truth is tested in the struggle toward it from the depths of human consciousness. The possibility of mutual recognition across the great symbolic constructions is integral to the claim of a spiritual advance each of them makes. Movement forward presupposes the possibility of movement and therefore of the conversational expansiveness that makes it a reality. In this sense, the conversation across the millennia that constitutes the drama of humanity does not have to be grounded beyond itself.[5]

We are already engaged in it even before we become self-conscious about its character. As a result, we cannot get back beyond the beginning of the differentiation we have absorbed, except by extending it in the direction of greater differentiation. We are limited to what we have received. But that is sufficient to constitute a world of common experience to the extent that we have received the same source. Recognition is possible across the religious boundaries, not because they are translatable into something else, but because they are redolent of the same revelatory Being. They are different glimpses of the same reality, but the reality itself underpins their unity. The movement by which advances occur and through which mutual recognition is possible is the one movement of responsive unfolding of the transcendent Being, whose invitation is the source of the movement. Convergence centers on the Beyond toward which the conversation is drawn. Instead of looking toward a unity that can be placed under our control, the conversation of spiritual traditions can best be understood in terms of the revelatory outbursts from which they derive. They cannot be translated because they are not descriptions of any reality apart from them. Rather, they are aspirations toward a Being whose disclosure occurs in no other place than with the momentary glimpses in which immanent reality is structured by the pull toward what is utterly transcendent. We cannot afford to forget that the conditions for spiritual illumination extend into the possibility of communication between the various carriers of the revelatory touch of God. Nothing is changed because we ask a second order question about a first order experience. Just as there is no system that can comprehend the process of the whole, there is no key to all revelatory transactions.

But this is also what sustains the inexhaustibility of their conversation. They are apprehensions of what cannot be apprehended, but whose self-revelation may be received. Each is unique, irreplaceable, and unrepeatable because it represents the glance of transcendence within the particular concreteness of the occasion. Multiple refractions of Being offer a glimpse of the unfathomable magnitude of the source from whence the illumination emanates. Truth is therefore present in all of them because they radiate the truth of Being over beings. The advance experienced in each of them is an advance in truth, a greater adequacy of participation in the transcending movement that draws all reality toward itself. But none of them is the encompassing truth that renders all of the others obsolete. Each is enriched through the encounter with the others, and all would be impoverished through the disappearance of any of them. At its deepest level, once the dogmatic defensiveness and insecurity have been rendered redundant, their conversation is not one that requires effort to sustain. The love of Being that draws each of them individually is also apprehended as the common love that draws them together in pursuit of the same transcendent touch.

Their authoritative claim to truth almost requires them to take account of the competing symbolisms that come to their attention. Naturally, the more differentiated spiritual traditions have a distinct advantage in their capacity to comprehend the other partners, but none can simply dismiss the challenge to their comprehensiveness. Some minimal acknowledgment and attempt to refute and encompass earlier as well as parallel streams of illumination are a virtual necessity. The articulation of the order of being is an encompassing enterprise, and that must include previous and rival articulations. However, a distinct phase is reached when the recognition of their mutual enrichment engenders an attitude of pervasive toleration. This is by no means an early achievement, however much its logic may be present in the structure of spiritual experience from the start. Tolerance implies a differentiated appreciation of the unencompassability of Being and the incapacity of all finite formulations to embody it. This awareness may be present in practical form all the way back to the earliest symbolisms, and we have good reason to suspect that it underlies the adaptability of cosmological theologies, but its theoretical formulation is the fruit of a more differentiated account of transcendent fullness.[6] Of course, loss of tolerance remains a perpetual possibility, and there is no guarantee that the realization of underlying unity will not harden into dogmatic battlelines. The concern here, however, is with the principle itself and the recognition that its roots lie ultimately in the toleration of Being for the limitations and the waywardness of the human partner of the drama.

The great enemy to tolerance in this true sense is what can only be characterized as its false alternative. We have already alluded to the tolerance of indifference but now that its true source in the openness of Being has become clear, it is worthwhile to sharpen the contrast. Sham tolerance is by far the most influential attitude toward the relationship between the world religions. It consists of a live-and-let-live magnanimity that reassures us of the irresolvability of the differences between them. The generosity of the disposition is disarming, so much so that we fail to recognize it as a cover for the most repressive dogmatism possible. Toleration in the name of unknowability appears to be a position that welcomes all traditions equally, with prejudice toward none. But the appearance is deceptive. Under the banner of invincible ignorance, all are permitted to speak, but none are permitted to be taken seriously. Not only does it not take a position on behalf of any truth, but it adamantly refuses to admit the possibility of truth. Under the guise of mutual toleration, we are asked to subscribe to a principle that renders the value of toleration moot. What is the purpose of tolerating different viewpoints and permitting their conversation if we have already resolved in advance that they cannot be permitted to reach the truth? The cost of toleration is too high if it requires us to dogmatically consent to a particular view of truth, viz. that truth is nonexistent.[7] Besides, the cost of entrance into the paradise of pluralist irrelevance is unnecessary.

Tolerance can be most fully grounded in the unattainability of Being, not in the unattainability of truth. The dogmatic assertion of the latter presumes that Being has been comprehended sufficiently to determine its inapprehensability as truth. Reversing the relationship, we reach not tolerance but its perversion. By contrast, tolerance is most fully grounded in our participation in the openness of Being. The limitless Beyond can be apprehended by us through the medium of finitude, but only sufficiently to recognize its transcendence of all limits. Such a glimpse is possible because of the openness to Being that constitutes each human being as the *imago Dei*. The tolerance owed the formulations apprehended by each one is due to the capacity to embrace the whole, albeit from the fragmentary perspective of a part. The character of individual participation in Being attaches even more evidently to the great symbolic elaborations in which the perspectival glances are unfolded. Every symbolic form is worthy of respect, not because they are all equally developed, but because they are all equally participative in the whole. While stepping forth as the apprehensions of the parts, they nevertheless are evocations of the whole. The encompassing character of each of the great spiritual traditions is no accidental feature. It arises from their essential trajectory, which is to participate through representation of the whole.

However, grounding tolerance in the mutuality of truth is no more than a beginning. Trivialization is avoided, but at the same time the stakes are raised considerably. If we are to understand the relationship between the great spiritual traditions as ultimately collaborative, then the quest for truth must eventually lead toward the sharpening of distinctions between them. They cannot all be equally attuned and equally misattuned toward the order of being. Even when each of them evokes the Being that none are capable of adequately encompassing, there are still legitimate distinctions that should be made, albeit from the finite perspective. Equidistance from Being can mean varying perceptions of the equidistance. Even their own self-emergence as distinct traditions involves the articulation of differences from the more inchoate traditions that preceded them. They cannot present themselves as advances in truth and attunement if they insist on the invidiousness of all such claims. Without succumbing to the relativity of all viewpoints, the spiritual traditions cannot maintain their own assertion of truth unless they are prepared to take seriously the rival claims of all others. Distinctions of rank cannot finally be avoided, and they can only be intelligibly made from within the spiritual traditions themselves.

The task is sufficiently formidable to discourage most serious attempts over the past two millennia. Our situation is different only in the inescapability of articulating their interrelationships. Contact and contiguity between the great spiritual traditions has historically been of a more limited nature. Particular episodes and locales brought the problem of parallel revelations to occasional attention. Never has the contact across traditions been so ubiquitous and constant as the global modern civilization has made it.[8] Familiarity with other civilizations has been an accelerating feature of modernity ever since its emergence in the voyages of discovery. Ease of travel, communication, and migration have made us increasingly aware of the diversity of cultural traditions, and the intensifying interdependence of global development has made the promotion of mutual understanding a more pressing requirement. Our present moment, poised at the dawn of the third millennium, raises ever more profoundly the question of the meaning of the convergence that is drawing us together. The challenge for the future is to find the means of spiritual interrelationship to match the increasing practical interpenetration of our world. We have been presented with the opportunity and the necessity of conversation across the great spiritual traditions, but we have yet to find the theoretical shelter within which a meaningful dialogue can be carried on. Indifference concealed by feigned interest is clearly neither a source of toleration or conversation.

Only a common pursuit of truth is capable of grounding a meaningful exchange. Mutual respect cannot avoid eventual consideration of the character of the differences and judgment of their adequacy or inadequacy for the common reality toward which they point. Distinctions must be acknowledged because it is only on their basis that the inner unity can be explored. From an amorphous relativism, nothing meaningful can be derived. We must take seriously the presence of a common reality in which all human beings participate and by which their experience is rendered communicable, rather than give credence to the fear that there is nothing generative of a bond between us by appealing to a superficial rhetoric of toleration. The harder way is the testing of respective strengths and weaknesses through conversation. Even a robust exchange is appropriate if the issue concerns the truth or falsity of existence. In the process, we will no doubt discover that what still separates us is far less than the reality that unites us in the common quest of being. The need for illusory harmonization fades away as the invincibility of our common humanity comes to the fore. In the process, we discover that the problems so apparently insoluble at the beginning of the exercise, especially the great question of a criterion of truth recognizable by all, assumes more tractable proportions. Conversation itself leads us toward the criterion embedded in the inquiry itself. Our quest for being does not have to await the discovery of the principle by which it is to be guided, since it is already contained in the movement that animates the search. We know of what we are in search before we enter upon it. This simple but profound realization can provide the means of illuminating the interreligious dialogue it already sustains.

Compactness and Differentiation

The relationship between the spiritual traditions is implicit in the drive toward Being, and the degree to which it becomes explicit varies with the extent to which the nature of the quest itself has been differentiated. Has it yet understood itself precisely as a quest for Being, or is it still at a more inchoate stage of self-consciousness? The level of transparence is pivotal because the participation in Being is not an autonomic process. It is engaged in deliberately and consciously. Attunement to the order of Being grows in adequacy to the extent to which its dimensions are more accurately delineated. Consciousness as the mode of our participation is pervaded by the differentiations of self-consciousness. Without the discrimination of that toward which we are headed and of the character of our communication with it, we can scarcely move in the direction we are inclined. Not that we are ever completely blind or immobile; otherwise, there would not even be the restless dissatisfaction that starts the process in motion. Nor do we ever reach the stage of illuminative union that would enable us to leap out of our creaturely condition of existence. But, between these poles of blankness and iridescence, we struggle along a continuum of more or less penetrating glimpses of the order in which we find ourselves. Understanding and communication across the great symbolic forms are possible because we recognize the equivalence of responses toward the same fundamental question. Variation is confined to the extent of differentiation of the parameters of the movement itself. None succeed in penetrating beyond them.

But the struggle toward greater self-consciousness of participation should not be considered largely the fruit of our efforts, whether of determination or perspicuity. A turning point occurs in the irruption of transcendent Being, which discloses itself through itself. This is decisive both from the perspective of the advance in participation it makes possible and from the illumination it casts over the movement of self-understanding. Transcendent Being can be known, it now becomes clear, only through the self-revelation of the Beyond. A qualitative leap beyond the capacity of immanent reality is required for the contact that floods us with its transfiguring presence. An unmistakable rupture occurs in the order of being as we recognize with varying degrees of intensity, but all with consciousness of the epochal break entailed, the incommensurability of the two levels of reality. A bridge can be built between them only from the divine side. Revelation is the indispensable moment that dramatically structures the relationship from that point on. The openness of the cosmos toward its divine source is still the fundamental background, but now the irreducibility of the Beyond has begun to become clear. Immanent longing for the transcendent may still be the pervasive feature, but it is now recognized as being generated by the touch of Being, whose apprehension can come in no other way than the glance of transcendent revelation.

Even the discovery of that necessity cannot be fully made in the absence of revelation. It is an inescapable aspect of the transcendent constitution of our existence that the illumination of its dimensions is also dependent on the revelatory events. Apart from the discovery of God, the adumbration of the full range of human nature cannot take place. Differentiation is thus not merely the history of man's increasing penetration of the order in which he participates; it is more properly conceived as the history of the episodic irruptions of transcendent Being, whose radiance irrevocably changes the order of things. Strictly speaking, there is no such thing as human history apart from the history of the encounters between God and man. To the extent that the most momentous events consist of breakthroughs from a level of reality beyond anything known in our ordinary experience, the differentiation of self-consciousness is punctuated by theophanic outbursts. In retrospect the illuminations may be recognizable as elaborations of what is already known, but the luminosity that makes the apprehension possible cannot be accounted for without remainder. Even the retrospective continuity that is recognized is in some sense prepared by the preceding flow of revelation within an immanent reality that has never completely forgotten its originating divine touch of creation. Wherever we turn, we never seem to gain the purely natural unfolding of consciousness by which the odyssey of self-discovery and self-realization might become the preserve of routinized human instrumentality.

We are thrown back on the revelatory process and the moment of its transparence as the decisive breakthrough of self-consciousness. Theophanic irruptions, the self-disclosure of the Beyond, are indeed the events that have structured our history. To the extent that the emergence of the world religions has been the single most significant development of meaning, then we may regard their emergence as the turning point of history. The justification for regarding them as such is that, even today, they constitute the limits of the horizons of meaning within which we live. Modernity, which has sought to absorb them within itself as external phenomena, has succeeded only in missing their import. It has not succeeded in replacing them, and the reason is clear. Mundane rationality is capable of organizing only the world of beings; it is neither capable nor receptive of the transcendent glimpse by which their permeability toward Being is apprehended. The durability of the great symbolic forms of the world religions is not coincidental. It derives precisely from their formative relationship toward Being. Only a further illumination of the transcendent is capable of extending them and, once they have emerged, they have the durability of marking a distinct limit in the glance of eternity within time. Insofar as there is any absolute turning point within history, we are justified in regarding the theophanic outbursts as the legitimate contenders. They structure history into a Before and After by which even the differentiation of history itself arises.

Historians have long been fascinated by the question because the study of the past virtually invites reflection on its structure. A pattern that has impressed several generations with its significance is the occurrence of parallel irruptions of transcendent revelation between 800 and 200 B.C. This is the period when the prophets in Israel, the mystic philosophers in Greece, the Vedists and Buddhists in India, the Taoists and Confucians in China, and the Zoroastrians in Persia were all engaged in the opening of the soul toward the extracosmic revelation by which universal humanity is constituted. It was a period of such momentous significance in terms of the break with the cosmological myth, the discovery of rationality, and the emergence of universal human nature that Karl Jaspers named it the axis time.[9] All history seemed to revolve around it, and we recognize the source of the great symbolic forms that endure architectonically up to the present. A particularly striking convergence seems to occur around 500 B.C., at least in retrospect, when we contemplate that Confucius, the Buddha, Heraclitus, and Deutero-Isaiah were contemporaries. The pattern could not be merely coincidental, since the moment seemed to have inaugurated the decisive opening of history toward universality. Jaspers may even be forgiven the enthusiasm of denoting the

epochal contemporaneity as the "axis time" because such outbursts do signal a decisive differentiation of order. Of course,
reminder is needed that the axis designation omits such momentous irruptions as the Mosaic revelation and the epiphany of Christ
as well as the experience of Mohammed, but the inclination is not
false. Each of the theophanies is axial, but neither individually nor
in aggregate are they reducible to a mundane pattern of occurrence. The axis is precisely the shattering of the cosmic realm as
the scale of measurement of reality.

They converge in rupturing the compactness of the cosmological form of experience. Unity is the primary experience of the
cosmos within which we find ourselves. It is one order whose
consubstantial wholeness indicates that all levels of reality are
connected from the most ephemeral to the most enduring. Only
the cosmos as a whole is the comprehensive embodiment of order,
and everything else gains its position by participating in the imi-
tation of the cosmos.[10] Just as order in the cosmos is mediated
hierarchically from the highest visible divinities to the lowliest
elements of nature, so too can human society live in order by
analogically reflecting the hierarchical mediation of the cosmos.
Just as the cosmos undergoes its cyclical redemption from disorder
and the rebirth of new order by returning to its first day of
creation, so human existence can participate in the same rhythms
of regeneration from decay by fitting within the New Year renewal of the cosmos. Cosmological order, as it developed in the
ancient high civilizations or as it perennially exists among all
archaic societies, is an enchanted world. It is a world "full of
gods" in which any event can become the occasion for a hiero-
phany and in which magical transformations can break out at
any moment. Not only is nothing simply what it is, but rational
speculative unfolding is impossible. The most poignant feature is
surely the degree of unself-consciousness concerning the source
of its order. Everything must be depicted in tangible visible terms,
since there is no differentiation of the mind, soul, or heart as the
seat of its symbolic profusion.[11]

All of that unexamined unity is ruptured, not by the breakdown of order that compels men to think about their situation, but only by the concomitant irruption of transcendent Being, whose revelation is, of necessity, wholly inward. The instrument by which it is apprehended is illumined only in the radiance from the Beyond. Apprehension of the radical otherness of the transcendent casts varying degrees of negativity over all other immanent transmitters. Divinity withdraws from the cosmos as it is concentrated in the revelation of Being. Mediation by the hierarchy or rhythms of the cosmos can no longer occupy central place, when the incompatibility of the God with all intrascosmic embodiments has been more or less dramatically discerned. The move is not from polytheism to monotheism, since both variants are discoverable at every point in the cosmological myth. Indeed, the consciousness of the gods as all derived from a common divine cosmic substance is its overriding emphasis. What is decisively new is the irruption of transcendent Being. The encounter with an utterly different order of reality is the signal event. Having once felt its unmistakable touch, the derivative character of all other reality can never be eliminated. All of the epochal spiritual outbursts move in the direction of this fundamental distinction from which all other differentiations follow.

The line by which the implications are unfolded is never smooth or uniform. It can be expressed as an utter gulf between the transcendent divinity and the rest of reality, as in the Mosaic definitiveness of the I AM, yet never succeed in extending beyond the confines of the Chosen People to the chosenness of each individual human soul. The break with the divine reality of the cosmos may be far less radical, such as in classical philosophy, in which the movement of the soul toward the Beyond is differentiated, but no countermovement from the transcendent can be conceived of a divine source whose paradigmatic ikon remains the cosmos itself. Friendship between man and God is, according to Aristotle, impossible. A fully transcendent and self-revealing God, indispensable for such a relationship, has not yet been experienced by him. The break with the cosmic reality can be so tenuous that the movement toward the Beyond is still expressed hierarchically, as in Confucianism, or has been concentrated into itself as the Way, which is simultaneously the way of the cosmos and the way beyond it, as in Taoism. Or the transcending movement can remain so tied to the struggle against the cosmos that it can only be conceived in terms of the dichotomy of illusion and liberation, as in Hinduism. By contrast, the focus on the movement itself can become so intense that it can become its own justification eclipsing all other reality, as in the Buddhist attainment of Boddhisatva. Even when the maximum differentiation is beheld in the self-revelation of transcendent Being within time, as in Christianity, there is no guarantee that the full amplitude of differentiation will be maintained. Islam arises, to a considerable extent, out of the demand for simplification of the mystery of the incarnation, and Gnosticism flourishes because of the perennial demand to overleap the distance that separates us from its consummation.

Permanence of Pluralism

The situation of the world religions is, to put it mildly, complex. Two distinguishing features stand out. First, they each originate in the break with cosmological form, albeit of varying degrees of completeness. Second, the break, once it has occurred, seems to endure with the shape and limitations imparted to it from the beginning. A durability attaches to the concretization each of them has assumed. The breakthrough of differentiation is what endows them with spiritual strength, and the mystery of the interpenetration of the particular circumstances seems to form the core of their immovability. The paradigmatic case is perhaps Judaism, which has caused such notorious difficulties that it is not even universally classified as a world religion. Despite the radicalness of its break with the myth and the manifest originality of the revelation, it is virtually the only spiritual outburst that does not give rise to a spiritual movement per se. Rather it generates a people, an *ethnos,* whose trajectory is fraught with universal significance, but whose transformation into a religion spells the deathknell of its existence as a people. The peculiar compactness of the Judaic form afflicts both Jews and the state of Israel all the way up to the present. But the general case is not unique. An immobility or fixity attaches to the shape of differentiation that draws its durability precisely from the spiritual universalism of the breakthrough.

Pluralism is, in other words, an irreducible feature not just of our world, but of *the* world. Humanity is widely dispersed in space and time and is constituted by theophanic experiences of varying degrees of differentiation. The result is the plurality of spiritual outbursts and corresponding symbolic forms we observe in the history of order, whose mysterious emergence can never be penetrated as a whole. In the absence of any systematizing viewpoint, we are compelled to agree with Eric Voegelin that "The order of history emerges from the history of order."[12] Indeed, the only order of history is the history of the related and unrelated illuminations by which the order of Being is apprehended and realized in human existence. A certain undeniable pressure exists within each of the spiritual irruptions to move toward the incorporation of all others. The emergence of an absolute within time, albeit precariously glimpsed in the moment of its revelation, is enough to suggest the prospect of its extrapolation toward the whole of reality. But the overwhelming experience of history points us toward the contrary realization. However universal the implications of each theophany, the reality is that traditions emanating from other theophanies remain impressively resistant to absorption. Revelatory breakthroughs are capable of effecting dramatic transformations in the existing symbolic order, and conversion is a constant feature of human experience. Yet the sheer persistence of parallel and rejectionist traditions seems to set definite limits to the movement. The diversity and durability of the distinct traditions, despite the often impressive communication between them, can only lead us to conclude that ineliminable pluralism is a feature of order itself.

A context in which contact across the world religions was relatively limited could readily overlook this realization. Unfamiliarity with the spiritual appeal of other traditions could lead to an underestimating of the difficulties of mass conversion, and the lack of success of missionary movements could be ascribed to the relatively early stages of the effort. Only with prolonged experience does it become evident that the prospects for any decisive shift among the world religions are comparatively slight. Conversion can occur most readily when a more differentiated revelation encounters a far more compact tradition, as in the missionary success of Christianity among African animists. But the encounter between comparably differentiated forms yields a far lower frequency of conversions, as the paucity of Christian success among Buddhists and Taoists illustrates.[13] The reason is not hard to discern. Differentiation, once it has occurred, establishes the firm conviction of an advance that is often so strong that the possibility of a further differentiation cannot readily be admitted. A kind of congealment of experience, reinforced by institutional investments and the rigidities of symbolic constructions, seems to attach to the revelatory encounter with the transcendent. This unsurprising preservative response draws its strength from the realization that what is at stake is the very achievement of differentiation itself. High civilizations have a durability because of the self-consciousness of their height.

On the other hand, they are not irrevocably closed to one another. The very universalism of their impulse and the awareness of their own movement out of compactness link them inextricably with the common human search for order in existence. Far from existing in splendid isolation, their character as illuminative movements draws them into the conversation of mankind. The search for truth compels them to take account of the counterclaims of others, at least to the extent of developing the techniques for their dismissal. Once the fatal step is taken of considering what the other has to say, the conversation is irrevocably engaged. Today the pervasiveness of the mutual awareness intensifies the need to discover a means of sustaining a meaningful exchange. When all the reservations have been made and the expectations of major shifts sufficiently dampened, we still have to find a way of continuing the conversation. We are thrown back on the common ground that unites them—the search for truth—as the only source from which authoritative criteria of distinction might be derived. How is it possible to conceive of the diversity of spiritual traditions as all fundamentally true, yet not refuse to confront the unavoidable question of the variations in their apprehension of the truth? Is respect for the integrity of each compatible with distinguishing between the adequacy of their differentiations? In short, how is it possibly to render judgment without being judgmental?

The answer to these questions lies in a deeper appreciation of the conceptual apparatus that we have already intuitively adopted. Advance from compactness to differentiation seems to imply the obsolescence, if not the irrelevance, of the earlier forms for the later. The model of scientific progress intrudes again on our imagination as we recognize that no contemporary physics course returns to the study of the Egyptian or Greek attainments in the discipline. It begins with the latest state of knowledge and regards its historical predecessors as superseded. However, in the philosophical disciplines, the pattern is reversed. We always go back to the beginning and to the classic expositions, in the conviction that they have not been and probably cannot be surpassed. Progress means something quite different in disciplines defined by the asking of the same questions, not by the development of new ones. The great and classic sources are such because they represent the most definitive responses of their particular kind toward the same questions. It is not so much that our knowledge develops as that it is enriched. Each of the unsurpassable articulations is a source of illumination that could not otherwise be replaced. We have no alternative but to return again and again to the great evocations in which the questions have been unfolded if we wish to gain any sense of the richness and depth they sustain. The same is true of the world religions and, in general, of the symbolic forms in which the human search for order has been carried forth. Even the secure possession of one of the most robust and differentiated traditions is not sufficient. A distinct quality of impoverishment still attaches to it so long as it exists in ignorance and isolation from the richness unfolded across the range of perspectives. Only by contemplating the range of alternatives do we ever acquire a sense of the character of differentiation entailed. Advance in differentiation is neither univocal nor final. It never replaces the whole from which it has emerged.

This is because differentiation is always from within the whole. It affects a more restricted realm of experience, not the larger context of the movement itself. This means that the most comprehensive experiences and symbolizations are the earliest—the ones in which the whole is encompassingly depicted. Differentiation of transcendent Being does not directly affect the symbolization of the cosmos itself, although it is replete with indirect consequences for the way it is represented. Adjustment of the depiction of the divine presence within the cosmos is required, to ensure its correlation with the illuminative encounter with its transcendent source. If the world is not evacuated of its gods, their stature is at least diminished in light of the differentiation of the transcendent divinity beyond them. But we do not dispense with the need to represent the whole, and the only symbols available to us are those derived from the primary experience of the oneness of all things. They may have undergone a purification of their unseemliness, now evident in the luminosity of Being, but we have no other means of identifying the wholeness of the cosmos in which we find ourselves. This is why we observe the persistence of cosmological forms, albeit in opaque and degraded variants, all the way up to the present. Architectural depictions of the wholeness of the cosmos cannot be more reassuringly presented than through overarching domes, nor can the possibility of ascent toward its divine regions be more effectively portrayed than by columns, obelisks, and rockets. Nor is the magic of the first day of creation quite forgotten in our annual celebrations of anniversaries, birthdays, and millennial new year festivals. We may have forgotten the hierophantic cosmos that gave rise to such symbols, but we have never quite ceased to live within it.

Cosmogonic myths, with their recounting of the emergence of order through the successive unfolding of the cosmos, remain an abiding necessity. We cannot avoid symbolizing the whole in which our experiences take place. To do so requires that we reach beyond the range of what can be experienced as we extrapolate toward the Beginning before there was a cosmos and, when differentiation requires it, project the movement forward to the point when the cosmos will be no more. Myth is the ineradicable medium through which such reflections can be unfolded. The ingredients go all the way back to the early paleolithicum, when the earliest symbol using evidence of human life was indicated by the construction of spheres and crosses, for the whole and its organization in the four cardinal directions.[14] All of the great spiritual breakthroughs are accompanied by a correlative refurbishment of the mythic materials in line with the revelatory advance. Christianity is no exception with its adaptation of the creation narrative and its elaboration of an eschatological vision. Preservation of the illuminative experience itself is crucially dependent on the elaboration of the whole in such a way as to preserve a balance between its transcendent orientation and its continuing immanent presence. The exodus within reality does not mean the exodus from reality.

A similar, although less evident, indispensability attaches to the range of historic differentiations. Each represents a unique variation along the spectrum from compactness to differentiation. As such, they generate a rich trail of symbols by which the tension between transcendent Being and its immanent presence might be depicted. If we think of the cosmological myth as one end of the continuum, in which Being remains indistinguishable from the world of beings, and Christianity as the other extreme, in which the possibility of Being as present has been fully differentiated, all of the other symbolizations represent the range of intermediate possibilities. Despite their status as intermediate, they provide an insight into the form of representation by which the various modes of transcendent presence might be embodied. The inexhaustibility of the experience cries out for the profusion of symbolizations by which the multifaceted quality of the interpenetration of divine and human might be adumbrated. The outstanding illustration of this pattern is surely the Christian absorption of the Hebrew Bible as their Old Testament. Despite the realization that the revelation of Christ supersedes the Mosaic dispensation, the very richness of the experience seems to call for its elaboration in terms of the range of Old Testament prefigurations. Far from diluting or confusing the Christian revelation, the Old Testament exemplars sharpen attention for the uniqueness of what is entailed in Christ's transcendence of all of their limits. Without the astonishing profusion of historical and prophetic elaborations by the people of Israel, there is a decisive sense in which the revelation of Christ could not have been received.

This is an awareness that permeates the New Testament writers themselves, as they ransacked the Bible for the prefigurations that would provide the elements of an apprehension of who Jesus is. The centrality of the Hebrew Bible continued to expand in Christian civilization as successive Christian societies sought to work out what it meant to be the People of God, while also retaining their hold as a concrete political organization.[15] Nowhere is tension more fully exposed than in the Old Testament, and the Christian differentiation between church and state did not obviate the symbolic richness available for adaptation in the Hebrew Scriptures. We are not endowed with an unlimited stock of symbols from which we can, at will, shape whatever meaning we wish. The symbols that hold evocative power in human existence are not even the fruit of man's pure imaginative exertions. They arise from the encounter with Being and partake of the power of that exchange. Neither purely human nor purely divine, the symbols that emerge from the participatory glimpse have the same intermediate status as the experience itself. Poets are so much aware of this problem that they do not simply create metaphors. They come to them from we know not where; they are not strictly ours. In the same way, we cannot casually discard the richness of the historic unfolding of God's revelation to man merely because we have gained the conviction of entering its fullest differentiation. On the contrary, the need is even greater to preserve the symbolic richness as the only way of even inadequately depicting the inexhaustible depth of what we now behold more fully. This realization is what underlies the inclusive disposition of Christians to adapt and adopt indigenous traditions around the world.

Inclusion Without Destruction

The question provoked by all such interactions is whether the more differentiated form can incorporate the less without doing violence to it. At the heart of the question of dialogue across the traditions is the issue of imposition of meaning. If the terms of the discussion are set by the more differentiated symbolism, as they inevitably must be in the absence of any independent viewpoint, is there any way of avoiding the deformation of compact forms incapable of meeting the criteria of the more differentiated? Misunderstanding seems almost built into the relationship in which the more differentiated symbolisms view the compact forms only as foils for their own increase in luminosity. Whatever incorporation occurs is more in the nature of rummaging for booty that can be carried away from a defeated enemy. Despoiling the Egyptians was not just a pastime for the Israelites. A similar incomprehension attaches to the Christian devaluation of Judaism as the dead letter of the law. But that pattern does not account for the deepest level of the relationships. It is noteworthy that the Israelites understood themselves through the elaboration of the central Egyptian symbolism of the firstborn. Israel become the firstborn in place of Pharaoh. And the rich integration of Judaic symbolism into the Christian redemptive account could not present a deeper example of the process of enlargement.[16] The question then becomes not so much a warning against spiritual imperialism, but a far more fascinating inquiry into the possibility of one spiritual tradition understanding another more completely than it does itself. Again, it is not so much with a view to exposing its obsolescence, but with a view to its elevation within the more comprehensive differentiation achieved.

Is there always something illegitimate about the transformation of one tradition into the old testament of another? Or is it possible to preserve respect for the full integrity of the less differentiated while absorbing it within the greater amplitude of differentiation of the latter? Under what circumstances is it permissible to read Christianity into the Hebrew scriptures? Or find philosophy in Confucian or Taoist thought? The answer is only if the former is already contained in the latter. No violence is done so long as the interpretation does not involve the distortion of the more compact formulations in a direction inimical to their own tendency. So long as the Hebrew prophets already point in the direction consummated by the advent of Christ, then it does them no disservice to read them within that perspective. Indeed, the Christian conviction is that such a reading completes them. In the same way with all of the dialogue across the range of compactness and differentiation, the possibility of rereading without injustice is assured by the degree to which each is a whole containing all of the others. Christianity can include the Hebrew Bible because the Bible already contains Christianity. In general, we may say that one symbolic form can absorb another when the more inclusive represents the highest possibility of what is contained in the other.[17] Moreover, the exchange does not simply take place in one direction. The discovery of a more compact equivalent enhances the transparence of what has been differentiated, through the luminosity emergent from within the more concrete conditions of existence. Celebration of Christmas at the turning point of the new year deepens the meaning of the winter solstice, but it also enriches the symbolic means of depicting the radiance of transcendent Life emergent within mortality.

It is true that the relationship can be apprehended only from within the perspective of the more differentiated viewpoint. From the perspective of the less differentiated traditions, the relationship remains opaque. Buddhists may be able to comprehend Confucians, but not vice versa. Christians can understand Muslims without provoking a challenge to their own conviction, but the reverse is hardly the case. Understanding may still take place in a purely formal or external manner, but not the deeper apprehension that takes the full measure of the reality presented as intended for me personally. No doubt this situation is a source of some dissatisfaction in a world bent on universal communication. But it is no more than an instance of the general pattern of what is entailed in any intellectual advance. What is perspicuous, once the advance has been achieved, remains impenetrable to those who remain in the earlier condition. The unidirectionality of spiritual communication is only remarkable because of the widespread modern expectation that communication of indifferent and inconclusive matters ought to be relatively facile. It is a feature of an historically unfolded, pluralistically centered humanity that communication across the spiritual traditions remains problematic. Nothing is assured, although the perspective of maximal differentiation offers the best prospect.

Frustration at the limitations imposed by our human dispersal recurrently generates the fantasies of a Tower of Babel by which they might be overcome. However, such illusory projects of escape do not constitute the greatest danger. Rather, the danger lies in the despair that is equally predictable in the shattering of the dream of unification. Ours is not a condition in which all men address one another in the same tongue, but that does not imply that we ought to abandon the labor of seeking to reach a common understanding. It may indeed be that such communication is difficult to attain, but just as understanding across the barrier of languages remains eminently possible for the persistent, so the prospect of mutual understanding across the division of spiritual traditions is open to those with the dedication to make it their task. Nothing, however, will be gained by refusing to concede that the most adequate language for such understanding remains the most highly differentiated. Despite all the current enthusiasm for multiculturalism, the fact is that such inclusivist aspirations toward the integrity of all traditions is uniquely expressive of the Christian experience.

The opening of universal humanity as a sphere of discourse has its origins in all of the spiritual outbursts, but its consummation is in Jesus's drawing of all men to himself (John 12:32). It is in Christ that the transcendent openness of every human being toward the divine presence becomes fully visible. From that realization emerges the assurance of the divine will for all men to be saved and the confidence of discerning the outlines of the movement within all of the spiritual unfoldings of the human heart (I Tim. 2:3–4).[18] Their patterns may still conceal the full differentiation of the divine action within history that culminates in Christ, but the fundamental impetus remains constant as the self-outpouring of God that makes possible our loving participation in the Beyond. The full differentiation of the transcendent Being incarnating itself within being may have to await the mysterious fulfillment of revelation, but the structure of the tension toward Being from which it is grasped remains universally in place. Full differentiation is dependent on the transcendent irruption, but its punctuated reverberations in the continuum of theophanic encounters richly prepare the soil for its reception. However, as the utterly unanticipated gift of Being, Christianity is the bearer of a special responsibility to communicate the transcendent luminosity to a world aching to receive it. More than simple prosletyzation, the obligation calls for the deeper movement of lifting what is best within each tradition to a level beyond itself. Recognition of the headship of Christ over all humanity, Voegelin observes, "means that one has to recognize, and make intelligible, the presence of Christ in a Babylonian hymn, or a Taoist speculation, or a Platonic dialogue, just as much as in a Gospel."[19] In the process, Christianity itself does not remain unchanged. It discovers its own, more expansive possibilities that must remain latent so long as it has not yet followed Jesus in pouring itself out in love of the other. The most differentiated revelation does not escape the finite medium through which it is absorbed. Fullness in principle still stands in need of the concrete unfolding of the possibilities of participation in Being available only through the plurality of spiritual traditions. Discovering Christ in all other symbolisms also means discovering all of them in Christ.

Modernity as Intuitive Unity

Mutual understanding across the traditions is possible because of the inner mutuality of their presence to one another. Each contains the whole reality of man's participation in Being and therefore gives access to the full range of differentiations through which it is articulated. Change or development presupposes that the movement of differentiation can be apprehended as being true from within the perspective of compactness. The continuum is permeable in both directions. No doubt the full articulate acknowledgment of differentiation cannot be made without departing the compact starting point; however there would be no movement at all unless it was possible to sense the direction to be pursued from the most inarticulate beginning. The image of a universal rational nature, standing apart from all historical and cultural unfolding, has effectively been demolished. We know there is no neutral anteroom to history to which human beings are capable of repairing when they wish to communicate unrestrictedly. Enlightenment reason is one of our definitively shattered illusions. As a result, communication, despite the widespread evidence of its occurrence, has become one of our most insoluble puzzles. Having dispatched transcultural reason, we have failed to recognize the possibility of a culturally embedded rationality capable of a range of elaborations from compactness to differentiation and therefore underpinning the possibility of communication across the gamut of historical traditions. Communication is not as effortless as on the Enlightenment model, but it is not as impenetrable as the irreducibly pluralist alternative would suggest.

Even when the full differentiation of Being cannot be articulated, the order of reason it sustains can be apprehended as its intuitive unfolding. It is not necessary to behold the full elaboration in order for the authoritative implications to be apparent.

Human beings have always exercised reason without contemplating its source. What the movement of differentiation does is render explicit an order that is implicitly present to all human beings everywhere. The unfolding of transparence with its dramatic irruption of transcendent Being is not a negligible development, but neither does it fundamentally alter the tensional condition of existence from which it emerges. That underlying continuity is what creates the possibility of communication, albeit of a tenuous and inarticulate nature, across the millennia and traditions. We recognize the meaning of human existence in every context, although our capacity to say what that recognition is undergoes development and decline. This prearticulate community that all human beings share is what makes possible the formation of a common world even in the face of plural differentiations. Various capacities for reflection do not radically affect the underlying imperatives that drive them. Reason exercises its imperious pull even on those incapable of identifying it.

The situation, however, is fraught with turbulence. We have seen the disorientation generated by the modern ethos that severs itself from the experiential movement of its differentiation. The rationality of science and the self-evidence of rights can be sustained so long as no searching questions are raised about the reality to which they are applied. One cannot afford to press the limits of scientific method too hard, either in terms of the origin of reality, the relationships among its levels, or the prospects for its transformation. Science works so long as it restrains itself strictly within the confines of the given. The self-evidence of rights works so long as no one is compelled to elaborate on their meaning or source. In a world of technical mastery, the unmasterability of human beings protrudes as the great misnomer. The schizophrenic collapse of the modern world is avoided only by refusing to be drawn beyond the limits of its competence, thereby preserving the mysterious tension of its emergence from spiritual depths that it is incapable of adumbrating. How is the situation different for non-Christian and, in general, non-Western traditions? Surely they are as capable of the same attitude of steadfast avoidance of all ultimate implications? In some respects, they would even seem to posses a certain advantage in never having known the full amplitude of differentiation. Operation on the basis of intuitive trust comes more readily to societies that are still more compactly connected to the cosmos.

Perhaps this reduced susceptibility to the Western demand for certainty and transparence accounts for some of the readiness with which Asian civilizations have been able to adapt to the conditions of technological success. But there is also another inexorable tendency. Just as fidelity to the full requirements of rationality draw modern civilization toward acknowledgment of its sustaining spiritual order, so the same submission by non-Western societies to the requirements of reason pull them inevitably in the direction of differentiation of their spiritual compactness. It is impossible to acknowledge the parameters of scientific method without also being pulled toward the recognition of the transcendentally structured reality in which it operates. Acceptance of the language of human rights creates an inexorable movement toward the acknowledgement of the unique transcendent openness of each human being before God. One cannot simply pick and choose between the implications. Having entered along a path, the hierarchically organized cosmos of more paternalistic societies cannot ultimately stand before the insistence on the inexhaustible value of each human being.[20] More is at stake than an opening toward the chaotic uncertainties of modernity. Behind both the reluctance and the dampening of the more robust rights expressions in the East lies a less frequently acknowledged awareness that further extensions might decisively subordinate their own spiritual traditions to a secondary role. Civilizations that have existed for millennia, secure in the supremacy of their own spiritual differentiations, cannot too readily enter along a path that will suggest their decisive derogation in importance. A tension of almost insoluble dimensions is set up by the decision to thread along a path of rationality whose presuppositions point toward a more differentiated order of existence.

The problem is one without a solution in principle. We cannot conceive of the elimination of the Christian underpinnings to modern reason, nor is it conceivable that the other historic differentiations of order will embrace the full amplitude of the Christian. The latter is a possibility unforeseeable within the modern West itself. Instead, we must understand the situation as being fraught with a complex of tensional pulls that can be acknowledged but not resolved. The most abiding one remains the undertow of modernity from and back to Christianity. Just as modern civilization can be best understood as the product of a Christian differentiation from which full self-awareness has withdrawn, so the non-Western societies drawn into its orbit can be best comprehended as variations on the possibility of anonymous Christianity as well. Affirmation of the full differentiation of Being, with all of its consequences for transcendent revelation as the redemptive divine presence within time, may not be possible. But the order of rationality derived from it exercises undeniable authority. The relationship is unstable, as it is with the culture of modernity as such, but the instability is not of the same kind.

In many respects, the other spiritual traditions remain more receptive to the Christian completion of differentiation, since they are themselves constituted by the participatory movement. As parallel experiences of the formative divine revelation, they can more readily apprehend the equivalence of the Christian symbolization. All of the spiritual traditions of the world converge on the acknowledgment of the divine source of the order of existence. They indubitably reject the assertion that man creates his own values and therefore is called to freely choose the order to which he is to submit. The nihilistic suggestion of secular rationality is adamantly rejected, and, with it, the crucial acknowledgment of man's openness toward Being is firmly guaranteed. But the full unfolding of that intimation toward the Christian elaboration is equally resisted, and this is not just the result of native partiality. A fair accounting of the great spiritual outbursts would lead toward the conclusion that they are *sui generis*. Each of them comprises a nonidentical perspective on the mode of openness toward transcendent divinity. They may be equivalent, but they are not interchangeable. Part of what sustains their resistance to further differentiation is the awareness of the unique luminosity of their respective perspectives. The mystery of the opaqueness of other spiritual breakthroughs from viewpoints of lesser differentiation merges with the mystery of the richness of diversity thereby created. At the very best, the conjunction of the spiritual traditions of the world would still have to be one in which their individual uniqueness is preserved.

Surely this recognition is the ideal speech condition for their continuing conversation. Nothing can be lost of what has been touched by the Spirit in the mysterious unfolding of history. Yet, at the same time, the movement toward their maximal transparence for Being cannot be held captive to particular attachments. The tensional pull in which each of us exists individually and all of us exist socially cannot be avoided in relation to our global circumstances. Just as we cannot abolish the irresolvable conversation at the individual and social levels, so we cannot avoid it at the global level either. The conversation across the world religions must continue, and we cannot expect to arrive at a conclusion; otherwise, its sustenance would be in jeopardy.[21] This is the opposite of the false tolerance discussed earlier, which fails to sustain any meaningful conversation because it has already decided the discussion is futile. Interreligious dialogue is conversation that is unending, not because it is fruitless, but because its superabundance cannot be contained within any formulated conclusion. It is not that the conversation becomes the final substitute for the traditions themselves—much like the idea that talk about religion is often assumed to be the same as religion—but that the conversation between them is the deepest exemplification of the drama of eternal Being in time in which they participate.

Far from being a regrettable necessity imposed upon us by the practical convergence of the modern world, the conversation of world religions is the fullest elaboration of the mystery of our history. There we behold not a single line of revelation, but the contemporaneous presence of all of the lines whose transmission has ensured their survival up to now. Instead of treating it as an opportunity to step outside of the tensional unfolding of our attunement to order, as in the phenomenalistic study of religions, we must regard it as the opening of the deepest avenue into our mode of participation in Being. This is the significance of the millennial mutuality of the world religions. But it will be lost if, in the name of a fake tolerance, we remove the incentive for substantive conversation. Only if it is rooted in truth does the conversation acquire a purpose for engagement, and only if the truth is unattainable can its inexhaustibility be guaranteed. The human pursuit of the ground of existence must now be conducted with reference to the range of spiritual traditions emergent over history. That is the meaning of a world whose practical convergence not only makes communication possible, but whose theoretical implications direct us authoritatively toward the movement of differentiation from which they have emerged. Convergence around the great modern intellectual achievements in phenomenal science and the moral-political recognition of rights already constitutes a remarkable first step into the wider conversation of sustaining experiences and symbols. To withdraw from that historic invitation at this moment would not only mean rejecting an opportunity for immeasurable enrichment, but would also mean turning our backs on a modern world precariously poised on the untested assumption of its harmony with all of the diversity of human cultures within it.

The practical convergence already constitutes a signal contribution. Not only does the ubiquity of modern science and the language of rights frame a working order of cooperation, but they point toward the inner convergence of the human community itself. The authority of scientific method exercises a remarkable primacy, but most astonishing is surely the degree to which the far more problematic achievement of a common moral and political discourse has been effected. Respect for the inviolable dignity of each individual is the coin of integrity all over the world. It is not just the cultural prerogative of Americans or Europeans, but the universal vocabulary by which dissidents, political prisoners, and the aggrieved everywhere assert their case for justice and the higher law by which government itself is to be judged. Enshrined in the U.N. Declaration of Human Rights, the liberal respect for individual dignity has become an effective moral language not merely because of its practical accessibility, but because it has encapsulated the authoritative truth about human life. The genius of this liberal consensus is to have compressed the transcendent openness of personality into a few evocative public principles. As such, it is capable of drawing on the resonances of the transcendent illuminations in all of the spiritual traditions without becoming too explicitly identified with any of them. The origination of this language in the Christian West is only of historical significance. Yet neither in the West nor elsewhere can the unarticulated depths from which the resonances emerge simply be allowed to atrophy from neglect. Continuous attention to the inarticulate sources from which the convictions arise is an indispensable means of their preservation. To the extent that the convictions have become worldwide, their meditative enlargement cannot neglect the convergence of all the spiritual traditions supporting them.

The movement of differentiation is what has made possible the emergence of the modern world, with its narrowing of authoritative forms of thought. Its survival depends on the preservation of the memory of that emergence in the movement of differentiation. All of our difficulties arise from the forgetfulness that assumes science and rights stand on their own self-assertion. Incoherence eventually throws us back on the recognition of the presuppositions about being and its illumination by Being, as we have seen. The realization that the limits of rationality are attained through the limiting revelation of Being within time—through the epiphany of Christ—does not shed light on its significance for all outside that historic orbit. Are non-Christians condemned to a reduced exercise of rationality? No, but the representative significance of the Christian events must be elaborated. They must be understood as an unfolding of what the other world religions already contain and toward which they point. Then the convergence of our world around the minimally evocative rationalities of science and rights can be rediscovered in the full amplitude of their differentiating spiritual foundation. We no longer have to worry about the compatibility of rational science and political rights with non-Western traditions or suspect that our profession of them is a tacit form of asserting our cultural superiority. If science is valid and human rights are universal, then they must be recognizable in some sense from all the available traditions, especially those constituted by the opening of differentiation.

Nothing less than the authoritative truth of the modern world is at stake in the conversation across the world religions. Do they give rise to different rationalities and different conceptions of the rights of human beings? Are we held in an irretrievably pluralist fracturing of meaning? Or is there a common world? Only the conversation in which the great spiritual traditions exemplify their community can demonstrate it. The practical convergence, in a common understanding of scientific reason and the imperative of rights, suggests an underlying spiritual community at work. If the norms of rationality and morality were only a matter of expediency they would not have the conviction and durability they demonstrate. The canons of science and rights function as authoritative forms of truth. They are acknowledged universally. This means that the truth of the underlying movement of differentiation that sustains them is also implicitly acknowledged. How is this possible from the perspective of the less differentiated spiritual traditions? It is only possible because the validity of the movement can be apprehended from the perspective of the less differentiated forms. They are not heteronomous modes of existence. Rather, there is a continuity in which all that is to be differentiated is already contained in the more compact experiences. Indeed the movement of recognition implies the predifferentiated presence. What the surface convergence of our world in the exploration of nature and the affirmation of human dignity has done is to call attention to the much deeper convergence in the spiritual unity of mankind. Acknowledgment of truth at the level of method and norms cannot avoid its extension to the affirmation of the core experiences of reality from which they arise. It is not that modern civilization has made the world one, so much as the oneness of human existence has made the convergence of global modernity possible.

It is in the conversation between the great spiritual traditions that the continuity is exemplified. To be a genuine conversation, however, it must not be derailed by misplaced sensitivity toward the advantages and disadvantages of the respective partners. A distinct advantage attaches—there is no point in avoiding it—to the perspective that is most differentiated. It can understand the positions of all others, and the others cannot comprehend it to the same degree. Christianity can lay claim with most justification to this distinction, just as its differentiation has spawned the highest rationality of modernity. But far more than the hegemonic rule of science and rights, we may regard the role of Christianity as the most inclusive and preservative of all other traditions as well. From the perspective of fullest revelation, it can appreciate the richness contained in the profusion of symbols over the millennial encounters between the human and the divine. It can understand most profoundly the impossibility of containing the fullness of Being in any of the finite avenues toward his presence. The God who could only reveal himself through himself, Jesus Christ, can be endlessly pointed toward by all other theophanic movements. Just as the advent of Christ is contained in all of the opening toward transcendent Being, so each of the spiritual traditions can understand itself most completely in relation to that kenotic movement of divine love. To be a Christian today means to be open toward the recognition of the divine presence outside of Christianity. They are exemplifications of a mode of participation that, although not concretized, are in principle contained within the Christian horizon. In the same way, the truth of Buddhism or Islam or Taoism is to be apprehended in opening toward the other traditions in which the reality most deeply realized within each of them is exemplified in its other unrepeatable possibilities. The complementarity and inclusivity of the world religions is not a postulate awaiting our demonstration. It is already a reality within the heart of God, whose transcendent self-donation makes possible our discovery of it.

Notes

1. We might reflect on the consistency of the survey data accumulated by George Gallup that indicate the ubiquity of life-altering spiritual experiences, even in the absence of any religious frame of reference or interpretation. See George Gallup, Jr. and Jim Castelli, *The People's Religion: American Faith in the '90's* (New York: Macmillan, 1989).

2. See Samuel Huntington, *The Clash of Civilizations and the Remaking of World Order* (New York: Simon and Schuster, 1996).

3. Some sense of the scale of the challenge may be gauged from the comprehensive account of fundamentalism across the world religions recently furnished by Martin Marty and R. Scott Appleby, *Fundamentalism Observed: Fundamentalism Project vol. 1* (Chicago: University of Chicago Press, 1994).

4. See the essay "On the Essence of Truth" and others in *Pathmarks*, trans. William McNeill (New York: Cambridge University Press, 1998).

5. The term "drama of humanity" has been used by Brendan Purcell to identify the fascinating intersections of meaning in the search for order within history. Brendan Purcell, *The Drama of Humanity: Towards a Philosophy of Humanity in History* (New York: Peter Lang, 1996).

6. The turn toward mysticism is always a later development within a context in which symbols have degenerated into dogmatism. One particularly finds the mystical turn within moments of spiritual crisis in which the need to return to the ineffable divinity beyond all symbolization is most evident. We have already referred to the great mystical enterprise of Jean Bodin at the height of the French wars of religion in the sixteenth century. A parallel case is provided by Henri

Bergson in his *Two Sources of Morality and Religion,* trans. R. Ashley Audra and Cloudesley Bereton (New York: Holt, 1935).

7. This is a point that was made most forcefully in a classic essay by Wilmoore Kendall, "The 'Open Society' and Its Fallacies," *American Political Science Review* 54 (1960): 972–79.

8. Saint Thomas wrote his *Summa Contra Gentiles* to prepare missionaries who were to dispute with other religions, and he reflected on the problem of communication across the barriers of pluralism in its opening. "Thus, against the Jews we are able to argue by means of the Old Testament, while against heretics we are able to argue by means of the New Testament. But the Mohammedans and the pagans accept neither the one nor the other. We must, therefore, have recourse to natural reason, to which all men are forced to give their assent. However, it is true, in divine matters it has its limits." Bk. I, Ch. 2.

9. Karl Jaspers, *The Origin and Goal of History,* trans. Michael Bullock (New Haven: Yale University Press, 1953).

10. For an account of this order, see Voegelin, *Israel and Revelation* (Baton Rouge: Louisiana State University Press, 1956), Chs. 1–3; *Ecumenic Age,* Ch. 3; H. and H.A. Frankfort et al. *Before Philosophy* (Baltimore: Penguin, 1949); Mircea Eliade, *The Sacred and the Profane* (New York: Harcourt Brace Jovanovich, 1957), and *From Primitives to Zen* (New York: Harper and Row, 1977).

11. One of the most striking examples of the limitations under which reflection must labor are the Homeric epics, in which there is no psychological or interior language, even the term "corpse," to indicate what remains after departure of the spirit. As a consequence, whenever any of the heroes must undertake some particularly significant action, the interior preparation can only be depicted by means of an external intervention of a divinity. See the analysis in Voegelin, *The World of the Polis,* Ch. 2. An equally amazing case concerns the "Dispute of a Man, Who Contemplates Suicide, with His Soul." It is an Egyptian text that recounts the man's perceptive analysis of the moral crisis of his society, yet utterly fails to recognize that his own capacity for diagnosis is precisely the noetic instrument by which a renewal might be undertaken. It is to be found with many others in James Pritchard, ed. *Ancient Near Eastern Texts Relating*

to the Old Testament (Princeton: Princeton University Press, 1950), 405–07.

12. *Israel and Revelation,* ix.

13. On the missionary aspect of Christianity, see Stephen Neill, *A History of Christian Missions* (New York: Penguin, 1964).

14. See the work of Marie König, which reminds us of the source of the symbols and ideagrams by which we still represent the whole. *Am Anfang der Kultur* (Berlin: Mann, 1973) and *Unser Vergangenheit ist älter* (Frankfurt: Fischer, 1980).

15. One among many instances is the consistent attempt to understand America from the colonial beginnings onwards as the "New Israel." See the anthology of Conrad Cherry, *God's New Israel: Religious Interpretations of American Destiny* (Englewood Cliffs, NJ: Prentice-Hall, 1971).

16. One of the Pyramid Texts has the Pharaoh greeted by the gods with "This is my son, my first-born." To this is juxtaposed the formula of the Mosaic revelation, "My son, my first-born, is Israel" (Ex 4:22). See the discussion in Voegelin, *Israel and Revelation,* 390.

17. See, for example, the discussion in Simone Weil, *The Intimations of Christianity Among the Greeks* (New York: Routledge, 1998).

18. St. Thomas Aquinas, *Summa Theologiae* III, q. 8, a. 3, "Whether Christ is the Head of All Men."

19. "Response to Professor Altizer," *Published Essays, 1966–1985,* 294.

20. The extent to which the full individualist implications have not been absorbed from the liberal forms is perhaps most evident in China. Suppression of the Tiananmen Square uprising was possible, not only through the power of the Red Army, but more broadly by the reluctance of a paternalistic society to countenance the open challenge to authority. One suspects that the striking image of a lone demonstrator deflecting a line of tanks was too unsettling for popular consciousness to bear. Even Japan, the most progressive of all Asian societies, still demonstrates the extent to which a robust airing of political disagreements, especially by way of party competition, has not yet been fully absorbed within their ostensibly American constitution.

21. The peculiar situation in which the liberal political tradition finds itself—characterized by the universal acknowledgment of its legiti-

macy, yet riven by its incapacity to provide a rational account of its principles—surely has something to do with the sense of having solved the problems of politics. The conversation, by which meaning is sustained, cannot continue on the presumption that there are no further questions to be discussed. I have tried to address this problem in *The Growth of the Liberal Soul.*

Christ as the Heart of Civilization

THE CENTRALITY OF CHRIST is seen most clearly in relation to the great civilizational threat. This is the distorted perception of reality that occurs when human beings lose their hold on the balance of existence. Exaggerated expectations of fulfillment or dejected extremes of despair unhinge the equilibrium so crucial to the functioning of our reason. In such disorientation, we realize how frail an instrument of guidance our reason really is. It ultimately depends on the broader spiritual setting to enable it to fulfill its rational nature. We know that disequilibrium has been the prevailing problem of the modern world, and we are more cognizant than ever of the necessity of finding the balance of aspirations and realizations enabling us to live. What we have not yet discovered is that the way toward the elusive balance can only be found through the full differentiation of the tension of existence provided by the revelation of Christ. Far from constituting a source of imbalance, the eschatological finality of Christianity uncovers the full amplitude of mundane existence. Only through the otherworldly fulfillment of Christ is light finally dispensed on the fullness of life within the world.

The civilizational significance of Christianity lies, as we have suggested, in the stability it imparts to historical existence. Quite apart from the soteriological good news, there is a distinct achievement of order within this life. Differentiation of the limiting participation in transcendent Being not only illuminates the movement of theosis, but also sheds light on the limiting structure of human life as a whole. Reason acquires firm spiritual supports. A clarity concerning the boundaries of the human condition has the effect of removing the major deformations of reason. As a result, the spirit of rational enterprise is unleashed without substantial danger of excessive inflation or deflation. The result is visible in the resolute articulation of limits within which the full potentiality of life in this world can be realized, enlarged, and communicated to all mankind. Of course, balance is always the fruit of a perpetual struggle against imbalance and is never a permanent achievement, as we know only too well from our own experience. But the basic parameters that restrain the misdirection of reason have themselves been articulated in the course of this civilizational development, which, by definition, has attained a degree of stability impressive by any historical standards. Christian civilization, including its modern secular expression, has a staying power precisely because it has articulated the limits of rational perception. Its global preponderance is less the fruit of hegemonic expansion than of the authoritative power of the rational equilibrium it differentiates. The source of the existential rationality behind the rationality of efficiency lies in the transcendent revelation of Christ.

Gnostic Alternative

Contrast with Christianity's great imbalancing opponent provides the most convincing demonstration of this equilibrating force it provides. Acceptance of limits and the readiness to strive unceasingly against them is a fine line to walk, and it is not surprising that it is more often missed than found. But, whatever the difficulty, it is the one avenue toward the fullest realization of the possibilities of existence. On it depends the progressive movement of the human race, which must simultaneously avoid the overreaching ambition that destroys itself. There are many ways, as Aristotle remarked, that the mark can be missed, but only one in which it can be hit. Yet the multiplicity of distortions all derive from the same root in their unwillingness to submit to the discipline required to reach the goal. Indiscipline has its source, not primarily in the unruliness of temper that will not accept a master, but in the prior disposition of revolt that sets its own will above all others, including the will of the whole. St. Augustine refers to it as pride, the assertion of human primacy before all other reality. Even God cannot supplant the self-will at the center of the soul that has chosen its own way irrespective of the consequences. Persistence in revolt is the great imbalancing force of human existence because it cannot be deflected by a rational consideration of the costs. Revolt and irrationality go together, and the symbolic elaboration of its thrust is the great alternative to the Christian redemption of disorder.

This symbolism has for two millennia been known as Gnosticism. It has been so closely related to Christianity that it can, with considerable justification, be regarded as the quintessential Christian heresy. Features of Gnosticism are certainly discernible in most of the great heretical movements over the two millennia of Christian history. Some have even gone so far as to suggest that Christianity spawns Gnosticism as its inescapable double. While there is a certain plausibility to this perspective, it should not allow us to overlook two other decisive factors. First, the advent of Gnosticism as a syncretic, mytho-speculative movement of escape from the cosmos antedates the time of Christ and the early Church. Second, and of more crucial import, Christianity itself is the great antidote to Gnosticism because it teaches us how to live fully in the world while fully acknowledging our home beyond it. Christianity represents the definitive elimination of the spirit of revolt because it is the most complete expression of submission to the will of God mysteriously present in existence. God himself has submitted to the same imperative of order, definitively establishing it and revealing it within the unfolding of reality. Balance has been perfectly achieved in Christ between the movement toward transcendent Being and the condition of immanent existence that is the only possibility known to us. Yet the sentiment of revolt has not been eliminated. We find it present within ourselves, in the impatience with the necessity of enduring the imperfection intervening before its abolition in the blinding return of perfection.[1]

The propensity to run toward the final consummation is almost inevitable in any movement of spiritual illumination. Eschatological, apocalyptic, and millennarian expectations are a feature of the spiritual outbursts in which revelation is received and perennially renewed. The glimpse of Being that illuminates existence in every moment tempts us to overleap the distance that separates us from the enchanting goal. But something more is needed to make us persist in the project of consummation, even if it means jeopardizing the only condition in which the momentary glimpse of transfiguration obtains. The additional element is revolt. It is resentment at the limitations imposed on us as the price of our mysterious participation in transcendence. Irrationality erupts in the abyss of revolt that will not endure the condition of being a man and insists on jumping immediately into the state of divine being. The outbreak of irrationality, which is itself the mystery of iniquity, cannot be rendered intelligible. That is its character. It defies all reason because the futility of its aspiration remains impervious to dissuasion. This is why spiritual revolt is the great disturbing factor within human history, destroying not only our hold on spiritual life, but ultimately even the very possibility of life in this world as well. Only the healing touch of transcendent Love, pouring itself out for us, is capable of breaking through the blindness that robs us of the capacity to see through reason.

The deadliness of the Gnostic leap into perfection is seen in its evacuation of the possibility of human life. What would it mean to have realized our complete and total fulfillment right now? This is the prospect that has opened up the post-Hegelian speculations on the end of history. It is, of course, the promise contained in all of the ideological movements of immanent transfiguration. But it is only when we contemplate the end point toward which they and, by extension, the modern world is directed that we apprehend the full blankness of what they contain. The end of history, as Alexandre Kojève most profoundly delineated for us, spells the end of human life as we know it.[2] All that we are is constituted by the restless striving toward goals that, as soon as they are reached, turn out to fall short of the satisfaction envisioned. We move restlessly and ceaselessly from one achievement to the next, the former turning out to be only the means toward the latter, which in turn reveals its own provisionality towards a further impetus, and so on. Infinite progress driven by unfillable longing turns out to be the mystery that guards human life. It preserves our openness toward the transcendent Being that alone can answer our insatiable hunger and, at the same time, ensures against the attainment of any entombing resting place within this life. The restlessness of the spirit driving toward eternity is simultaneously the preservation of our earthly vitality as well. Nothing can be more oppressive than perfection, as the utopias of our imagination forever attest.

It is one of the curious ironies of our secular civilization that the preservation of its most impressive accomplishments is crucially dependent on their inconclusiveness. Nothing is more damaging to science than the suggestion that we are entering an era in which all of the fundamental questions have been resolved. This may have been the holy grail that drew the great efforts of discovery forward, but its attainment would spell the end of all scientific life. No more would boundless curiosity set us out in search of an ever more comprehensive understanding of the world in which we live. Inquisitiveness and the thrill of discovery would disappear. Without a boundless field of inquiry to stir our imaginations and provoke our pursuit, there would be nothing to preserve even the capacity to extend our scientific reach. If all knowledge is known, then, in a certain sense, knowledge is no more. It cannot be activated as a movement of discovery; it is routinized as the transmission of what is incapable of progression. Life—not only intellectually, but in all its other dimensions—would no longer resemble the thrusting, striving, and enticing vitality we recognize as the core of human existence. If ever our satisfaction were achieved, we would be no more. Instead, we would be compelled to revert, as Kojève so preceptively observed, to a purely animal level in which thinking has no place, since all has been reduced to the mechanical. We might go through the motions, as he explained, in preserving a kind of snob formalism, but this would be merely be an external cover for the hollowness at our core. We shudder at the suffocating finality of all utopian dreams and are grateful that we have not been blessed with such perfection.

The most militant recent expressions of the perfectionist impulse in totalitarian ideologies may have passed, but the temptation remains a permanent possibility. What could be more plausible than the extrapolation from perfection glimpsed to its consummation? Only the definitive differentiation of the transcendent distance can guard us against the possibility. We must be able to apprehend the gulf between immanent existence and its transcendent fulfillment. The impossibility of finite being adequately embodying infinite Being must remain inescapably clear, if only to guarantee against the possibility of confusion between them. Then we recognize the incapacity of the human to become the receptacle of the divine. Only through the free gift from the divine side is a bridging of the distance conceivable. In its own terms, this world and all that is in it is clearly incapable of the transcending perfection of Being, and there is no danger of confusing the two. Far from devaluing existence in this world, such a differentiation grounds the value of immanent reality at its deepest level. Now it is free to unfold its own dynamic, secure in the knowledge that there is no possibility of exhausting its innermost nature as an image of eternity within time. Since there is no possibility of time encompassing the transcendence of eternity, the endless fecundity of finite existence rolls forth as the analog of true infinity. Existence in this world is fully accepted on its own terms and yet recognized in terms of its highest aspiration. That is, mundane reality points toward the Being it reflects, but is ever incapable of attaining. Transparence toward the infinite is the highest realization of finite existence.

The differences between ancient and modern varieties of Gnosticism are less significant than their similarities. They both point irrevocably in the same direction: the devaluation of earthly existence. Ancient Gnosticism is extracosmic, seeking an escape from material imprisonment in the cosmos through flouting the norms of society, or an ascetic revolt against life, or varieties of ascensional experience. It is not that such variants are unknown in the modern world, but their recurrence is within a more intracosmic direction that points toward an immanent eschaton. Yet, despite the expansive focus on development, they too yield the dead end of a static condition of existence as their telos. A hatred of life remains their deepest impulse. They will not accept existence on its own terms and thus resolve to rage against it, even if it means their destruction. We see the symptoms of the Gnostic sentiment in many of the features of our age. A civilization showing many signs of fading vitality—from declining birth rates to the withdrawal into private cocoons—can be just as deadly as the titanic destructiveness of its militant ideological phase. As much as ever, we are in need of the reminder of the inexhaustible depth of life because it contains within it the promise of eternity. Faith in the future and the courage to expend ourselves in its creation can only come from individuals who recognize such mundane striving as emblematic for something higher, which can neither be realized nor eliminated from our experience of existence.

Christ as the Balance

The balance that sustains the full vitality of life depends on the full differentiation of Being. This provides the deepest understanding of mundane reality, which is beheld without illusion for what it is, but at the same time is contemplated in its full finality beyond itself. Life in this world is not merely confined to its parameters. It is pregnant with implications for participation in Being itself.

Through the theophanic intervention, the luminosity of existence has been opened up as a participation in the drama of the God who becomes man in order to redeem the human world for himself. What is at stake is not mere survival, but life itself. It can be lost through the overreaching that prompts us to step outside of our stature in the order of being and thereby slip into the abyss of all that lacks reality of any kind. As a result, life here is ennobled or elevated beyond its mere biological-psychological significance. To the extent that we lose sight of this transcending dimension of existence, we are also losing our grip on what most deeply affirms the value of mere physical and emotional and factual existence. The imperative of balance could not be more heightened, and neither could the line through which it is to be found more clearly delineated.

Life is to be accepted on its own terms. It is incapable of providing the uninterrupted, peerless satisfaction we crave, but neither is it for that reason to be burdened with the concupiscent drive doomed to disappoint. Within that modest range, our earthly existence is capable of the highest actualization of life through the receptive opening toward transcendent Being. But that transcendence remains dependent on acceptance of our creaturely status. The way toward reception of the transcendent fullness lies through complete submission to the mystery of the whole in which we find ourselves. No murmuring against our fate is permitted if we are to become the vehicle for ineffable divine Love, whose deepest reality consists in the same outpouring of itself toward all creatures. Not only is this world affirmed, it is enhanced as the royal road toward the truth that contains it all. Revelation of the divine gift of self freely offered to all men and shining on the whole of existence becomes the beacon transforming and drawing all things to itself. The irruption of transcendent Being within time not only saves all that respond to it from the fatality of genesis and perishing; it sanctifies the process of becoming through which the transfiguring event of intervention takes place. Suffering, life, and death are no longer the impenetrable barriers of our existence. Now they assume the radiance of utter abnegation of self by which the translation into the being of Being takes place.

A dimension far beyond this transcendent finality of revelation, however emerges with the advent of Christ. The preceding meditation might be drawn from the Sermon on the Mount, as the account of how those open to the drawing of God ought to conduct themselves. The injunction toward perfection is reiterated because that is the way of the Father. Throughout, the refrain is repeated that the motivation for going beyond what we are strictly bound to do arises from the superabundant generosity of the Father who "makes his sun to shine on the good and the bad" (Matthew 5:45). The opening toward unconditioned Love requires the unconditional self-donation of love. There is no point at which we might hold back in expending ourselves in service toward others; not even their hardness and opaqueness can be sufficient reason for not doing more than we are expected to do. It must be toward all and for all and with all. Only then will we become the kind of men and women who are capable of becoming children of God, vessels of the transcendent Spirit that lives in us too. But we forget that the Sermon on the Mount was only the beginning of the teaching of Jesus, not its culmination. Beyond the reception of the luminous teaching is the recognition of who the teacher is. The Sermon reaches its apogee in the recognition that the utter submission of self that it calls forth is undertaken most perfectly by God himself becoming man in Jesus.

Another level is attained through the recognition that the fate of perfect submission is undergone by Being itself present within the world. Not only is the full acceptance of the order of existence apprehended as the way toward Being; it is also revealed as the way of Being. A dimension over and above the revelatory movement toward the Beyond is contained in the recognition of the participation of the Beyond in the full realization of existence. It is best expressed as redemption. Not only is the path of self-submission before the mysterious order of Being unmistakably clear, but its realization has been definitively attained within time as being effective for all other beings. The sacrificial surrender of Christ to the divine will accomplishes what is lacking in the submission of all other beings throughout creation. Not only is a decisive rupture marked within time radiating its light in all directions, but all finite existence has been definitively raised up toward the redemptive participation beyond all immanent expectations. The transfiguration toward which all reality unattainably aspires has been differentiated as the culminating fulfillment of the eschaton. Indeed, the eschaton has become present in the death, resurrection, and ascension of Jesus. Finite reality already exists in the tension that is transparent for its transfiguring fulfillment. No higher possibility can be conceived for immanent being.

Gnostic Loss of Illumination

The limit of transcendent revelation illuminates the limits of mundane existence. No deeper penetration is possible. The great Gnostic alternative aims at comprehending the mystery, but in the process ends by abolishing it. Nowhere is this more evident than in the drama of good and evil through which human life is unfolded. Gnostic subsumption of the human struggle to the extra-cosmic clash of divinities carries all the appearance of piercing the veil of mystery surrounding existence. But it is no more than an appearance. The reality is that projection of the moral contest outside of ourselves does not illumine it so much as reduce it to a power play. Good and evil as such disappear because we are not intimately involved in either of them. We are merely the passive victims of the cosmic battle being transacted over our heads. Gone is any profound sense of the realities of the two because they have been removed as dimensions of our experience. We do not see that goodness is that which is self-justifying above all else and that evil is the permanent possibility of our fall away from it. The "mystery" of evil may be solved, but it is hardly any longer evil because it has been transformed into objective forces of the divine cosmic process. Evil as radical unintelligibility and, therefore, radically without a cause or explanation disappears from view. It is no longer the rupture within being chosen for the sake of darkness itself. Goodness as the healing power of love whose sacrificial depth is capable of overcoming it cannot, as a consequence, be perceived either. Instead, all is reduced to the most elemental clash of powers.

Once evil has been transferred to a problem to be solved, redemption also disappears in its full mysterious unfolding. The power play of divinities replaces the Father who so loved the world that he sent his own Son to die for it. Inexpressible love in the glance of Jesus, turned simultaneously toward the world and in utter submission toward the Father, is covered over. We are left with the flatness of explanation that grasps nothing. In the mystery resolved, the deepest apprehension of reality escapes. Nothing can be known of the redemptive power of love as the inexhaustible sacrificial presence that is the surest warranty of the final victory of good over evil. As a consequence, the deeper insight into human existence is lost. Not only is the radical unintelligibility of the collapse into evil removed from sight, but the even more impenetrable luminosity of goodness through which the defeat of evil is assured disappears from view. Without the transcendent mystery of the divine redemptive outpouring of itself, the possibility of beholding its reflection in human existence has been lost. This is why the Gnostic apprehension of human life—a perspective whose symptoms we notice all around us—represents a distinct impoverishment of existence. It may step forward in the name of advancing illumination of the mystery behind the mystery of redemption, but it ends by losing sight of the transcendent fullness glimpsed in the sacrifice of Jesus on our behalf. No explanation in terms of theological necessities can surpass the real explanation of love in which we are held with infinite tenderness despite the inexcusability of our turn toward rejection. Love itself is the great explanation that cannot be transcended.

The unsurpassability of the spiritual perspective is recognized whenever we must deal honestly with the deepest questions of existence. All great art is built on this recognition. If it wishes to get to the heart of the matter, it must foreswear all distracting inclinations to resolve the issues at a more intermediate level of power, convention, or artifice. Sooner or later, all hearts know they must make that transcendent choice in moving toward love or toward withdrawal. Invocations of extraneous factors are all beside the point, which is itself utterly simple. But its truth is utterly penetrating. In the extremity of existence, the path toward life is to be gained through the willingness to sacrifice self in realizing love. The other way of inversion leads toward nothing but the emptiness whose fascination remains nevertheless ineliminable. At the center of the drama is the luminous moment when the light of love pierces our darkness and we are drawn up toward it. We respond with love to the love showered upon us and, in that opening, begin to play our part in the redemptive sacrifice of self by which all things are led back toward their transcendent source. The outpouring of love makes us sharers in the redemptive movement. All great art is implicitly Christian in the sense that it moves inexorably toward the unfolding of the deepest mystery of our participation.[3] Limits limned by the movement of love cannot be breached. Any attempt to overstep them succeeds only in losing sight of the most penetrating source of luminosity. It is love that finally illumines existence.

This is why, for the Gnostics, the radiant center of love must become the ultimate target of their rejection. Gnosticism is not only anti-Christian in the generic sense that all such rival spiritual movements must become oppositional. It is anti-Christ in the sense of his specific rejection. Despite the closeness that existed between Gnostic sects and the Christian community over history, there has never been much danger that the Church would be taken over by the Gnostic spirituality. In its implications, Gnosticism is pointed irrevocably against Christ. He must decline in significance when he has become merely emblematic of the larger divine-cosmic drama the gnosis expounds. The turning point is not his redemptive death and resurrection, but the future triumph of the forces of liberated divinity in their cataclysmic struggle with the imprisoning forces of the cosmos. Christ slips from being the Son of God to becoming a son of God, albeit a leading exemplar. Salvation is gained not by receiving the fruits of his atoning sacrifice, but by entering into the same battle indicated by Christ against the darkness of material existence. We are set on the course of becoming another Christ, but not deriving the strength to do so from him. We must become the other translucent Christ far beyond the humble, loving servant of his revelation within history. The supersession of Christianity is most evident in the significance imparted to the new Christs of the liberation. Having transcended him definitively, we will no longer stand in need of his mediation. The determination to surpass Christ in attainments inevitably leads toward his rejection. Gnosticism ultimately renders Christ obsolescent, once man possesses the gnosis that enables the ascensional movement of liberation to be realized. However much Gnosticism may live around the boundaries of Christianity, there can be no ultimate reconciliation between them.

The reversal accomplished by the Gnostic "advance" is nowhere more in evidence than in its decline from Christian morality. In place of the loving generosity lavished on all God's creatures, we witness the harsh assertion of self-interest fueled by the resentment of our fate in this material universe. Power replaces love as the abiding theme. What matters is the difference between the Gnostics and the ignorant—between those who possess the secret knowledge that furnishes the means of cheating the ruler of this world and those deprived of it. No attempt is made to save the reprobates who refuse the call of higher knowledge, thus confirming their true natures as remnants of the powers of darkness. Pride, superiority, and indomitability are the determinations that mark the features of the godded men who will lead the way toward the final liberation of the truly divine souls in existence. As for the others, they are irreparably condemned to the grossness that is their true nature. A sharp division between two types of human beings replaces the mysterious intermingling of good and evil in all human hearts. Now the battle lines have been drawn, and victory belongs to the supremely resolute. Harshness has replaced the face of love presented to the world and to all men, and in that realization we can see the change effected by the Gnostics. Far from an advance beyond love, it shows more clearly than ever that the decline from love leads away from the light. In attempting to surpass the only source of luminosity available, the Gnostics have lost themselves in the outer darkness.

The feature is well known in the antinomian character of the Gnostic movement. Death is recognizably the outcome of a movement that turns its back on all that is good in this world, utterly refusing to be led by its promptings. Cutting themselves off from the tangible intimations of goodness we receive in our earthly existence, the Gnostics imagine they have stepped into a transcendent dimension of unlimited light. But they have only succeeded in locking themselves even more firmly in the hell of their own closed imaginations. The pattern is recognizable in the Romantic affinities to Gnosticism. Romanticism in part draws its strength from the same sources. A deep-seated resentment against the finite conditions of our existence, constrained within the imperfections of convention and nature, is combined with a limitless aspiration to overstep the limits in the attainment of a bliss transcending all imagination. Predictably, the result is not the attainment of either earthly life or the movement toward its eternal completion; it is the railing without benefit against limits that remain impervious. But the darkness at the Gnostic core is revealed in its extinguishing of the only hold on life that is possible for us. Everything is destroyed in the maelstrom of annihilation generated by the madness of revolt. We see this in the death-dealing choices of the Romantics, who not only kill themselves but communicate their own disease of destruction to all else. Nothing can stand comparison to the transcendent glimpse attained in the moment of self-immolation.[4] The nihilism of revolt we recognize as a feature of modern history draws its strength not from the spirit of rejection, but from the perverse will toward transcendence that will brook no limits. Even the necessity of submission to the tensional expansion of existence as the way of transcendent participation is not enough to staunch the madness.

What is less well understood is what the Christian tradition has known from its beginning—that is, that Christ is the one who rids us of the Gnostic possession. In him we see the only way in which submission to the order of immanent existence can yield the opening toward transcendent life. It is not by the antinomian raging against all order, but by the humble and complete abnegation of self before the impervious divine will. Suffering and the finitude from which it derives is not an impenetrable obstacle to our fulfillment, but the most precious gift available for the self-transcending movement toward Being. Christ does not reject earthly existence, but submits perfectly to its conditions. Suffering, he shows, is not the unrelieved dead end we instinctively take it to be. Rather, it is the flower of redemption through which all that is inverted and evil is subsumed in the offering of self on behalf of all. We do not know or perceive how that transformation of all reality is to take place. But, in Christ, we intuit the means by which it is accomplished. He is not only the perfection of human existence open to the redemptive will of the transcendent, but also the fullness of divine being that redeems all of human existence through his participation in our fate. No more luminous account of the mystery of the human condition is possible. Christ is the great prize of our spiritual life, lost by the Gnostic overreaching and found only through submission to the humble path the Nazarene himself trod. In contrast to the Gnostic rejection of suffering as the way, Christ is the one who shares its higher meaning of redemption with all mankind.

A measure of the degree to which our contemporary religiosity is infected with the Gnostic illusion is the extent to which spirituality has become defined by self-fulfillment. The gnostic pattern of spiritual short-circuitry is at work in it. Feel-good narcissism and consumer gratification are well-recognized features of the contemporary spiritual landscape. But what is less well understood is their filiation with the oldest of all rivals to Christianity in Gnosticism. It is sensed, but rarely understood, how deeply contrary to Christianity the spirituality of immanent success really is.[5] Attainment of the means of our satisfaction undermines the redemptive thrust of the Christian message. Congregations already satiated beyond their expectations and thus perfected in their spiritual lives are hardly in need of a redeemer. No wonder there is little call for preaching on the wickedness of the human heart or on the ineradicable proclivity for evil within each of us. As a consequence, there is even less need for reference to the redemptive power of suffering. Lives neither in need of repentance nor prone to the afflictions of the body and mind are hardly receptive ground for the Christian message of healing. The perfect have no need of a savior, and the same is true of those who have lost all cognizance of their imperfection. But with this evisceration of the Christian message, there also flows away the depth of insight within which reason can unfold toward its limits. The field of rationality is correspondingly shrunk toward a mundane realm of existence closed off against all illuminative glimpses from the Beyond. It is no wonder that a spirituality reduced to secular self-fulfillment and self-esteem can offer little in the way of guidance to a reason condemned to endlessly organizing the achievement of mundane efficiency. The possibility that suffering might not be something on which we would want to turn our backs can no longer penetrate, because it is no longer transparent for the transcendent love that redeems and renders it redemptive toward all others.

Self-contradiction

What is perhaps most remarkable is that, even when the Gnostic ramifications are made abundantly apparent, little notice is taken of implications of a style of religiosity that has become virtually a commonplace. A good, recent example is the work of the contemporary self-avowed Gnostic, Harold Bloom. His *Omens of the Millennium* has been something of an omen of its own, not least of all for the unabashedly favorable reception it has received in the popular and religious press. The work is an extraordinarily forthright expression of the Gnostic faith. Bloom singles out the major contemporary developments of a quasi-Gnostic character, which he sees as harbingers of a new spiritual age. They are the growing interest among all segments in angels, the widespread fascination with the spiritual significance of dreams, the explosive proliferation of near-death experiences, and the generalized absorption with the turn of the millennium itself. Bloom's scholarly insight consists in pointing out that such contemporary novelties of New Age spirituality are not as original as they take themselves to be. On the contrary, he correctly insists, they have affinities with the lore of esoteric speculative and practical disciplines that go back before the first millennium. To anyone steeped in this exotic and occult literature, as Bloom is, the parallels and, no doubt, the continuities are obvious. While there may be some originality in religious symbolism, the scholar is generally better served by assuming the reverse. Then he or she will be led to uncover the evident lines of transmission by which our latter day theosophists develop their accounts of Metatron, the revealing angel of gnosis, the yogi-like character of out-of-body experiences, and the alchemical techniques by which the perfecting of our inner reality is attained, together with the function of symbols in manipulating thoughts, dreams, and the metempsychosis of souls. A far more extensive panoply of spiritual practices and extrapolations is to be found in the work of Jung and his disciples. Indeed, Jung's work was so encompassing that it still remains a reliable guide to the esoteric spiritual traditions of the world.[6] But what even Jung did not do, at least explicitly, was to take the step of overt endorsement advocated by Bloom. The latter has stepped outside of the pseudo-objectivity of the scholar to openly propose a return to the great Gnostic tradition as the road into the millennium.[7]

It is striking, especially as an indication of the unfettered context of the conversation, that Bloom pulls no punches in the program he advocates. He knows that this sets him diametrically at odds with the great revealed traditions, not only of Christianity, but of his own Judaism. Yet he bluntly asserts his desire to see the millennial revelations replaced by the Gnostic family of sub-traditions that promise the consummation of divinity within existence. The tension of existence—fully differentiated by Christianity, but present in all the revelatory symbolisms—would be abolished as man resumes the divine stature that is his birthright. All of the omens of the age of perfection are derived from a transcendence of the limitations of our present earthly condition. Whether it is the ascensional association of angels, the transphysical powers of communication linked with telepathy, the boundary expanding experiences of the migration of souls and contact with the dead, or the tangible suggestions of resurrection radiating from the near-death experiences, the common theme is their transcendence of the limits of our present earthly condition. Bloom speaks forcefully on behalf of the transformational hunger that fires the variants of New Age spirituality. But, unlike the wooly inclusivism that characterizes our contemporary yearners, he has the intellectual hardness to affirm its antitraditional bias. Bloom is indeed quite insistent that the real task is the removal of the ancient revealed religions. Not only do they stand in the way of man's advancing spiritual prowess, but the God of the Bible has betrayed his own ineliminable injustice through the history of the twentieth century.

The hard edge of revolt is imparted to the soft New Age contours through the conjunction with the Gnostic core of resentment. What makes Bloom an unusual voice for contemporary spiritual fantasies is not only the scholarly depth he brings to the task, but the unmistakable note of invective nurtured by the Holocaust in which God allowed his people to be virtually destroyed.[8] It is the sense of aggrievement against God that gives Bloom the determination to embrace the full amplitude of the Gnostic stance. Revolt is the crucial driving force for the overt rejection of the Hebrew and Christian god, in favor of the Gnostic divinity lying beyond him and promising the consummation of the longings so imperfectly fulfilled in this life. New Age aspirations for transfiguration are not in themselves enough. The full Gnostic elaboration, through which they acquire an intellectually coherent and credible articulation, requires the additional factor of revolt. Even murmuring against God—that perennial human failing—is not enough; the revolt must be carried to its full-blown expression for the resolve of self-salvation to take shape. The complex is strikingly illustrated in Bloom's call for the New Age speculators to embrace their full Gnostic ancestry. It is in marked contrast to some of the other Jewish responses to the Holocaust, including the founding of the state of Israel, which is premised on the conviction that political survival requires a state, precisely so that Judaism might not be abandoned.[9]

However, what is most remarkable about this most self-disclosing of all of Bloom's books is the warmth with which it has been received. Of course, a certain cloying adulation is to be expected; when celebrity scholars are reviewed by self-perceived celebrity publications, a common iconoclastic thread weaves them ever closer together. More unexpected is the broadly uncritical reception the book has received elsewhere. A perusal of the mainline reviews reveals a torrent of gushing admiration for his great leaps of spiritual adventure, his opening of vast new vistas for a society awash in new spiritual ferments, as well as the obligatory acknowledgment of his astonishing erudition. What is notably absent is any hint of the need to take issue with the portrait of Jewish and Christian faith presented in Bloom's interpretative sweep. The suggestion that the God of the Old Testament might not be the loving, caring savior of his people or that the Jesus of the New Testament might not be the way of salvation seems brushed aside as an assault on orthodoxy so commonplace as to be no longer worthy of serious consideration. It is indicative of the confusion and deterioration of the Biblical faiths that a prominent public rejection can be made without even provoking a faint-hearted defense. Truth has been so thoroughly eliminated from spiritual life (indeed this is virtually the definition of our New Age fluidity) that the popular press no longer considers it any part of its job even to point out where disagreements are involved.

Despite the charms of this unchallenged tolerance, one of its most significant costs is the decline in intellectual penetration. As we have seen, reason is inextricably bound up with the character of our spiritual orientation. Nowhere is this more evident than in our incapacity to mount a serious analytic consideration of the visionary extravaganza propounded by Bloom and admired by many. We dare not, for example, do the one thing necessary to expose the Gnostic fallacy: call their bluff. It is a measure of the insensitivity of an age besotted by false spirituality that it lacks any credible sense of the issue of authenticity. Who any longer has the directness to ask whether we are being presented with the real thing? If the core of the Gnostic claim is the promise of vaulting into the state of perfection—now fully present within us and only awaiting the acquisition of the gnosis that effects its realization—then we are surely entitled to ask whether the spiritual advance does indeed take place. Assertion of the transition to the status of godded men virtually compels scrutiny of the pronouncement. It is especially worthy of attention when the claim to have overleaped the human condition is accompanied by the assurance that no further exertion on our part is required to complete the process. Perfection, if it is entitled to call itself such, cannot fall short. To what extent then is the claim to have reached the summit of spiritual truth borne out in a life of undiminished nobility, goodness, and love? Do we in fact behold the transformative witness of unconditioned love, retrieving and redeeming all that comes before it? Is this the Suffering Servant of Yahweh, whose transcendent perfection would not permit it to crush the bruised reed or quench the flickering flame? Or do we see nothing more than the arrogance of conceit surfeited with the sense of its own superiority to everything?

It is indeed difficult to maintain that the vast expansion of man's mastery over the spiritual dimensions of existence—virtually matching the control achieved through the physical sciences—constitutes a decisive moral development. Interpretation of dreams, access to angelic powers, and the ability to peer over the boundaries of life itself seem more in the nature of instrumental acquisitions. What is the specifically moral contribution they make, if they can be used well or badly? They are still as much in need of the core enlargement of the heart that draws us out of ourselves in love and toward Love. Power is one thing, but it should never be confused with the holiness whose value outweighs all else. What good is it if a man gains the whole cosmos and loses his own soul? It is the growth in divine goodness rather than the growth in divine power that forms the core of existence. To the extent that the Gnostic flight toward translucent corporality is really a flight away from the irreplaceable ascent in love, then it is nothing but an escape from ourselves as well as the cosmos. Anything that draws us away from this central task of our existence, even if it is accompanied by angelic wonders, is to that extent the loss of our true self rather than its gain. Even the imaginative elaborations of Gnostic perfection cannot erode the central perspective within which human life is weighed. Are we becoming better than we were? Is there that advance in virtue or excellence by which alone we can measure our growing participation in the Being that transcends all else? At the end of the day, it is not power or accomplishment that constitutes the measure of anything. It is whether we have loved as we should.

Nothing betrays the mendacity of the Gnostic position more than its indifference to the moral struggle.[10] In many respects, Gnosticism is developed to avoid or overleap the conflict between good and evil within us. But the desire to jump into another condition does not materially affect our situation. Without attention to the rigors of resistance against evil, we do not magically leap into a state of perfection, but instead leave ourselves more vulnerable than ever to the blandishments of selfishness, cruelty, and vice, which we are no longer even able to recognize. The situation could hardly be worse. Having lost sight of the growing realization of goodness as the imperative outweighing all else, we have simultaneously become incapable of detecting our own drift downwards into the abyss of indifference and self-satisfaction. It is no wonder that Gnostic movements eventually wreak havoc on themselves and their world. In some sense, this is their intention. They wish to invert the entire established order of things. But they do not wish to extend the process into the destruction of their own spiritual selves. In this last bastion of connection with the world of ordinary experience we behold the irrationality of the Gnostic conviction, precisely at the point at which it cannot quite close off the awareness of itself. The Gnostic mindset knows that it has not attained the spiritual perfection it claims. Rather, a cosmic aggrandizement of power has been mistaken for the goodness to which it is irrelevant.

Perfection, as St. Augustine understood, is the Achilles heel of Gnosticism. He should know, having spent years under the influence of one of the most powerful ancient forms derived from the monk Mani. Augustine's *Confessions* contain one of the classic analyses of the process by which the Gnostic position, so seemingly impregnable against all obvious objections to it, nevertheless cannot quite avoid the inner crumbling of its certainty. The expansiveness of Augustine's personality could not be contained within the confines of a system, no matter how peerlessly consistent. He recounts the major attractions of the Manichaean outlook. It answered the questions of suffering and evil in existence that remained insoluble under all other perspectives, including the Christian. But its signal attraction was that it provided initiates with a sense of infinite superiority to all merely cosmic realities and simultaneously relieved them of the burden of the moral struggle by which we and the world are improved. Convinced of the absolute purity of the true inner sense and cognizant of its detachment from all external reality, including our own physical and social existence, the Manichaeans were left with nothing to do but contemplate their superiority to the unrelievedly evil regime around them.[11] It was a quintessentially dualistic system of good and evil realities, with all of the benefits and defects inherent in such a construction. Impervious to all objections posed from outside it, since all such resistance must come from the evil morality of this world, the unravelling could only occur from within the hermetic closure of the system itself. Augustine recognized the static nature of the faith in which he lived. It allowed for no possibility of progress, since neither intellectual nor moral advance was possible within this world. The attraction might have remained firm for lesser minds, but not for the omnivorous restlessness of an Augustine. A faith in which limitless spiritual and intellectual development was impossible simply could not answer the deepest longing of his nature. The transcendent fulfillment that Gnosticism sought to grasp with such premature eagerness proved incapable of enclosure within the fixity of determined revolt. Intimations of transcendent Being eventually broke down the walls of incarceration in illusion.

The difficulty of dislodging the Gnostic disposition is considerable, but it is not impossible. Nothing that happens in the external world can be adduced against it, certainly not the deadly consequences in terms of the utter devaluation of earthly existence or the static achievement of perfection that installs a living death. All of the normal values have been inverted, so that death itself is welcomed as the release toward true life. Presence of the symptoms of inversion in our own society in terms of the devaluation of life, the ennoblement of suicide, and the casual disregard for the marginalized are all warning signs of the pervasiveness of Gnostic influences. Life that does not seem to amount to much can be inconsiderately tossed aside. Yet, despite the impregnability of the mindset that has already preassigned the significance of all evidence introduced against it, the closure is never quite complete. An opening of vulnerability remains in awareness of the degree to which the vaunted achievement of perfection falls short of the transcendent aspiration behind it. In this sense, our situation has not changed in the slightest over the past two millennia. We are still in need of the illumination of Christ as the fullness of transcendent openness within existence. Missing from the diffuse reception of Bloom's latter-day Gnosticism is the penetrating glance of perfection realized in the God-man.

The imperative is evident in Bloom's own critique of the superficiality of the contemporary Gnostic developments. He is fully capable of identifying the shallowness and the hollowness of their claims to have reached an exalted state of humanity through the attainment of certain experiential states. Common sense still prevents him from making too much of the New Age claims of angelic visitations or out-of-body experiences. Besides the endemic possibility of charlatanism, there is the more serious possibility of misconstructing the significance of experiences that are real. Bloom is enough of a literary critic to retain awareness of the extent to which all experience is already linguistically constructed. There are no pure experiences as such, just as there are no purely original revelations. Everything has its literary-historical context of affinities and attenuations. But he is then immediately misled when he gravitates toward what he considers the deeper textual sources of the contemporary phenomena. This is due partly to the natural excitement of the scholar in uncovering the hidden sources, but by far the greatest factor is Bloom's own personal proclivity in the same direction. He wants the ancient Gnostics to be true, as they represent the most compelling expression of his own deepest intuition. As a result, they are not subjected to the same searching examination, and he fails to recognize the superficiality that still attaches to their admittedly more impressive formulations. Despite their evidently greater depth than our evanescent contemporary fantasies, the historic Gnostics still fall short of the deepest illumination of the human condition. A static mode of escape masquerades for the only tangible possibility of advancing participation in Being. They miss the transcendent submission to finitude revealed in Christ.

Christ as Limit of Luminosity

No higher viewpoint is available to us. Rationality is the fruit of the differentiation of Being that has historically unfolded through the revelatory encounters. We cannot penetrate to a deeper apprehension of the movement toward transcendent Being than the glimpse of limitless Love that is luminous in Christ. Virtue cannot extend any further than the utter self-abnegation we behold in the crucified Savior. Nor can we sense a more perfect realization of transcendence than in the victory he accomplishes over sin and death. All cosmic and extracosmic heroes pale in comparison with the theophany of limitless Love. What higher perfection can be worthy of attainment or emulation? No powers, skills, or miracle working can compare with the wonder of transcendent Being making itself present to us and thereby showing us the way by which we ourselves might become like it. Everything else seems paltry as a mode of reality. A definitive principle of truth is attained that, for us, represents the limits of differentiation. The alternative is the turn away from such luminosity, which points us back toward the compactness of confusion, but is in reality the decline into darkness rejecting the tension of existence. Imagining that we are capable of standing apart from it and thus determining for ourselves the order within which we will stand accomplishes little. It only guarantees the loss of the only transcendent illumination from which our reason might be directed.[12]

Some sense of this necessity, of standing within the order from which we might behold where we are, is still inchoately present in the speculations of Bloom and our contemporaries. Indeed, what there is of luminosity still trades on its presence. The component of legitimacy in the complaints against the revealed theologies arises from the sense of their opaqueness. By far the most poignant aspect of Bloom's account has to do with the sense of unfulfilled longing arising from his engagement with the orthodox traditions. At the most elemental level, they failed to communicate a sense of transcendent Being to him. Whatever there was of revelatory force within them had lost its transparence; now they came across as the detritus of encrusted dogmatisms irrelevant to human experience. Beyond the element of Promethean revolt, a large part of what sustains him is the longing for direct contact with God. Religion is of value only to the extent that it makes the immediate experience possible. Without that pivotal event, nothing else of its theology can carry any weight. The vivifying source of all faith is the participatory moment by which we are assured of the touch of Being itself. Bloom is enough of a spiritual searcher to have been led by a very profound sense of that ineluctable presence. This is the secret of his appeal, just as he recognizes it as being the evocative force behind all the great transmitters of theophany within history. Distortion only sets in when Bloom himself resolves to step outside the possibility of illumination, by imagining that the illuminative events can be comprehended by him. At that point, he becomes a Gnostic.

But the extension is by no means inevitable. It can readily be resisted from within the unfolding of the illuminative events themselves. All that it takes is a greater movement of love of the light that allows us to travel toward it without quenching it in the overreaching ambition to contain it. Again Christ provides its fullest exemplification. In order to participate in the luminosity of Christ, we must be prepared to submit ourselves as perfectly as he submitted himself to the Father. Despite the strong bias against the orthodox tradition, Bloom can never quite escape its authoritative influence. What there is of truth in his exhortation consists of the promise of the vivifying divine fullness beyond the dead letter of law and dogma. His reflections trade on the enlarging movement of spiritual perfection, even if the reality ultimately escapes the attempt to grasp it within his control. However, even the illegitimate extrapolation from the true sense of transcendent openness to mystery—submission to the ineffable divine will—takes its origin from what it already knows it should follow. If hypocrisy is the complement that vice pays to virtue, then truth is the unacknowledged presupposition for deception. Dissolution of the falsehood requires only the recognition of its futility to initiate the process of collapse. Gnosis is finally deficient in its claim to illumination. Rather than reaching a higher perspective beyond the common lot of humanity, it falls away from the only opening toward Being that is available to us. Even Being itself, when it entered time, did not advance in any other way. We know God only by submitting our wills utterly to his. Any other avenue draws us further away from the true touch of the transcendent.

Clearly, there is no way to prove the Gnostic wrong. None of us has access to the kind of external viewpoint on reality required to definitively judge the accuracy or inaccuracy of the respective accounts of the whole. Our perspective is inextricably within. But we are not without resources, in the form of intimations of the direction in which the fullness of Being lies. Reason, or the sense of truth and order, is crucially dependent on discovering the right intimations and faithfully unfolding them toward their differentiating limits. A battle between competing orientations toward the whole is the arena within which the emergence of rationality succeeds or fails. The possibility of reaching any kind of consensual convergence on the context of reason derives from the presence of the same intimatory longings in all human beings. Without that prearticulate community, there would neither be a common humanity nor the possibility of a public world. Patient fidelity toward the deepest intuitions informing our experience can provide, if not the means of settling the great metaphysical divergences, at least the possibility of evoking the recognition of the convergence toward which we are implicitly drawn. Settlement, even of a provisional nature, is possible because of the common structure of recognition. Spiritual perfection is not to be attained in any other way but the growth in love. Self-donation to others counts more highly than all the wonder-working powers of the cosmos.

Ordinary life itself seems to conspire to point us in the same direction. Celebration of the value of earthly existence suggests that it is at its best when viewed within the movement toward what is beyond.[13] In this sense, it ceases to be ordinary. It is suffused with the mysterious ultimacy of Being and radically incapable of being viewed in mundane terms. This is, of course, the most pervasively overlooked feature of human existence. Each of us lives within an enchanted world despite the prevailing tendencies of our instrumental culture to rub the mystery away. But life without the halo of ineluctability would not only be unendurable; it would be impossible. Nothing is more striking about human life than the degree to which its ordinary unfolding from birth to maturation to death is invested continuously with transcendent significance. This is why all of the important events are marked with ceremonies large and small, public and private. In themselves, the symbolic amplifications add nothing to the tangible achievements or transactions of births, marriages, graduations, anniversaries, celebrations, deaths, and remembrances. But in another sense, they constitute for us the whole reality. We are almost incapable of effecting the practical finite increments through which our lives are constituted without invoking the larger significance beyond them. Ordinary life is a myriad transparence for the boundary of Being that remains forever beyond its grasp yet never beyond its presence. The undertow of existence itself converges with the opening of the soul inwardly to point toward participation in transcendent life as the highest realization of existence.

The truth of the inner intimations are confirmed in the fullness of life they support. At the most basic level, this is manifested in a trust in existence. As opposed to the Gnostic insecurity generated by an obsession with the precarious hold that all things have on reality, we are furnished with a confidence that, somehow, the invisible sustaining order is to be relied upon. Anxiety is one of the hallmarks of the Gnostic impulse. To the extent that it marks our preoccupation with risk and the endless efforts of avoidance and insurance that our fertile minds bring forth in response, we are once again in the region of Gnostic symptomatology. The effective antidote is not greater certainty, but the recognition that the divine ground on which everything depends cares about us. A world cut off from its transcendent source gives way to the high anxiety that robs ordinary life of its sustaining confidence. Highly sophisticated analyses of the sentiment do nothing to assuage a sense of dread that arises from nothing specific at all.[14] No matter how thoroughly we plan for the eventualities and accidents of existence, we cannot reach a sense of peace. Gnawing away at the heart of our vast security arrangements is the fear of what is indefinable and therefore cannot be secured against. How different the tonality of existence is when it is grounded in an order of being that can be trusted unconditionally because it is the order of Being. Nothing has changed in the vicissitudes and uncertainties of human life, yet everything has been changed in the quality of experience. Where before the dark shadow of nothingness had enshrouded everything with death, now the radiant glance of Being enlivens everything we encounter. Removed from the dread of what is not, we can live life to the fullest in every moment.

Attention flows naturally toward the celebration of life's turning points with a significance larger than life. Intuiting the infinity that lies beyond all finitude, the tangible realities of existence can readily assume the transparence toward what they are not. Nothing we experience is infinite, everlasting, complete, or fulfilling, yet they can be unreservedly embraced both for what they are and for what they adumbrate. They are not required to deliver more than they can promise, nor are they to be mistrusted as the illusory sirens of our destruction. Rather, life is to be lived to the fullest on its own terms. This is the undergirding faith that sustains the most vigorous and extensive unfolding of the human creative impulse. If we were always to stop and weigh up the multiple possibilities for disaster along the way, then humanity would have risked and accomplished nothing. Commitments would not be made, children would not be born, great endeavors would not be undertaken, and civilization would not be built. The whole vitality of existence depends on a confidence that life itself does not alone provide. It may draw us toward it, but the source is to be found only by the inner opening toward its self-revelation. The glimpse of transcendent Being is the assurance of the order in which we find ourselves. The Gnostic disposition ruptures the connection between the two because it is unwilling to participate within a relationship whose mystery remains even after the revelation. However, mystery is not pierced, only eliminated. Disorientation is complete as we cut ourselves off both from the immediate disclosure of Being and its mediated presence within the order of reality as a whole. Gnosticism encloses itself within a fantasy.

The alternative remains the illuminative glance of which reality is capable. It does not reach the all-penetrating viewpoint from which the whole can be comprehended, but it does attain the luminosity that is possible without overreaching toward the impossible. From the perspective of ordinary life, that is more than enough. Not only does it sustain the underlying trust on which its vitality and momentum depends, but it projects a shaft of light that assures us of the transcendent significance of all that we do. The investment of the transient, with resonances of the eternal, is not merely an empty aspiration of the finite self. It is answered by the inviting revelation of transcendent Being itself. We do not merely enact the drama of our existence. Life is a partnership in which Being itself bends toward us in drawing us up beyond the possibilities of finitude to a participation in the life of God himself. What, from the mundane perspective, had been no more than the sum total of the explanatory factors converging on each of our finite actions suddenly is illumined for its significance within an order of being of surpassing moment. We do not simply trudge incrementally towards our finite end. Rather, we carry within us an inexpressible depth of mystery that renders all that we do potentially revelatory of Being itself. Human life becomes transparent for what constitutes it, yet transcends it. Ordinary existence is itself theophanic.

The turning point, as we have tried to suggest throughout this meditation on the dawn of the third millennium, arises when the drama of our participation in Being intersects with the revelation of the participation of Being in the drama of our existence. Then not only are the intimations of transcendence confirmed, but they are beheld as actualized within concrete historical reality. A dimension of definitive valorization is imparted to immanent reality in the recognition that it is mysteriously united with transcendent Being itself. The Incarnation is rightfully the center of history. In its inexhaustible mystery, we behold, without comprehending, the degree to which creaturely existence is open to the life of the Creator, and the fullness of divine reality simultaneously embraces the reaches of finitude. Something new and unheard of since the beginning of the world has been introduced, and its depth cannot be sounded throughout all of the time that remains. Our own clouded secular valuation of worldly existence still lives from the resonances of that pivotal revelation within history. As with anything that enters history—even the birth of God himself—it must submit to the imperfection of the possibilities of communication. But, even despite the nonuniversality of the acceptance of Christ, he remains the definitive realization of the intimations of revelation scattered across human consciousness from beginning to end. Ordinary life can no longer be viewed as ordinary so long as it is continuous with the incarnational mystery.

Of all of the revelatory outbursts that emerge in history, it must be the limiting case. No further differentiation is possible beyond the differentiation of Being itself. The epiphany of the transcendent God within time must illuminate the ultimate parameters of participation in order within existence. It is, in this sense, also the definitive revelation of the order of immanent being as well. This is why philosophy after the advent of Christ must of necessity be Christian philosophy. It is the differentiating limit of the order of virtue through which the actualization of the transcendent dimension of existence is reached. The one who is the fullness of Being must embody the mode of fullest human participation in Being. He is the highest realization of mundane existence because he is the fullest manifestation of transcendent reality within the world. No fuller revelation of divine presence is possible within a human being or toward human beings. Instead, the radiance of human nature expands through Christ, both toward its eschatological completion as well as its abiding temporal paradigm. Its transfiguring finality is already manifest as a perfection immanent within existence, both in Christ and in all who are open to his Spirit.

Fullness of Life

This paradigmatic significance of Christ has long been remarked, even among those who could not affirm the recognition of his divinity. Less frequently considered is the connection between the transcendent fullness manifest in Christ and his normatively authoritative role. How was it possible for Jesus to be Christ if he was not also God? No one else has lived as perfectly, not so much in the sense of leading a virtuous life, but in the sense of revealing the fullest ramifications of what virtue requires. Beyond the sheer nobility of goodness that we behold among the most exceptional human beings, he showed the necessity of a further outpouring of self to the point of extinction on behalf of those who are least worthy of the effort. Not merely the resistance to evil, he showed the route of representative suffering by which it is overcome. The inexorable unfolding of right requires not that we stop at the actualization of goodness, but that we continue the direction to the point where its victory is assured through the complete outpouring of self. Our purpose here, he revealed, is not just to live within obedience to the divine will, but to surrender ourselves to the task of God himself—in suffering the revolt of evil and, through suffering all of the consequences, bring about the kingdom of God on earth. As the fulfillment of the kingdom he first went about announcing, Jesus disclosed the eschatological love of God as the reality mysteriously emergent through all time. He established his divinity not primarily through the wonder working miracles, but through the fullness of divine Love present within him. Familiarity has too often obscured the utter novelty of this conception of love that Jesus himself struggled to single out as the mark both of the Father and of his discipleship. It is unlike any other conception of love within history, despite the primacy it has subsequently come to occupy, because it can derive only from the irruption of Being itself within time. In Christ, we behold the transcendent divine love that is the transfiguring power beyond all creation.

But it is more than an epiphany. The decisive additional dimension is the recognition that, when Being enters time to redeem it through the movement of transcending itself, the action is effective of redemption. We not only behold the participation of the human in the divine; we witness the moment in which it is accomplished for all human beings everywhere and at all times. Christ is both the radiant center of history and the point of its maximal transfiguration. We do not know how or even clearly why this is so, but we do know that, when the transcendent God has taken action, its effect is infallibly completed. The only mode of conclusive divine action in history is what is undertaken by God himself. Therefore, the definitive communication of the divinely willed order of being can be effected only by God's irrevocable intervention within time. Only the one who is God can completely and perfectly and finally incarnate the order of transcendent Being within existence. Action completed by Being is of the same mode. Over and above the illuminative glimpse of transcendent Love in Jesus, we extrapolate toward its conclusive eschatological meaning of redemption.

This world is simultaneously luminous toward its beyond and toward its consummation. Whatever slight impatience may be imparted through the imagination of its culmination, this is decisively outweighed by the serenity with which temporal existence is accepted as its indispensable condition. A world within which Being itself dwelt bodily, and indeed lingered for a full span of human life, has reached its highest transparence toward divinity. Far from constituting an imbalancing anticipation, this transfiguring impetus is surely the mode in which the mystery and burden of earthly existence can be most fully supported. It enables us to understand and acknowledge the full reality in which we presently find ourselves. This world is a succession of fleeting satisfactions that are no sooner attained than they either prove to be inadequate or slip away from our enjoyment. Yet the joy and fulfillment of which this life is capable are real and are not to be casually cast aside. How then is it possible to embrace them with balance? The answer is within the differentiation of the transfiguring tension effected by Christ, in which we can recognize finite existence in all its immanent transcendence. Such a life is (as the Greeks suspected, although they did not fully recognize) the most pleasant. It can be embraced unreservedly and enjoyed without qualification, because not a shadow of regret enters into the consideration of its evanescence. Neither burdened with too much expectation nor discarded with excessive disappointment, life within the eschatological movement attains its highest possibility. Not only is it valued for its own sake, but it is even more welcomed as the harbinger of that toward which it points. Nothing is lost and nothing occurs without meaning in a world irradiated by the divine Love. Far from an otherworldly faith, the opening effected by Christ takes the full measure of finitude because it discloses the full participation in infinity.

Our capacity to rationally unfold, as well as enjoy, the reality within which we find ourselves is crucially dependent on the preservation of that maximum differentiation. Without it, we flounder in the spiritual disorientation that obscures the nature of reality for us in ways that reason itself is powerless to correct. Rational self-discipline can compel us to describe the world just as it is, unaffected by hope or despair, but that is an attitude we are incapable of sustaining over life as a whole. The coloring of our metaphysical tonalities, either toward illusionary expectations or toward abyssal bleakness, sooner or later seep into our way of looking at things. This is why we so frequently oscillate between enthusiasm and dejection. Equilibrium is virtually unattainable in the absence of a balanced vision of the whole. Our present postmodern moment seems more than ever in need of that elusive glimpse of transparence it knows yet is powerless to reevoke. An ordered life hinges on the recognition that life in this world is to be pursued with hearty confidence, but that we must not place our ultimate confidence in its capacity to provide our fulfillment. How is it possible to give ourselves utterly to the civilizational task of building up all that is good in life and yet withhold our ultimate allegiance from its often dazzling self-importance? The task is not easy, yet the life of reason depends on it. We know that the development of this world calls forth the expenditure of all our energies, yet at the same time we know we cannot afford to abandon ourselves utterly to the exigences of its achievements. We ultimately remain and retain that unabsorbed opening toward the transcendent.

The imbalance of excessive immersion in the struggle of mundane existence has been the historic distortion of the past two centuries. Ideological madness has been its most dramatic manifestation, culminating in the convulsive emergence of the totalitarian states. But the problem has more widely afflicted the modern world since its inception. Residues of the trauma of great collective exertions are visible in all of the modern societies, from the colonization of the Russian landscape, to the vast westward settlement of America, to the mass migrations and population upheavals of modern warfare, to the gigantic technological enterprises in which we are perpetually engaged. In all of them, the individual appears a largely disposable element. That is the symptom of the disconnection from transcendent Being known only through the human soul. Even when we are not pressed so relentlessly into the service of great collaborative projects, the sheer complexity, ceaselessness, and comprehensiveness of modern life seems to exhaust all possibility of contemplation. Eventually, of course, the relentless self-expenditure on mundane accomplishments wears itself out and the enthusiasm for immanence evaporates. When the magic of development disappears, the modern world, as such, is at an end. All of the prodigious energy poured into its construction and extension, from the transference of unlimited expectation toward limited projects, dries up.

At this point, the disposition to turn our backs on this world can become incredibly strong. Our postmodern self-characterization is replete with such overtones, although the decisive rejection of mundane existence has still not been taken. Presentation of an alternate direction is indispensable to such a move. So far, none of the available suggestions have captured the social imagination as the compelling truth. However, there is more than a slight possibility that the refurbished Gnosticism advocated by Bloom might represent the cusp of the next wave of spirituality to wash over us. Not only does he accurately identify the prearticulate rumblings in this direction bubbling up from the assorted New Age preoccupations in the culture, but the Gnostic proposal reconnects such musings to the most powerful evocative alternative to Christianity over the past two millennia. The durability of the Gnostic imagination resides in its profound appeal. As we have suggested, it resolves the most impenetrable questions of existence while surpassing Christianity in its promise of immediate perfection. But it draws us decisively away from the task of working in this world, as well as from the work of moving toward our substantive spiritual perfection. In the name of enlightenment, it turns away from the expansive elaboration of reason in immanent and transcendent aspiration. Whether in its ancient extracosmic orientation or in its latter-day intracosmic variant, the impulse is the same. Gnosticism is a movement of escape through the flight from the cosmos or into the inner world of wonder-working marvels. Neither the work of the world nor the work of the soul any longer count for anything. Bloom's contribution is to have shown quite clearly the direction in which the vague postmodern intimations of spirituality ultimately point.

Yet neither the activist nor the escapist varieties of Gnosticism can decisively affect the reality within which they occur. Their distortions can, for a time, deflect human beings from their attunement to the order of Being within existence. But the self-conceit of mastery eventually exhausts itself through prolonged exposure to its unreality. Then the drama of man's existence can resume its mysterious unfolding in tension toward the Being that has generated it, guarded it, and greeted it at every moment. In that opening toward Being in which the recovery of reason from closure takes place, humanity glances around for the marks of the same disclosure within the historical process itself. That is the point at which the encounter with Jesus occurs as the recognition of the definitive revelation of the divine presence giving itself within our hearts. The great mystery of the reality in which we find ourselves suddenly opens before us, with consequences for the defining balance of existence within which life can be lived to its fullest. In Jesus, we recognize that the drama in which we participate is not merely our realization, but that its deepest level is glimpsed in the recognition of its subsumption within the drama of God's participation in our existence. We are not so much participants in Being, as Being is itself participative in us. The Love of Being reveals itself as the Being of Love. The moment of that intersecting luminosity within history marks the turning point of the drama in which the process of its unfolding becomes transparent. No longer a matter of mysteriously playing a part whose intimations are sensed but never apprehended, now we recognize our calling as the responsive unfolding of the role whose meaning is definitively glimpsed within the divine drama itself. Maximum differentiation means that the process is penetrated as far as it can be while still remaining a drama. Any further revelation would dissolve the structure of the drama itself, as the Gnostic deformation demonstrates abundantly. By reconnecting with the revelatory outburst in which the limiting differentiation of reality has occurred, we discover again the historical epoch within which we live. It is still properly numbered from the birth of Christ as the point at which the structure of existence has received its fullest illumination. When all the distorting alternatives have slipped away under the weight of their incoherence, we recognize that we continue to live in the only unsurpassable historical differentiation of order. We enter gladly into the third millennium of Christ.

Notes

1. The connection between Christianity and Gnosticism is a complex question. Voegelin has emphasized the intimacy of the connection while recognizing the prior existence of Gnostic currents. See his *New Science of Politics* (Chicago: University of Chicago Press,

1952), *Science, Politics and Gnosticism* (Washington: Regnery, 1997), and *The Ecumenic Age* (Baton Rouge: Louisiana State University Press, 1974). Jaroslav Pelikan also emphasizes the connection with the definition of dogma, *The Emergence of the Catholic Tradition (100–600)*, Ch. 2. Standard works include Hans Jonas, *The Gnostic Religion* (Boston: Beacon, 3rd. ed. 1978); Kurt Rudolph, *Gnosis: The Nature and History of Gnosticism*, trans. Robert McLachlan Wilson (San Francisco: HarperSanFrancisco, 1987); N. Deutsch, *The Gnostic Imagination: Gnosticism, Mandaeism and Merkabah Mysticism* (Leiden: Brill, 1995); and the collection of Gnostic texts known as *The Nag Hammadi Library*, ed. James N. Robinson (San Francisco: Harper and Row, 1990); as well as the more complete collection in Bentley Layton, *Gnostic Scriptures* (Garden City, N.Y.: Doubleday, 1987). Useful recent studies include Elliot R. Wolfson, *Through a Speculum That Shines* (Princeton: Princeton University Press, 1994) and Gerard Hanratty, *Studies in Gnosticism and in the Philosophy of Religion* (Dublin: Four Courts, 1997).

2. Alexandre Kojève, *Introduction to the Reading of Hegel*, trans. James H. Nichols, ed. Allan Bloom (New York: Basic, 1969), 159–60. Also Barry Cooper, *The End of History* (Toronto: University of Toronto Press, 1984), 303.

3. A good, recent example is the catalog produced for an exhibition at the National Gallery of Victoria, Melbourne, *Beyond Belief: Modern Art and the Religious Imagination* (Melbourne: 1998). See also Gregory Wolfe, *Sacred Passion: The Art of William Schickel* (Notre Dame: University of Notre Dame Press, 1998).

4. One might think of the ambiguity of love potions and poisons, death, and erotic consummation in such a treatment as Richard Wagner's *Tristan und Isolde*.

5. An exception is the book by Philip Lee, *Against the Protestant Gnostics* (New York: Oxford University Press, 1987).

6. For Jung's own Gnostic tendencies, see *Memories, Dreams, Reflections*, ed. Aniela Jaffé (New York: Vintage, rev. ed. 1965), and for a splendid example of his exploration of esoteric spirituality, *Mysterium Conjunctionis*, trans. F.C. Hull (Princeton: Bollingen, 1963).

7. Bloom understands the distinction between Gnosticism and gnosis.

"When the knowing represents itself as mutual, in which God knows the deep self even as it knows God, then we have abandoned belief for Gnosis. This book is essentially about Gnosis . . ." But when he goes on to describe the character of gnosis, he explicitly distinguishes it from an experiential knowledge of God and draws it back into the framework of Gnosticism. "Gnosis grants you acquaintance with a God unknown to, and remote from, this world, a God in exile from a false creation that, in itself, constituted a fall. You yourself, in knowing and being known by this alienated God, come to see that originally your deepest self was no part of the Creation-Fall, but goes back to an archaic time before time, when that deepest self was part of a fullness that was God, a more human God than any worshipped since." *Omens of the Millennium* (New York: Riverhead, 1996), 182–3. It is also noteworthy that Bloom assimilates the home-grown religious movements of America to the same Gnostic pattern. See his *The American Religion: The Emergence of the Post-Christian Nation* (New York: Touchstone, 1992).

8. The loss of Bloom's relatives in the Holocaust is enough to convince him of the shortcomings of the God of Judaism, Christianity, and Islam. "That gives one a God who tolerated the Holocaust, and such a God is simply intolerable, since he must be either crazy or irresponsible if his benign omnipotence was compatible with the death camps. A cosmos this obscene, a nature that contains schizophrenia, is acceptable to the monotheistic orthodox as part of 'the mystery of faith.'" *Omens* 23–24.

9. One should not, of course, overlook the poignancy of Bloom's disappointment with God. "Prophetic religion becomes apocalyptic when prophecy fails, and apocalyptic religion becomes Gnosticism when apocalypse fails, as fortunately it always has and, as we must hope will fail again. Gnosticism does not fail; it cannot fail, because its God is at once deep within the self and also estranged, infinitely far off, beyond the cosmos." *Omens,* 30.

10. One is struck by the narcissistic quality of the experience, which Bloom reveals as well as anyone. The story of his own "nihilistic depression" is movingly sketched, but one has to wonder about the means of his deliverance. It came when, after reading Jonas's study of *The Gnostic Religion,* Bloom immersed himself in the work of Emer-

son and found there the answer to his search. He quotes the passage that most struck him: "That is always best which gives me to myself. The sublime is excited in me by the great stoical doctrine, Obey thyself. That which shows God in me, fortifies me. That which shows God out of me, makes me a wart and a wen . . . " *Omens,* 24–27.

11. "It flattered my pride to think that I incurred no guilt and, when I did wrong, not to confess it so that you might *bring healing to a soul that had sinned against you.* I preferred to excuse myself and blame this unknown thing which was in me but was not part of me." *Confessions* V, 10. See also Peter Brown, *Augustine of Hippo* (Berkeley: University of California Press, 1967), Ch. 5, "Manichaeism."

12. It is not surprising that the other transcendent faiths, Judaism and Islam, also discovered the necessity of struggling against the Gnostic temptation if they were to preserve the spiritual differentiations they had reached. See Scholem's account of the reaction against the extreme antinomianism of the messianic Sabbatai Zevi, *Major Trends,* Eighth Lecture. For Islam, the discussion of Sufism by Fazlur Rahman illustrates the same tension that threatened to erode the moral-theological truths, *Islam* (Chicago: University of Chicago Press, 1979), Chs. 8–9.

13. Charles Taylor has drawn our attention to the centrality of ordinary life within the modern worldview, but he fails to exhibit the capacity for transcendence that renders it worthy of such celebration. *Sources of the Self* (Cambridge: Harvard University Press, 1989). A quite different, but parallel, elevation of ordinary life is contained in *The Autobiography of Saint Thérèse of Lisieux: The Story of a Soul,* trans. John Beevers (New York: Doubleday, 1957).

14. The problem was well understood in the ancient world, as the writings of the Stoics attest. Aristotle puts his finger on the core of the problem in his explanation of why economics cannot be considered a part of politics and thus central to what constitutes the life pursued for its own sake. Men mistake unlimited acquisition as the goal of life because they have failed to discover what makes life itself worthwhile. "But the fundamental cause of this state of mind is men's anxiety about livelihood, rather than about well-being; and since their desire for that is unlimited, their desire for the things that produce it is also unlimited." *Politics* 1258a.

Index